Richard 'Ricky' Hatton was born in 1978 and grew up in Hattersley, Greater Manchester. As a young amateur fighter he won several British titles and boxed at the World Junior Boxing Championship in Cuba, before turning pro in 1997. He went on to be champion of the world four times at light welterweight and welterweight, was awarded an MBE for services to sport in 2007 and is widely seen as one of Britain's greatest ever boxers. He lives in Gee Cross with his girlfriend, Jennifer, and has three children, Campbell, Millie and Fearne.

WAR AND PEACE
MY STORY

RICKY HATTON
with Tris Dixon

MACMILLAN

First published 2013 by Macmillan
an imprint of Pan Macmillan, a division of Macmillan Publishers Limited
Pan Macmillan, 20 New Wharf Road, London N1 9RR
Basingstoke and Oxford
Associated companies throughout the world
www.panmacmillan.com

ISBN 978-1-4472-4389-2 HB
ISBN 978-1-4472-4390-8 TPB

1 3 5 7 9 8 6 4 2

A CIP catalogue record for this book is available from the British Library.

Typeset by Ellipsis Digital, Glasgow
Printed and bound by CPI Group (UK) Ltd, Croydon, CRO 4YY

Visi
and
new

To Jennifer, Campbell, Millie and Fearne

CONTENTS

PROLOGUE

It was not supposed to end this way.

I was in the Manchester Arena and the fans were singing my name. That part was right, at least.

They chortled 'Walking in a Hatton Wonderland' with the same vigour and passion that they always had, and as I left the prize ring for the final time they cheered and applauded.

My face was black and blue and swelling rapidly, and I had lost for just the third time in my career.

They always say that comebacks are ill-advised but I never did listen to them much. It was my life, my career, my decision.

Although I knew it was going to be an emotional night, I could never have guessed exactly how incredible and unique it would turn out to be. You have to be a professional boxer to actually appreciate what it means to come out to a crowd of 20,000 raucous fans like that. I know you have your trainer and your team behind you, but you don't share the love with your teammates like you do in other sports; it comes all on you, only you and all at once.

There was an eruption when I stood on the stage waiting to walk to the ring, and I prepared to hold my head high as my music, 'Blue Moon', kicked in.

In that instant, I'm stood there alone and I prepare to step through the wall of noise that awaits. Walking to the ring, it's hard work. It's lonely, it's isolated, and the euphoria brought on by the roar of the crowd sinks under the pressure and feelings of dread. The place comes alive. A wave of flash bulbs blast at me and the arena spotlights shine directly into my eyes. I'm blinded but steady myself, gather my thoughts and think of my girlfriend Jennifer and my children, Campbell and Millie.

I need to hold it together. I've come so far. I can't crack now. I look into the baying masses. I bite down so hard my jaw clenches and shakes. I bang my gloves together: 'Come on, Ricky lad.' I emerge from my personal darkness and the noise begins to fill my soul while simultaneously popping in my ears.

It is deafening. There is no other way to describe it. It means more to me than it ever has done. Not too long ago I had been suicidal. I'd had knives at my wrists and I couldn't get any lower. Compare that to walking out in the Manchester Arena with all of these fans screaming for me, willing me to do well. I have come a long way – it means everything to me.

People have always asked me what my best achievement was in boxing and it was never anything to do with what I did in the ring – it was the fanbase that followed me. For somebody to have fought depression for a number of years, to hear that roar that night after more than three years away from boxing . . . I had to hold the tears back as I walked down the ramp. It sounds a little bit soppy but I just felt like dropping to my knees and saying thank you. To hear that roar one last time was more than I could have ever hoped for. I was getting teary-eyed, saying to myself, 'Come on, Ricky, keep it together. Come on, son, you can do it.'

The noise was somehow intensifying with every step I took. I began to think about all of the people I had let down. This whole fight was about redemption and making people proud of me again.

Then there was my baby girl, Millie. I didn't want her to read in the papers the rubbish my son, Campbell, had to about me and my private life. I didn't want that. I wanted her to read about how well her dad was doing. I was also thinking about my parents, who I'd barely spoken to in two years, and how I felt I'd been let down by those people who were closest to me.

When it came down to the actual fight, against a very good former world champion in Vyacheslav Senchenko, it was hard for me to try and channel my emotions and say, 'This is great, this is what it's all about.' Beforehand I just thought the world was against me and I was just going to show everyone. I had so much fury inside me, more than I did when I fought Kostya Tszyu. The fact no one thought I could beat Tszyu, that was my fury. 'I'm not just a ticket-seller,' I was thinking, 'I'll beat him.'

But this was different. National hero, getting flattened by Manny Pacquiao, then retiring, the personal problems that I had and all the rest of it . . . How I felt for Senchenko was, 'What did I do to this world to have it fucking happen to me, this whole weight that seems to have fallen on my shoulders?' Stick it all in a ball and I thought that's what Senchenko had coming at him. 'It's going to be fucking painful for him,' I thought.

As I stood at the bottom of the ring steps, having lost four-and-a-half stone, after all the issues that I'd faced and everything I'd been through, the love the fans still had for me was incredible. It was the most emotional fight of my career, and that includes Kostya Tszyu, Floyd Mayweather and Pacquiao. That is something that will never leave me.

I could have picked an opponent I would have flattened but I didn't. I went straight in at the deep end and I wouldn't do anything differently. I've always been a hundred-per-cent man, all or nothing, and that had not changed in my time away from the ring.

There was something extra that night, too. An air of uncertainty that everyone bought into. Some would have been saying, 'Why's he coming back? He doesn't need to.' Cynics would think, 'Well, we know why he's coming back.' But even avid fans of mine would have been sat there not having a clue what was going to happen, wondering if I was going to be the same as I was at my best. Was I going to come back better or stronger? Should I really be doing this? That added to the atmosphere. No one knew what was going to happen. When I won my first world title against Kostya Tszyu it was an electric night, but it didn't compare to this.

I step under the ropes and into the ring and the crowd bursts. I have never heard a noise like it. It's gladiatorial. They want me to do well. I step onto the canvas and I can feel it shaking and vibrating under my feet with the sound. It is unbelievable. It is priceless. I look back out at the fans, fully embracing the bond we have always shared. I glance at Senchenko. 'You're having it tonight,' I think to myself. The fans clearly agree. He doesn't look back at me. I see individual faces in the audience. They scream and sing. Some of the fans are punching the air, pulling for me. I can feel their hopes pinned on me. They have paid a lot of money to come and watch me fight. They have come to see me win. It is what they expect.

I meet my opponent in the centre of the ring. I look at Senchenko, expressionless, hiding my nerves, disguising my anger, the fury that burns beneath and my eagerness.

The last time I had fought I had been destroyed in two rounds by Manny Pacquiao. It's all very well concentrating on the story away from the ring – redemption had been my mantra – but the last time I'd stepped between those ropes I'd been knocked out. Badly. Ultimately, it was not just the Pacquiao fight that sent me over the edge, it was an accumulation of things, but I was embarrassed about it and I had to face up to it now.

I've never said I will be the greatest fighter ever but one thing I have always been is a very proud man and I always took on the best. So as a man, it was very hard to come to terms with that knockout. I had been heartbroken last time I had been in the ring. And now there was self-doubt, too, with a lot of people asking me if my chin was going to be able to hold up to the same punches that it could before and I read somewhere that: 'This could be another blast out. He's obviously past it.'

I didn't want to make a dickhead out of myself. If I lost again like I did against Pacquiao then the fear of being a laughing stock comes into play, doesn't it?

To compound that, when I went for my boxing medical they said, 'Ricky, your blood pressure is sky high, you're half an inch away from having a heart attack.' And that was even once I got my weight down, because of all the stress from everything away from boxing. I was still having problems with my mum and dad, and the last three torrid years had been a horribly dark period for so many reasons.

My depression can be traced all the way back to the Floyd Mayweather fight in 2007, but even though I had been in training for the comeback, not drinking, doing what I needed to do, sometimes feelings don't go away. My blood pressure was through the roof and it was worrying.

Still, after eight rounds against Senchenko I think I was winning. Not everyone does, but I've watched it back and believe I was winning a close, hard scrap.

I'm a boxing historian and I have listened to old fighters who have turned round and said, 'We'll give it one more go.' And in the gym, in sparring, the padwork and the training, I was in no doubt that I was going to be better than I ever had been in my life. That's what those old fighters said, too.

I was sharp, feeling fast and me and my trainer Bob Shannon were both thinking: 'Jeez, there's not even any ring rust.' Training, though, is so different to the fight. The minute that bell went it was different. And after three or four rounds, I sat on my stool and thought, 'Oh Ricky. You haven't got it.' Reality set in.

Again I think of little Millie, Campbell and Jen, my new family, and so launch myself back into the fray each session, trying to make my point.

The fight gets tougher round by round. It becomes a battle and as we take turns landing heavy shots our faces begin to tell the tale of a hard fight. It's another violent story, another war. It's my forty-eighth professional contest and I've spent the best part of fifteen years dragging my body down to the right weight. I can feel all of the miles on the clock. The fighting engine doesn't fire like it used to. It splutters; stops and starts. That's how I'm fighting. It is not fluid and it's becoming painful as he starts to land long, raking blows that crunch into my face and pump my head back, jolting it so I can hear audible gasps from my crowd. That is never a good sound.

I walk back to my corner after each round and glance down to the middle seats of the front row at ringside. For every fight previously, Mum and Dad have been there, willing me to do well. They aren't there. Their seats are taken and it reminds me of the heartache away from the ring.

Jen is there, Campbell is at home and Jen's mum and dad have baby Millie. Former world champions need babysitters, too. But it just doesn't feel the same, emotionally or physically. Everything is different.

In the ring I wasn't quite getting out of the way quickly enough. I wasn't quite moving my feet away correctly; when I was throwing punches some of them were just missing by fractions and it was the little things like that. It wasn't like it used to be. The timing, the movement. They weren't there. So you knuckle down and try to go through with it. And you force it because it's not coming naturally. And then that works against you. I thought, 'If I haven't got it, let's just get to the final bell. Let's just get the win and do what we've got to do.'

Then, in round nine, he got me with a body shot. A left hand crunched into my side.

It is a sickening, painful shot that captures my breath. I'm drowned of oxygen and drop to my knees. The pain in my side is severe and it bends me at the waist. I try to breathe in, at first through my nose, then through my mouth. But I can't draw breath. I can't breathe. When you get hit on the chin you can get up, shake it off, but they always say you can never shake a body shot off and when I fall I can hear referee Victor Loughlin counting: '. . . two, three . . .'.

I'm still trying to take breaths, thinking I'm going to rise at eight. I can actually feel the crowd willing me to get up.

Victor's count gets to '. . . four, five . . .' and I can hear the crowd really shouting for me. 'Come on.' My nose is not able to bring any air inside. Then it is '. . . six, seven . . .' and it's even louder. Now they're pleading with me. 'Come on, Ricky. Get up. Get up.'

CHAPTER 1

In the Beginning

They called him Spider Hatton. His first name was Richard, too, but he was my great uncle. We have pictures of him dating back to the 1920s and he had a cherubic appearance about him, like he was too polite to wear boxing gloves. Yet by all accounts he could pack a punch and was a prominent figure on the Manchester fight scene. He was a throwback and apparently pretty good.

My family only found that out when we looked into it after I started boxing, because we didn't know where my talent came from. No one in my immediate family had ever boxed before. My dad, Ray, had played football for Manchester City, my grandad had played for City's B team before the war; so when I took to boxing like a duck to water it had us all baffled. We went back through the family tree and found where I got it from – Spider Hatton, the bare-knuckle fighter. I suppose bare-knuckle would have been right up my street, wouldn't it? He was actually my grandfather's brother, but my grandmother's father, Daniel, was also handy with his fists on the bare-knuckle circuit

9

in Ireland. As with most things in this sport, reputations give birth to legends, and they said that Eileen Slattery's husband Daniel – my great-grandfather – was one of the best.

I wasn't drawn to boxing when I was really young. My dad always had public houses and my mum, Carol, worked in a clothes shop in Hyde before she took on a carpet stall at Glossop market when one of my uncles died. But then I saw, and was amazed by, Bruce Lee on TV and wanted to be like him. You can guarantee that when *Rocky* comes on the TV every amateur gym is packed to the rafters the following night. Well, that's what it was like with Bruce Lee. I absolutely loved his films and so started kick-boxing. I did all right with it; I was only seven or eight and was as game as they come, but with me being short and stocky you could see my talent was with my fists and not my feet. I couldn't get near my opponents and the taller ones were kicking my teeth in. The coach said that because I was giving away so much height and reach I should give boxing a try, so I walked over the road to the Louvolite Boxing Club. Ted Peate was my first amateur coach, and I was there for the first two years of my amateur career. Within about two or three months I had my first fight.

Boxing is one of those sports where you get whacked on the nose and you either like it or you think, 'It's not for me, this game.' My first fight was an absolute war. I boxed a lad called Danny Reynolds, from Leeds, and it was toe-to-toe for three one-and-a-half-minute rounds. The crowd went mad, and if I hadn't had a strong stomach I would have thought, 'Sod that for a game of soldiers.' But I loved it. I was hooked. The harder the fight, the more I loved it.

At the Louvolite there was me, Stephen Bell and Tony Feno, two of my great friends at the time. Stephen went on to captain England as an amateur, and both would come to the big fights later in my career, but back then boxing was fun for us, we were best pals and called ourselves the Three Amigos. There are still old black and white pictures of us in the gym now. In the minibus we'd sing songs all the way down to the show, tell jokes and take the piss out of Ted. By the time we got to the show and we had to fight it was almost as if it was secondary to having a laugh with the guys; you'd expect that at a young age I suppose, we were only eleven or twelve. I loved going boxing and going to the gym, even from the start, but it was a social thing as much as a sporting thing for a while. That didn't last too long. As the fights ticked by, and people started to tell me they thought I was pretty good, I began to take it a bit more seriously.

Like my dad, though, and my grandad before him, I was playing football as well and I also supported Manchester City like them. I played right midfield and wasn't bad, featuring for my local team on the council estate in Hattersley. I went for trials with Tameside Boys, my county team, and was selected for them. By playing for Tameside I was picked up by Man City and was at the FA School of Excellence for two years. In my class at City were Jim and Jeff Whitley, who both went on to play for the club and were capped by Northern Ireland, and it always makes you wonder, could I have done it? I was okay and was always very fit because of boxing. I got up and down the pitch really well, was a good tackler and a decent passer of the ball. I was a Roy Keane-type player, always very aggressive, as you can imagine – and, as boxing keeps you thinking three or four moves ahead, I could always read the game well, pick a pass out. There were some players in my class who stood out a mile though, and I wasn't one of them. It was also clear to anyone watching that my real talent was with my boxing and I was forever working on that.

My dad had a pub, the New Inn in Hyde, where he built a gym in the cellar; I would spend hours down there practising punches, combinations, feints and footwork. The cellar had several small areas: if you went straight ahead and turned right there was a big room where all of the barrels were stored, beer, lager, ciders and so on; next was a little room where my boxing gym was; and through that a smaller room where all the spirits and bottled lagers would be. Then, if you came out of the gym and doubled back on yourself, by the staircase there was a long corridor that lead to three smaller rooms, where the pub football teams used to get changed before a game on a Sunday morning. There was also an extra room, full of clocks and things because there was a pigeon club at the pub. It was amazing in there, and it's fair to say there was a broad cross-section of people who came into the New Inn.

When I was training on a Friday night I would get people coming down to watch me now and then. The pub was supposed to be haunted, so I'd only go down there with my trainer because you believe in bad things at that age, don't you? But I had many happy times down there. It might have been the hardest game in the world but I was a bit of an anorak, even as a kid; while other lads from school and the estate were out on their skateboards, BMXs or mountain bikes, I was down there training. I suppose that's what you've got to do to reach the top, you've got to live it. One of the Louvolite coaches, Mick Lowan, brought his pads and came down to the cellar and spent hours and hours coaching me.

The gym I had in the cellar was just about the size of a small ring. On the walls we had fight posters of Marvin Hagler and Sugar Ray Leonard, and former heavyweight champions Leon Spinks and Mike Tyson. I had a corner where I would keep my skipping rope, gloves and hand weights, and there was a mat which, when I'd done all of my floorwork, I would lean up against the wall. The punchbag and floor-to-cciling ball would come down and be put away when me and Mick did the pads. I just ate, slept and breathed boxing – I was pretty much training like a pro from the outset. Even when I was due to fight on a Monday I was asking about possibly fighting on a Tuesday. More often than not I didn't get a fight but it didn't really matter to me, I just loved being around boxing, full stop.

When I trained down in the cellar some nights there was a steady flow of people coming to watch me train with a beer in their hand; some would go and get another pint from the bar and keep coming down for hours.

Even though I was so young I enjoyed it in the pubs, it was character building. You would look across the bar and think, 'Jeez, I don't want to end up like him.'

I think that's one of the reasons Dad never drank. I don't really know how that came about, but he had played football for City and it was just something he was never entertained by. I asked him one day and he just said, 'It's always been the case. I never really fancied it, wasn't into the nightclub thing. I was into sport. And when I was in the pubs and saw the sights across the bar I thought I'd made the right decision.'

Each to their own.

And Dad was always a grafter. He always worked hard. He had six or seven pubs, two carpet shops, and even before that he worked on the markets. He wasn't scared of rolling up his sleeves so that we could have the good things in life.

But in a local there's always the little old guy who sits in the corner by the dartboard, and as a kid I would challenge the regulars to games of darts. There's a fella who thinks he can pull women every five minutes and another fella who's the next Maradona, or so he thinks. They're characters you get in every bar up and down the country.

It was great, and I had a very good upbringing in the pub; later, when my dad started up a carpet shop, I was going out to people's houses and fitting them, dealing with the public.

The area where I spent my childhood often got headlines for the wrong reasons. The exact house where the Moors murderers, Ian Brady and Myra Hindley, lived several years earlier was just two hundred yards away from where we lived. It was destroyed in 1987. My younger brother Matthew and I used to go to primary school with the son of the infamous serial killer Dr Harold Shipman, who murdered more than 200 patients after moving into the area in the 1970s. Greater Manchester was in the headlines again in 2012 when two female police officers responded to a call in Hattersley only to be attacked by Dale Cregan, a fugitive who was on the run and who phoned in a false call-out to ambush the women – using guns and grenades. Some of the nicest people in the world come from the area but sadly it's not known for that.

Boxing has always helped people in the poorer sections of society, and some boys in and around Hyde ended up being taken to the gym to iron out kinks in their behaviour, but there really wasn't any of that with me. I think I only ever had one fight at school. That was in the first year, and no one wanted to fight me again because I flattened him. My teachers always said I was never any trouble; good as gold, they said, and they were right. The thing was I was bone idle. If my son, Campbell, had the same attitude as I used to have, I'd wring his bleeding neck. I was more interested in boxing, football, City, anything. I just wasn't into schoolwork, studying or exams. I thought I didn't need to do it because I was going to be a boxer; I was going to be a world champion. It was a stupid attitude to have because at twelve or thirteen I didn't know if I was going to make it as a boxer, and I certainly didn't know if I was going to become a world champion. I just farted around and if I hadn't made it in boxing I'd have had no exams or qualifications to fall back on; I could have been in a whole heap of trouble.

I still flirted with football because as an amateur boxer not many of the other kids would fight me. At the start of my teens I had won the schoolboy championships two years on the bounce and had knocked everybody out in every round. I ended up getting byes into the semi-finals and finals because I couldn't get fights. I was going up and down the country weighing-in at as many shows as possible to try and give myself the opportunity of getting matched. That meant my attendance dropped at football training. I was missing sessions, and Manchester City let me go as a consequence, saying, 'We're impressed with what we've seen, Ricky, but we haven't seen enough of you because of your boxing. We'll keep an eye on you.' That made my mind up. I packed it in for a couple of years, only to make a brief footballing comeback when one of my friends started a team, Hattersley Youth, on the estate. But I'd set my heart on boxing by then.

I had moved from the Louvolite and was now at Paul Dunne's Sale West Boxing Club. Paul used to work with my grandad, my mum's dad, for a security firm and my grandad said to give Paul's gym a go and it went from there. I still trained in the pub and in my own time, too, and I could turn my hand to almost anything in the ring. Sometimes I would box and move – using combinations, defence and footwork – the next minute you would see me ripping into my opponent. I would get that red mist, the eye of the tiger, from a very young age. The minute you get caught with a shot, ideally you go into survival mode, go defensive and tuck up. That wasn't me. If they cracked me with one, you could see steam come out of my ears and I sometimes forgot the main rule of boxing, which is to hit and not get hit. My attitude, which was totally wrong, was: 'If you hit me, I'll hit you back harder.'

By this time it seemed my whole family were into the carpet business. My Uncle Paul, Uncle Ged and my late Uncle John all had carpet shops. Then, when the pubs started to open beyond 3 p.m. on a Sunday they became very hard work, opening really long hours, so my dad gave up on the pubs and gave carpets a go like the rest of the family. It went well for him – and I started to help here and there at R Carpets in Gorton. At first I used to go in at weekends. I think it helped my boxing because I would be chucking underlay on the van, throwing grippers on, putting carpets on and lifting them on the rack; there was a lot of lifting and I think physically that stood me in good stead.

It was logical that I'd start carpet fitting, I suppose, and if the boxing didn't work out it was a trade to fall back on. At least I'd be earning. My dad used to say to Pete, who was the main carpet-fitter, 'Take Ricky out. Show him a few bits.' At first I was just putting the grippers down, then I would put the underlay in and then I started to learn to fit the carpets. I was probably Manchester's worst ever carpet-fitter to be honest with you. I was cutting them short, cutting through wires, I was terrible – I'd spend all day on my hands and knees and get home with dozens of plasters on my fingers and must have cost my dad a fortune. In the end he bought me a shop to look after in Hyde and put me in retail. As it turned out, if I was bad at carpet fitting, I was worse as a carpet salesman. It's just as well I had the boxing to fall back on because I wasn't much cop at carpets.

As a family we weren't very wealthy but we didn't ever

want for anything. Life was good, we were extremely close and if we needed football boots or trainers, we had them; it was the same for boxing gloves and kit, and we always had family holidays. We went to Tenerife, Benidorm, Magaluf, Torremolinos, Turkey and Egypt; we were very fortunate and saw a lot of the world at a young age. We went to Disney World in Florida twice, where it was all very expensive – and some kids will never go – so we were very lucky.

It wasn't all about pricey foreign holidays, either; we went to Blackpool a lot, too. We had some great times there. My dad's mum and dad – Nan and Grandad – had a caravan in Blackpool and we would go three or four times a year. It was me, my younger brother Matthew, Mum and Dad, and Nan and Grandad. We would go to Pleasure Beach, the Sandcastle – I've taken my own son and there's loads of fond childhood memories there. The good times always go through your mind, and when we're queuing up to go on the rides they come flooding back to the surface, like my lunch almost does whenever I've had to go on them.

Now, although I was always pretty quiet as a kid, my brother Matthew had a right mouth on him. He also has a dry sense of humour and will take the piss out of you without you knowing he's doing it. He used to mouth off and wind other kids up, and when it went tits up, he'd shout, 'Rick, sort this out.' I cleared up a lot of his trouble. He was a little shit; worse than that, he ended up supporting Manchester United.

It was in the New Inn, he was only about eight years of age, and one of the customers came and said, 'What team do you support then, Matthew?' He didn't know who he supported so the fella gave him a United badge. It was the size of a one-pence piece and Matthew was so impressed with this 'medal' he ended up supporting United.

We've had our arguments like all brothers do but we were very close when we were younger. He took a shine to boxing, too.

I was getting into the sport more and more seriously. It didn't always go my way, of course; I also lost fights. I was eleven years old when I thought my world was coming to an end. Robbie Grainger was a good fighter from Liverpool, and he'd beaten me on points. It was close but I thought I deserved the decision; I ended up boxing him a couple of years later and beat him. Then I was beaten by another lad from Liverpool, Tommy Lewis; I'd defeated him the first time but lost the re-match. There was a balcony over the ring that night and the changing rooms were upstairs. I took it so badly I didn't want to go downstairs, let alone go home; it was my second loss and my mum had to come in and get me because I was up there sulking and crying. 'Pull your face up,' my mum – who was my biggest fan – said.

Sale West was a small Manchester club that had some good kids but never anyone who'd gone on to national titles or any-thing like that. A couple of lads went pro but never really did anything. It was in the community centre, a basic place, and I got on well with Paul Dunne from the start. Paul was a former pro who'd had thirty fights and won more than he lost. He had a thick Irish accent that was hard for me to understand at first but from the outset he taught me how to roll, how to box and how to weave, which in the amateur game is quite rare.

Even as a novice I had been catching shots and throwing body punches – and I used to knock people out on a regular basis with body shots, which is not something you see much of in the amateurs. As a schoolboy, people were saying, 'There's this kid from Manchester who can't half body punch.' I'd just been brought up that way. Paul guided me to eight national schoolboy titles, and he and his chief coach, Jimmy Taylor, took me everywhere. My dad was there, too – if I needed to get to a fight he was always good about taking me there – but usually Paul and Jimmy did most of the driving and we were up and down the country looking for as many opportunities to get fights as we could.

If I had a fight on a Monday, weighed in and then the fight didn't happen for whatever reason, then I would go to fights with some of the other lads on the Tuesday and weigh-in there and hope to get matched. Then, on Wednesday, another couple of lads from the gym might be fighting somewhere else so I'd jump in the car and go with them, then weigh-in and try to get a fight. Even if I wasn't matched I was such a boxing junkie that being on the road and being surrounded by the sport every night was my life. It was all I wanted to do.

I trained every day, with the sounds of Oasis filling the cellar or my headphones when I was in the gym or out on the road. The minute this Manchester band came bobbing along I was constantly listening to them. I liked Oasis from the start, with 'Roll With It' and 'Wonderwall', all the songs that would become classics. I had them on when I was training for the schoolboys, in the junior ABAs . . . I've always been a very proud Mancunian. I supported City and listened to Oasis and the moment I heard a Manchester band was doing all right I said, 'Okay, let's have a listen to them.' As much as I love City, and come derby day I always want us to knock ten bells out of Manchester United, later in my career, whether people were City or United fans, they would all come to support me. There aren't many fighters who can unite two sets of supporters but when I was fighting, I did it.

I had a little following, too. My mum and dad were my first supporters and, as I got older and the fights got bigger, we would take a load of regulars from the pub, fifteen, sixteen, eighteen people or so, as well as my wider family and some pals, and we would shoot off to Leyland or Nantwich or Wigan.

It was the ABA youth titles and early stoppage wins that set me apart from a lot of other boxers my age. I was mature in the ring and you could tell that from when I boxed a kid called Jamie Moore.

I was only about fourteen when we boxed in the schoolboys at Blackpool and whereas I'd already won a load of titles, Jamie was only having what I think was his eighth fight. He was a southpaw and dressed a bit like me, all in black – black vest, black shorts and black boots. I thought, 'Jesus, he looks a scrapper.' He looked at me, put his arms out and beckoned me in, saying, 'Come on then.' It was like looking in the mirror: 'This

21

fella is coming for a fight.' He meant business. Jamie came out and I threw a few jabs, then followed them with a left hook and was really impressed by the way he rolled under the punch. I actually spun round and thought, 'Eight fights? He must be a ringer. That was good.'

A little later in the round, I barged up to him on the ropes and fired a left hook to the body, forcing him to bring his hands down, and I pinged one over the top. Little Jamie went down, got up and I hit him with a few more so the referee gave him a standing count. Then I followed up, hit him with a load more and the referee stopped it. After the fight, and bear in mind I was only fourteen so I don't know who I thought I was, I said, 'Hi ya, Jamie, all right?' He said he was okay.

'I don't want to sound patronizing,' I carried on, 'because it was over in the first round, but I was quite shocked you'd only had eight fights. I'm pleased I caught you when I did because I was in for a hard night. Don't be disheartened. Stick at it.' I was fourteen and giving that kind of advice. I've been mates with Jamie, who went on to win the European light-middleweight title as a professional, ever since.

It was wins like that that meant I was hard to match. Even by the age of about twelve or thirteen they had started calling me 'The Hitman'. Ted Peate gave me the nickname because I was so aggressive. He would say, 'Jesus Christ. Look at him, here, the Hitman.' I looked like I wanted to kill everyone because I was so aggressive. It got to the point where other trainers and parents were refusing to put their boys in with me. There was an article in the old *Amateur Boxing Scene* magazine, which *Boxing News* used to bring out, after my coach called them, saying I was a nightmare to get fights for:

> Any club looking for an opponent for a 17/18 year old weighing 65kgs need only contact Paul Dunne. Paul is the Sale West coach and Richard Hatton is the boxer willing to travel anywhere and everywhere for a bout (Europe included). The club are experiencing great difficulty in finding opponents for this talented young boxer.

We were constantly putting adverts out like that, but we were hardly inundated with replies.

Paul Dunne started taking me around all of the professional gyms for sparring when I was about sixteen. We went down to the Collyhurst and Moston Lads Club with Brian Hughes and I used to spar with people like European champion Pat Barrett, Delroy Waul and Robin Reid when he was world super-middleweight champion. Pat was a real puncher and he knocked me down once with a body shot, a left hook to the body, and it was the first time I'd ever been down from one and I'd never felt pain like it. I was quite good for my age so Pat had to open up to keep me off – and rightly so – and he hit me to the body, nearly snapping me in two. I thought, 'Jesus Christ, that's a bit good. I need to be able to throw them.' I couldn't get my breath and was in real pain, and that's when I realized, really, that – with me being short and stocky – body shots could be the way forward.

I'd also go over to Salford and train at Billy Graham's gym, the famed Phoenix Camp. Carl Thompson, the WBO cruiser-weight champion, who was also there, said, 'Hey, Ricky, if you stay at this you're going to be a world champion. You can go all the way.'

When people like that started telling me, I really began to believe it.

CHAPTER 2

Learning a Trade

I wasn't like any other teenager; boxing was all I wanted to do. I trained and fought whenever I could, watched what I could and learned as much as possible about the sport. I was madly into two-time world champion Nigel Benn; round then there was him, Chris Eubank, Michael Watson and Steve Collins. I wanted to be Nigel Benn, he was dead exciting; every punch was a hook, he never took a backward step and was very aggressive – Nigel was everything to me. I actually went to his second fight with Chris Eubank at Old Trafford. I was about sixteen and I had saved and saved all of my pocket money for a ticket. I went with my Uncle Ged, an even more die-hard City fan than me. He was absolutely ruthless when it came to United but we always said we would go and watch City play there – and we'd go to watch a boxing match there – but that's pretty much it. I think I paid £50 for my ticket; it took me forever to save up: 'Wow, £50, I'm going to have a great seat.' I was right at the back and the fighters looked like two full stops. I was absolutely gutted, but I was

25

enthralled by Benn and like him I was very aggressive when I fought.

With Nigel Benn what you saw is what you got. When he was beaten by Michael Watson he tried to change his style a little and box more but Nigel was always straightforward, no frills, no holds barred and always on the attack. But the more I learned about boxing and its characters, the more I started to enjoy the subtleties of the game, and Roberto Durán, the legend from Panama, became my favourite. While he was exciting, he also had a fantastic defence and not a lot of people gave him credit for that. He was rarely nailed cleanly by a punch, he'd either pull away, try to take the sting out of the shot, get a shoulder on it or just get out of the way. He was very, very good defensively and he would fight anyone and everyone. He was also up in weight, down in weight, and when you think he first won the title at lightweight and boxed the likes of Ken Buchanan and people like that, it's incredible to think he moved up and was one of the fabulous four – Sugar Ray Leonard, Marvin Hagler, Tommy Hearns and Durán – at middleweight. He'd won world titles first at lightweight against the likes of Esteban de Jesús and Buchanan when he was nine stone nine pounds years earlier. Then he was fighting Marvin Hagler, one of the greatest middleweights of all time, up at eleven stone six, and he could still mix it up with him.

There was no YouTube then so I collected old VHS cassettes. When I was in the pub, the old farts would come in and say, 'Oh, this is who you wanna watch. Watch Jake LaMotta, watch Joe Louis, watch this guy or that guy.' It was nice, really, because everyone there knew I was a boxer and they all took an interest in me. 'Watch Larry Holmes's jab, watch Tommy Hearns's right hand,' they would say. So I would do more and more reading about the fighters and it was Durán I really warmed to. I got more and more into it. I'd put the tapes on and be amazed and think, 'Jeez, I want to find out more about this guy.'

Apparently, outside the ring, Durán ended up skint because he'd do things like see a tramp and give him the last money that was in his pocket. He gave everything away. I admired him; there were no airs or graces about Durán, he was a man of the people, as mad as a hatter, fought the best and went through the weights. What's not to like? He was a real fan favourite. Of course, as a teenager I was no Durán but I was doing okay.

I still got some excitement from going to see Manchester City play, of course, but it wasn't the same as with the boxing. I particularly loved the wizardry of Georgi Kinkladze, the Georgian midfielder who had so much flair and somehow managed to exhibit it in a team that did not have much success. Despite City struggling at the time, whenever he started running at the defenders, you just moved a couple of inches forwards in your seat because he was so good. When he got the ball you knew that something could happen. I thought, how great it would be to be a sportsman that excites people.

In June 1995, at the age of sixteen, I was rated as the tenth best amateur welterweight in the country, with my future pro rival Junior Witter at number three because he was a bit older than me, but by the end of the year I was representing England

and, of all places, it was in Blackpool, where I'd been on so many family holidays. I'd trained at Crystal Palace with the full England team, sparring with Alan Vaughan, a very good fighter from Liverpool who won the World Juniors, and with Tommy Peacock, who I would go on to fight for my first pro title.

When I boxed for England Schoolboys the first time I remember thinking, 'Wow, I'm coming out to the national anthem here, boxing for my country.' The penny actually dropped that I was quite decent. I made a pig's ear of it on the night, though.

It was a head shot. Typical me, I was excited. I had sold a lot of tickets, about three coachloads went down – including the regulars from the New Inn – and it was at the Winter Gardens. Germany's Jürgen Brähmer was a very tall southpaw, had a typical amateur style, stood upright, always led with the southpaw right and fired in hard left crosses. I flew at him, tried to jump down his throat, hoping to impress; I was giving him a bit of a seeing to, having no problems landing or catching his shots. But he was a good, quality fighter and he was waiting for that one time. That left came straight down the middle, my legs went wobbly and I went down. I got back up and he gave me a standing count and then he caught me with another three or four shots before the England coach in my corner, Ian Irwin, threw the towel in.

I went away, learned and practised. Fortunately, it was not long before I had the chance to right the wrong against Brähmer as we met in Sardinia in a multi-nations tournament a few months later – in June of 1996. He beat me on points this time but by comparison with our first fight it was nip and tuck. His height, allied with the computer scoring – which had only just come out at that stage – didn't help short, stocky fighters like me. He was better suited to it. This time I'd changed my tactics from Blackpool, used my head a bit more, and managed to push him fairly close.

Having won so many national titles boxing as a schoolboy, and for Young England, I just never thought anyone could beat me. Now this fella Brähmer had beaten me twice and, even though it was closer the second time, there was no doubt about the decision. I came back from Sardinia thinking, 'Bloody hell, I wouldn't fancy him again. He's the dog's bollocks.' I had been boxing at welterweight, and I felt so strong when I was knocking everybody out that I had never felt the need to boil myself down to light welterweight. Then Mr Brähmer knocked me out, beat me again and I thought, 'Jesus Christ.' It hadn't been so noticeable at domestic level but on the world scene, those fights taught me that I couldn't afford to give a couple of kilos away against that kind of quality opposition. It cemented my decision to move down in weight, and when I went to Cuba to fight in the World Juniors in November 1996 I did so at light-welterweight.

Cuba fascinated me and I loved it there – the old American cars, the ramshackle gyms and that everyone had the same passion as I did: boxing. I knew about Cuba's history. We went in a few of the boxing gyms and their amateurs are so highly regarded and successful it was incredible to see first-hand how they did it with such little funding – there were tyres and mattresses fitted to the walls and they used them as punchbags. They did loads and loads of shadow-boxing, partly because they hardly had any equipment, but that's why their footwork was always very good. The Cubans were always good on their feet.

I thrived there. In the championships, in Havana, I was the only one to beat a Cuban and the papers there gave me some headlines. 'The English Mike Tyson,' they called me, because I jumped all over Roberto Guerra Rivera. I won on points and it went down like a lead balloon on the night. As I left the ring they were pointing angrily at me, doing slit-throat gestures. It was a cracking fight though, and they warmed to me as the tournament progressed. I'd already beaten the fighter from Georgia, then beat the American Keith Kemp, but in the semi-final I was defeated by Timur Mergadze, the Russian who went on to win it. The fight with the Cuban, who I'd beaten, was a lot tougher than the one against the Russian, who I thought I'd handled easily enough. Four of the five judges had me ahead on total punches landed but I somehow lost 14–10. One of the journalists who covered it wrote: 'The truth of the matter is that but for the peculiar button-pressing antics of one of the five judges, the Sale West boxer would have been a clear winner.'

I was absolutely devastated because, having beaten the Cuban, then the American, I then thought if I'd beaten the Russian, and I felt I had, I was almost there. I thought I'd won the fight, Ian Irwin thought I'd won it. There was a kid from Venezuela, Richard Reina, in the other semi-final and he beat

Christian Meyer, a German switch-hitter who he'd stood on his head, yet Meyer got the decision. Subsequently, me and the Venezuelan got the bronze medals and the Russian got the gold with the German getting the silver. They actually got booed on the podium, while me and the Venezuelan were cheered and applauded – even though the Cubans had been smarting when I'd beaten their fighter, the fans went on and supported me. I felt for the lads who were booed because it wasn't their fault.

It was no surprise that Jürgen Brähmer won the gold at welterweight. I thought he was a special fighter and he went on to become the WBO light-heavyweight champion as a professional.

When I got back I disconsolately chucked the bronze medal in a drawer, shut it away and forgot all about it, I was that upset. It was only several years later, when I moved out of Mum and Dad's house, that I found it.

A few days later I went to Motherwell and boxed in an England–Scotland match, knocking out Kevin McIntyre – a future professional British champion – in one round and Paul and I decided I would enter the senior ABAs for the first time. I was eighteen. I fought Jamie Spence and a kid from Droylsden, Paul Sweeting, in our local area and I knocked both of them out. Then I ended up boxing a guy called Carl Wall from Liverpool in the North West finals; he had already won the ABAs a year or so earlier at light-welterweight, and we fought a really close fight at Everton Park. I'd heard that he was a bit chinny and it was probably the worst bit of information I could have had because I went out there like a headless chicken, wild and reckless, and when I went back to the corner at the end I thought I wasn't going to get the decision. It was on a knife-edge, and I scraped home 14–6 – he wasn't chinny at all.

In the quarter-finals I thought I'd be fighting London puncher David Walker, but he was defeated by a guy called John Gallagher, brother of fan-favourite British super-featherweight champion P.J. Gallagher. He was a bit of a scrapper and we had a good fight at the York Hall, Bethnal Green in London's East End, and then I boxed Wolverhampton's Gary Reid, stopping him in the third round of five two-minute sessions as it was back then. He went on to be a good pro.

I fractured my right wrist against Reid. I went to the doctor, had it X-rayed and we were in two minds about pulling out. It was just about bearable, although if I punched with any venom I would have really felt it. I believed that if I just played a bit with the right – used it sparingly as a feeling punch for my com-binations – and just loaded up on my left I might be all right. I didn't want to hand the ABA title to anyone on a plate or give them a bye in the final. Me and the other finalist, Michael Hall, an England international, were the number one and number two in the country, and it was down to us. I was practically one-handed and went left-hand crazy, double left hook, left hook to the body, left hook upstairs, left uppercut. By the end, I thought I'd won the fight quite comfortably. I had kept up a high work rate and boxed nicely, moving in and out, but when they announced the decision, 'The winner of the fight and the

ABA final, by the score of five points to four . . .' I thought, 'Fucking hell, he's got it, hasn't he?' No way did I think it was that close.

But I'd won it. I'd just got through. Winning the ABAs is the pinnacle for amateurs in England, if you take out the World Championships and the Olympics. The Olympics were still three years away and my heart was always set on being a professional world champion. It would have been nice if the dates had fallen right so I could have gone to what would have been the Sydney Games, and sometimes I wish I'd tried, but as a kid I had never dreamed of Olympic gold.

I had been proud representing my country and had travelled to Cuba, Russia and Bulgaria in the amateurs, but I really just wanted to follow my heroes in boxing, and that meant aspiring to be a professional like Nigel Benn and Durán. I hung up my amateur vest and headguard and decided, coming up to the age of eighteen, to turn professional. I'd known for ages boxing was the life for me, since I was a little brat at Hattersley High School telling my teachers I was going to become a world champion.

When the ABAs were on I'd done a hell of a lot of work in Billy Graham's Phoenix gym. It wasn't a plush place by any means; it was a proper fighting gym, which I liked – but I was more interested by who was in there than what it looked like. I was awestruck. And I ended up sparring with quality pros such as Peter Judson, Paul Burke and Ensley Bingham, and I was later the main sparring partner for Andy Holligan as he prepared to fight Shea Neary in a huge fight in Liverpool. It was a good old-fashioned spit-and-sawdust gym, with blood on the ring canvas and where you could hear the leather of gloves colliding with Billy's bodybelt almost non-stop. I instantly warmed to Billy and vice versa, and when I made up my mind to go pro there was no doubt who I was going to go with. At Billy's I was training alongside Carl Thompson, Maurice Core, Bingham, Steve Foster. I was amazed being around quality fighters like that, guys who I'd seen and knew off TV and who were featured in *Boxing News* while I was getting noticed in the amateur section. Sparring with champions at British, Commonwealth and world level stood me in good stead. My opponents were experienced amateurs at the time and I was a comparative rookie, but the sparring made up for some of that.

The Phoenix Camp was not too big, or posh. The boxers would come in one after the other, overlapping for a laugh and a joke. The atmosphere there was priceless. Billy had boxed as a professional welterweight and middleweight between 1974 and 1976. He lost just two of fourteen fights before turning to training and learning under Manchester icon Phil Martin.

I'd been with Paul Dunne from when I was thirteen so when I went to Billy you'd think I would have had to get used to a new trainer because they have different methods and different ways – it's sometimes like starting from scratch – but it wasn't the case with us because me and Billy had the same thoughts and ideas. With Paul at Sale West, I used to do some work on the bodybelt, a fifteen-kilogram leather body protector that the trainer puts on over his head and is strapped on behind him. After I'd been at the Phoenix a few weeks, Billy asked me to go on the pads with him while he wore the body-belt. There were more similarities than just the bodybelt in the ways Billy and Paul trained fighters, but that piece of equipment would become our trademark.

That was one of the things that made my mind up about who would train me. I went to several gyms and learned a lot from each of them, particularly from Brian Hughes and Pat Barrett at the Collyhurst and Moston club, but I just felt Billy was a little more suited to me because I was a body puncher. Of course, I'd been known for my body shots from the amateurs, and Paul Dunne, being an old professional and very old school, had taught me the professional way – how to bob, weave and punch – and a lot of my success in the amateurs came from practically knocking everyone out with body punches in the first round. When I went to Billy and he got the bodybelt out, that was Billy's area of expertise, and it added on to everything I was already doing.

As an amateur, I had a decent left hook to the body. That was my honey punch. But the more I worked with Billy the left hook to the body improved. Then there was the right hook to the body and we worked on changing the angles of my attacks.

As I went up through the ranks, my reputation as a body puncher grew and grew, and you could see my opponents were trying to do their homework on me. 'That Ricky Hatton, he likes that left hand to the body, to change the angles and slip to the side, to come in behind the elbow.' As time went on, me and Billy would have to work on a lot of different ways of getting the body shots in. 'Listen, people have got your number with this body punching,' he said. 'Add a few sneaky moves in, like going to the head first. Touch them upstairs, then change the angle. Jab, knock the head back, then change the angle again. Touch him to the left-hand side so he readies himself for it, then sweep round to the right.' Body punching is a real skill. Your arms are only so big, nowhere near as big as your body, so they can only protect so much of it. What we did, while Billy fine-tuned me on the bodybelt, was to work on both sides, aim at the solar plexus and then pivot round to land punches on the floating rib. There's a lot more to it than people think, but it's a fine art, and the bodybelt was our canvas.

It was fine-tuning and tweaking from where Paul had set the wheels in motion. It was like my apprenticeship with Paul was done and I'd found an equivalent in Billy.

Billy spent a lot of time with me from the beginning. 'You're not the biggest puncher in the world, but you throw your punches with every ounce of your body,' he would tell me. He explained that because of my frame and my stature some weight-training would benefit me, and I started lifting some weights in a small room upstairs above the boxing gym; heavy weights but not many sets or repetitions. He would work on me punching from my legs, turning my shoulder into my shots, moving forwards, shifting my body weight and slipping to the side. By punching with leverage, and with the added strength, it was suited to what I was doing.

In the gym I thought Billy was very clever. He had a reputation as being a bit of a conditioner, as all of his fighters were always very fit, but I thought people did him down saying that. Technically he was very good. Equally as important, I liked him straight away. He was a character, had a good sense of humour, was very knowledgeable about boxing and we kept talking about old fighters. He would ask me who my favourite fighter was and I'd always say Durán. We thought the same way, talked the same way, and when I was about eighteen he asked what I was like socially. I told him I liked to go for a pint and he went, 'Fuck me, I've got one of these on my hands.' But we chuckled about it and just clicked. We could communicate without talking, no matter what the situation was – and it was like that in the ring. That's how it was, all the way through my career.

I suppose I had first started going out socially when I was about seventeen, although I might have sneaked into the cellar of the New Inn at about sixteen and had a cheeky drink here and there. I remember a couple of days after school we would quietly nip down there and have a couple of bottles. It doesn't make it right, but it seemed like the normal thing to do. I wasn't out every weekend, far from it – it was a bottle here and there. I started going out more regularly at seventeen. There was one club in Hyde that I would go into and I stuck to that. I wasn't pubbing and clubbing, a man about town going here, there and everywhere, I wasn't like that. There were a few pubs I could get served in and I just went to them. I didn't venture much further afield then because boxing came first.

However, professional boxing is a business and the money

side of things still needed to be taken care of. As a ticket-seller who had boxed for England, won about seventy of seventy-five fights, had won the ABAs and was turning professional as the number one in my weight class in the country, I had earned an audience with the country's biggest promoters, Barry Hearn, Frank Maloney and Frank Warren – three very different individuals. I always liked Barry. We got on well and, even though I did not sign with him, he would always invite me to the darts, to Fish 'O' Mania and other shows that Matchroom Sport did; there were no hard feelings. Maloney was the most bubbly of the three, more of a character; I also got on well with him. He was up my street in that we could have a joke and a bit of banter. We've always been able to have a giggle.

Frank Warren was the biggest promoter around at the time and it was the biggest decision of my life. Warren was very smooth; there was a bit of an aura around him and a lot of sense in what he said and the way he explained things to me. He was promoting Naseem Hamed, and Carl Thompson (who Billy also trained). He'd got big contests for many of his fighters with top Americans, including matching Winky Wright with Ensley Bingham, another of my stablemates, and it seemed the right move. Frank was the main promoter, and because Billy had so many fighters in the same stable it was a no-brainer.

There were detractors, of course. Frank was with Sky Sports, who were growing into boxing, and people said, 'Well, you won't get the same audience. You need to go with terrestrial TV,' or, 'You're not going to be in as many living rooms and you won't do this and that . . .' There were some who said Sky wouldn't be in boxing five minutes and that seems ironic, now. My fanbase came from Sky so that's put that all to bed. What happened in my career would go on to tell every other British fighter who was considering signing to be on Sky not to listen to arguments about terrestrial TV – look what happened with me. From day one I was solely on Sky; Joe Calzaghe, Naseem Hamed, Chris Eubank and Nigel Benn had all been on Sky but they'd all had exposure on terrestrial TV first. Sky are now the biggest broadcasters in British boxing, and I'd like to think I had a part to play in that for them.

At the time Frank had everyone. He was flying high, the leading promoter in Britain by a country mile, and Naz was getting ready to make his debut in America. I thought it was the best move all round when I signed for Frank. It was May 1997, at the Midland Hotel in Manchester, on the eve of one of his big shows at the MEN Arena; Naz was going to fight Billy Hardy, Robin Reid fought Henry Wharton and Steve Foster, another gym-mate, boxed Winky Wright. I put pen to paper with my dad and Billy next to me; my dad and myself were new to the pro game so Billy would advise us a lot of the time in those early days. That was fine by me. We were all very close and Frank gave me free tickets for the Naz–Hardy fight. I had blond, spiky hair, and I've seen footage of the fight and I was ringside with these ridiculous six-foot spikes, done up to the nines, wearing the most horrific green shirt you've ever seen in your life. At the time I thought it was cool as fuck.

I'd signed my contract, was ringside at a packed MEN, and I remember thinking, 'I want to be here, one day.'

But you never believe it. You never think you will do what your heroes have done.

CHAPTER 3

Turning Pro

'There's been a discrepancy with your medical,' said a voice at the other end of the phone.

According to the British Boxing Board of Control, I would not be allowed to make my debut on a bill topped by Naseem Hamed defending his world titles against Juan Gerardo Cabrera at the Wembley Arena. Worse still, I thought my career was over before it could begin. The Board of Control said they needed to do further tests on my heart and until they did those they would not let me box. I was devastated – I had just been about to jump in my car and head down to the weigh-in; now, aged eighteen and before even throwing a punch as a professional, it wasn't certain I would ever fight again. I thought it was over and I couldn't believe it.

We made an immediate appointment to see a specialist. I was told it was a heart murmur that might have developed because I'd done so much sport from a young age, as I'd been kick-boxing from seven and boxing from ten. The doctors said it was something small that must have happened over the years and it would in no way hinder my career. So, after this short delay, I made my debut on 11 September 1997 at the Kingsway Leisure Centre in Widnes on a bill topped by Robin Reid, defending his WBC super-middleweight world title against tough Frenchman Hacine Cherifi. I was scheduled to fight in what is called a floating contest, meaning that if any of the main fights ended in an early knockout, I would go out and fill the time before a more significant bout. It turned out there were no such gaps in the show and, although I was gloved up and ready by 8 p.m., I did not fight until midnight.

Even then there was a delay. After retaining his title over twelve hard rounds, Robin collapsed with heat exhaustion in the dressing room, where the paramedics rushed to his aid. He was fine, but we had to wait for the medics to get back to ringside before me and my opponent from Doncaster, Colin 'Kid' McAuley, could start fighting – for a good fifteen minutes. McAuley, who had won eight of about sixty fights, sat on his stool while I shadow-boxed in my corner. As if you're not nervous enough on your professional debut anyway, I was just hanging about in the ring, trying to keep warm, thinking, 'Please just let's get the bell rung.' It was the last fight of the night so only a few friends and regulars from the New Inn stayed behind to see me. Oh, and the fellas sweeping up.

I knocked out 'Kid' McAuley with a body shot in the first round. He went down into his corner and Nobby Nobbs, his trainer, seemed to be counting with him so he would know when to stand back up. But he didn't, he tried to recover but threw up into his spit bucket. Sickening body shots became my calling card of sorts.

British boxing was buzzing as Naseem Hamed prepared for his big American debut in New York. He was matched with the brash local Kevin Kelley in a December mega-event at Madison Square Garden, and Frank Warren put me on the undercard. Billy couldn't come as he was working Ensley Bingham's corner in a British title fight against Nicky Thurbin on the same night, so I went on my own. Over there, I palled up with the British heavyweight contender Danny Williams; we got on really well, but I was shocked at how nervous Danny was for his fight. He'd had about ten bouts but suffered unbelievably with nerves. On the morning of the fight, I sat there chowing down eggs, bacon, sausage and beans – while Danny pushed a bit of porridge around the bowl saying, 'Urgh, I can't eat anything.' I was eighteen years old, big Danny was eighteen stone, and he said, 'Oh, Rick, I can't eat this. I can't do it.' I couldn't understand how a heavyweight as big and talented as him was so nervous before a fight. 'Don't worry, Dan, you'll be okay,' I said. 'Just get on with it, you'll be fine.' He put on a wicked performance; he was a hell of a fighter. He achieved so much, but considering his early promise, and even though he went on to beat Mike Tyson, I don't think he fulfilled his potential.

That said, things couldn't have been much worse for me out there. Without Billy I was more anxious myself; at the weigh-in I was about ten stone and half a pound, while my opponent, a Brooklyn welterweight called Robert Alvarez, weighed around ten stone seven. So they sent me around the corner to eat a few doughnuts and have something to drink, while Alvarez went running around New York to lose some weight. By the time I came back I was about ten-one and by the time he came back he was about ten-five and the commission said we could fight each other. He was naturally a lot bigger than me and he'd had four fights and won a couple. He was covered in tattoos and he dwarfed me; he had more hair on his chest than I had on my basin haircut and I was as white as you could imagine. You can guess how I felt: 'Oh Billy, where are you?!'

It didn't get any easier when I was being introduced by Hall of Fame ring announcer Michael Buffer at Madison Square Garden in front of a heavyweight legend, and former heavyweight champion of the world, George Foreman; only a few months earlier I'd been boxing as an amateur at the Salford Working Men's Club. It was the first time Michael introduced me to the fans; it wasn't the 'Let's get ready to rumble' introduction he did for the main event, and back then I was known as Richard Hatton, not Ricky Hatton. However, I won a unanimous points decision over four rounds and had Alvarez bleeding from the nose and mouth. Foreman, who was working for US TV giants HBO, said I looked a good prospect and that people should keep an eye on me.

I was sat at ringside after my fight to watch Naz in his thriller with Kelley; there was eighteen-year-old me, and there was Robert De Niro, Al Pacino, Jack Nicholson and any number of top celebrities. I was almost looking at them more than I was the fight, I was just in awe of the whole occasion. The last time I'd been in America, just a few years earlier with my mum, dad and Matthew, I had been in awe of Mickey Mouse and Goofy at Disney World in Florida. Now, just a month after my eighteenth birthday, I had one of the best seats in the house to watch what was a real war between Naz and Kelley, as they exchanged knockdowns before Hamed stopped the New Yorker.

It was a much more memorable night than my eighteenth birthday party, that's for sure, although I only had myself to blame for that. In typical Ricky Hatton fashion, that hadn't lasted very long.

We still lived in the New Inn at the time and my mum and dad held a bash for me in the pub. People on the estate could see me doing well, and when they put on that party for me it was packed to the rafters. I think I was very well thought of on the estate, and I felt that all of the customers were fond of me – and I enjoyed being around them. That night, we had a disco, a singer and a buffet. It was a happy time but, as you can imagine, two pints of lager at that age knocked me on my arse. I'm afraid to say I was in bed for half ten.

Less than a month after boxing at the famed Madison Square Garden I was out on a bill at the Whitchurch Leisure Centre in Bristol. People see the bright lights of Las Vegas and the big fights later on, and think, 'Hasn't he had it good, him?' I hadn't had it good. It's tough. It's not all caviar and skittles. I had to work from the bottom up and that is one of my best attributes, I always loved a challenge. Whether it was boxing at a small hall or in a big venue, I loved the challenge of the fight and nothing ever fazed me, and it's the best preparation you can have if you can say one day you've fought in New York, the next you've been in Bristol, then you're at Everton Park, the Liverpool Olympia or in Germany. That's part of the education.

And this was how it was going to be for me for a couple of years, at least. I would get tantalizing glimpses of the boxing career I wanted to have – that I believed I would have – when I saw the main-event fighters on the bill and the hype around them and the adulation they received. I knew the sport well enough to know that to get there I had to climb every rung of the ladder. I would have to work my way up, fight after fight. Life would be split between the gym and fights every month or so. It was a relentless schedule with no partying, as I stayed in shape, waiting on calls to appear on any bill possible. I needed to test myself every time in a different way, each time reaching that little bit further up the ladder, each time getting closer to my goal. I can look back at it now and see the progress I made, how each bout brought me a fresh challenge, but at the time it was a proper slog. It looks like a steady progression but at the time it felt like anything but. It was important though, I was learning the ropes.

At the Whitchurch Leisure Centre, I was picking Hull's David Thompson off with good shots and pretty much catching him at will, and by the time the last punch came he just thought it was better off being over. He'd been down four times before it was stopped in round one.

I took my seat next to Billy in time to watch Glenn Catley

beat Neville Brown in the main event that night in a battle that was good for me to watch. In my first three fights I'd had things my own way, and as Catley and Brown eyed each other up Billy tapped me and said, 'Notice how they hold, nudge each other, how they put the shoulder in and so on. That's how they do it.' Glenn gave Neville a right roughing up. 'Don't think it's always going to be easy,' Billy said. 'This is how brutal it's going to get.' My eyes just lit up, I'd always liked rough fights: 'Lovely.'

But I was also experiencing boxing on many levels and Billy even had me working in the corner with him for some of his other boxers because he said I was learning the game so well and had an old head on young shoulders. I was in the corner as a youngster for a lot of the fights of Ensley Bingham, Carl Thompson and Peter Judson. I got used to being around big fights, tough fights, wars. I was in the corner for the great Thompson–Eubank fights. I was boxing, sparring, training with good fighters, so when the time came for me, I was well pre-pared.

A couple of months later, I fought at Telford Ice Rink, down the bill against Plymouth's Paul Salmon. Richie Wood-hall beat Thulani 'Sugarboy' Malinga for the WBC super-middleweight title.

As I said earlier, I'd been sparring with Andy Holligan ahead of his huge domestic grudge match with Shea Neary, and I'd even injured his ribs so I was more than ready for my op-ponent, who was a novice if you compared him to the guys I was training with in Billy's gym. I caught Salmon twice in 107 seconds, flooring him both times, to win in the first; a left hook to the head downed him the first time, a right to the body finished him and he never boxed again, retiring with four wins against thirteen losses.

Next I went in with Karl Taylor at Manchester's NYNEX Arena, as it was then, as part of a huge bill headlined by the cruiserweight war between Chris Eubank and Carl Thompson. Naz also featured, as did Herbie Hide. Myself and two other rising Mancunians, Anthony Farnell and Michael Gomez, were on the show, and there was a lot of attention on the three of us. Taylor was not expected to give me a test but he was meant to give me rounds; generally he knew how to survive and mess you around and could look after himself well enough. He'd only won a dozen of fifty or so fights but he wasn't often stopped. Our fight lasted only 105 seconds – my body shots won it.

I was back at the Whitchurch Leisure Centre a month later, defeating one of Nobby Nobbs's boys, Mark Ramsey. He was okay, but I floored him twice, once in round two and again in the third, and won our six-rounder comfortably. In Mark's corner, Nobby was funny. Boxing has many great characters like him and, against both Karl Taylor and Mark Ramsey, if one of his fighters had me in a corner and swung at me, or just missed, Nobby would shout, 'Oooo, stop it ref, he's got him.' There's no harm in trying.

I was in Sheffield next, on a bill topped by the Thompson–Eubank rematch, and I banked another six rounds, this time against London's Anthony Campbell. He didn't have a great record but he could fight, and two bouts later he upset future world-title-challenger Phillip Ndou in three rounds.

I had been a pro for a year and had won seven fights. I'd received a signing-on fee from Frank Warren when we did our deal and I was on £3,000 per fight. Twenty-one grand a year, plus a signing-on fee; for an eighteen-year-old previously getting about £200 a week carpet-fitting, badly, I was having the time of my life. I'd ask the lads on the estate, 'Hey, mate, are you coming out? I've got some money.' I've never been arrogant but I have shared what I've had: 'Here's fifty for you, fifty for you, let's go out.' Before I knew it I'd done all my money and my tax bills were coming in. I had the same shitty red Metro for three years because I blew all my money, I couldn't even buy a new car. At the gym in Salford I used to have to park up the hill and take one of my mates with me to the gym to push it and bump-start it.

At one stage, when I was three grand overdrawn, my dad said it was the hardest career in the world and I was going to have nothing to show for it. He said, 'This can't continue,' so we set up a company, Punch Promotions, and I would be paid a regular wage from that, with my dad organizing it for me.

I was kept busy, though, and that's what good prospects need. Just a couple of months after defeating Campbell I was out in Germany, boxing Pascal Montulet. Just shy of my twentieth birthday, it was my eighth fight. I dropped Montulet with a left to his stomach and he took a standing count as I turned the screws, honing in on his stomach. He was not a bad fighter but I caught him with a big right uppercut and when he bounced off the ropes I stepped to the side and nailed him with a body shot. It almost lifted him off his feet. Although he bravely rose, the fight was waved off, and quite right, too. It was around that time that more people had started talking about me; I wasn't just steamrolling people, I was doing it in a certain manner, and with moves that were impressing observers.

That trip was more memorable for what happened outside the ring than inside it. Me and Billy didn't have a pot to piss in at the time, we used to ask Frank for a few quid first to see us through before we got anywhere. In the build-up to the fight at the hotel, I'd have a cup of tea and Billy would have a pint; we'd sign for the bill, and they'd stash the receipts on the top shelf behind the counter. We just had to settle up when we checked out. After the fight, we went back to our hotel where there was a nightclub in the basement. We started signing for cocktails, and the bits of paper were piling up on the top shelf. The next day, we got up early and asked to be put through to Frank's room. 'Sorry, he has checked out,' they said.

We asked for some of the other Sports Network staff. 'No, they have all checked out now.'

'Oh right. Can you give me a rundown of my bill, please?' Mine was about four hundred and fifty quid and Billy's was about a hundred more.

'What have you got on you?' Billy asked.

'About seventy quid. What have you got on you?'

'About two hundred quid.'

'Fucking hell,' we said together.

We had to pay the bill. We weren't checking out until the

following morning and we needed to think of something. We went downstairs, had another pint as we contemplated our next move, signed for it, and Billy said he would get his missus to phone the hotel room at four in the morning, get us up and we would sneak out of the hotel and go straight to the airport. We'd be all right. 'Okay, Bill, no problem,' I said. We went out all day and all night, signing for everything as we went along, with more and more receipts piling up on the top shelf.

'We can't pay that so we might as well go for gold,' I laughed. We were spending money like Donald Trump. We were back in the nightclub that night, signed more receipts, went back to the room at about 3 a.m., where we proceeded to raid the minibar. It got to 4 a.m. when we got the phone call to say it was time and we went downstairs in the lift. The lift door opened and Billy poked his head out and the fella at reception peered up. 'He's looking straight at me,' Billy whispered, trying not to laugh out loud. But when the man went into one of the rooms behind the reception I yelled, 'Billy, go. Go, Billy.'

We came running out with our cases flying behind us, sending a standing ashtray crashing in the foyer, and dived into a waiting taxi. 'Airport, airport!' we shouted, and the driver set off. Then, all of a sudden, the driver went round the block and started taking us back to the hotel. 'What's up? What's up?' we shrieked. 'You said go round the block?' he said. 'No, no, no. We said the fucking airport.' He got us to the airport, finally. I never boxed in Germany again.

I won for the ninth time as a pro in October 1998 in Atlantic City, New Jersey, by getting rid of Kevin Carter in a round on the Naseem Hamed–Wayne McCullough bill, and my future friend, Mexican legend Marco Antonio Barrera, boxed on the same show, stopping Englishman Richie Wenton with a body shot in three rounds. Me and Billy went out that night, all night, and it must have been about ten in the morning when we staggered into the hotel and saw Frank Warren as he was going to breakfast. I yelled, 'Frank! All right?' He looked over, saw this twenty-year-old leaning everywhere, and he must have thought, 'Jesus, look at him and Billy holding each other up. That's meant to be my future champion.'

The celebrations continued as 1998 neared a conclusion, and the Boxing Writers' Club announced me as their Young Boxer of the Year. It was a prestigious award and near enough everyone who had earned it had gone on to win world titles. Although I was in distinguished company alongside the likes of Randolph Turpin, Terry Downes, John Conteh, Barry McGuigan, Frank Bruno, Nigel Benn and Naz, and it was nice to get the award, I didn't really realize what it meant until I got back to the hotel in London that night and saw the roll call of champions. It hit home that it was some achievement.

I had, however, a nightmare before Christmas and it came against Paul Denton on 16 December at the Everton Park Sports Centre. Farnell and Gomez were also on the bill again. I was expected to beat Paul handily and although he had lost more than he'd won, he was better than his record suggested. By the time I boxed him, Scotland's former world lightweight champion and Sky Sports commentator Jim Watt was calling me the most exciting prospect in the country. We had a scrappy fight, bumping heads regularly, and in the second round the skin around my left eye split open. It was a good learning contest, as it was the first time I was cut badly.

Billy worked on the cut between rounds but Denton had long arms and would pull and push to try to stop me smothering him with my attacks to the body. When I did throw punches he kept his hands high and his elbows tucked in to guard his body. 'Don't worry, keep calm. You've been cut,' Billy said. 'There's nothing you can do about it. Just get on with it. Stick to your boxing and don't let it affect you and that's the only thing you can do, really. The more you worry about it, the more it will affect your performance and you're more likely to get hit on it again.' Billy was very good.

Our heads kept thudding together and, although I had Denton in a bit of bother at the start of the third round, the fight carried on as it had done to that point, with me looking to attack and him looking to spoil, hold and cover, hoping the cut would cause the referee, Keith Garner, to stop it. By the sixth I just wanted him gone. I steamed out of my corner and floored him with a left hook, the first punch of the round. He went down and could not recover his feet in time.

It was another loss for Paul but he was one of those journeymen who was actually very good – it depended on which version showed up. At the weigh-in we were both a little over ten stone so he was in good shape, whereas if you fought Paul at short notice when he was at eleven stone and not in the best condition, he was not the same. That night he was awkward, he could hit and I had been too eager to impress. His record might have been 'win some, lose some' but he could be a tough task and I wanted to do a better job than other fighters who had boxed him before. We'd had a really tough fight, and, while the decision was not in doubt, my nerves were jangled because of the cut.

There was only a small pocket of fans watching me but they were making their voices heard; back then my fans probably could have filled a couple of minibuses, but after that stoppage you could hear them singing, 'There's only one Ricky Hatton', and, as I celebrated in the ring with Billy, they chanted, 'Hitman, give us a wave.' It was really just my mates who went to watch me. Whether they were from the New Inn, Hattersley or around the area, the night would consist of them coming to watch me, me winning and then all of us going out on the piss. People from the Hattersley estate, or Hyde, in the area were saying, 'There's some young kid here called Richard Hatton. Oh, we'll watch him. Let's keep an eye on him.' It was going to be a hell of a ride for all of us, my mates, my family, the area, my fans and for me; if you'd said to us back then that in a few years' time there would thousands upon thousands going over to Vegas, or that I'd be boxing at Manchester City in front of 58,000 fans, we all would have thought you were crazy. But it was the same mates who went to Widnes, to Bristol, to Everton and who went to Vegas; the number just snowballed after each fight.

My performance against Denton on Sky had not been as impressive as I'd wanted it to be. I was rarely up to the high standards I set myself but I'd managed to catch Paul unawares with that left hook. At the time, I thought it was useful that I'd learned how to put being cut to the back of my mind and focus on winning the fight and getting on with it. When I was stitched up – it took five stitches – some of the Vaseline was not removed. It was not until many fights, and several war wounds later, that we would discover that Vaseline was still inside the skin. Consequently, in the early part of my career I became well known for getting cut, always on the same eye; people thought I wasn't going to make it because cuts were always going to be a problem. I went to see a specialist in Harley Street in London; he cut it open and found a filthy mess inside. The Vaseline had hardened and, because it was near the surface, every time I got hit on it the cut would open up – it didn't even need to be a good punch.

Right after the Denton fight, though, me and Billy decided that we would need a cutsman to help, so he could concentrate on what he needed to do in the corner. You only get a minute in between rounds and he wanted to give all of his attention on the advice and strategy – you don't want to worry about cuts on top of that in just sixty seconds. I learned from my mistakes in that fight – that I was too aggressive early on. I had to be more careful because there were no longer any headguards to protect that part of my face, unlike in the amateurs. Over time, instead of locking heads, I learned how to put my head on my opponent's shoulder rather than by his head when in close; if I shifted my body weight to throw a left hook, I would make sure my hands covered the side of my head. They were little things that I picked up with experience because, when you are as aggressive as I was as an amateur and you take that head-guard off for the professionals, you can't be as free as I was with my head.

The cut healed well enough on the surface, and I was chomping at the bit to get back out and fight by the time I fought my first unbeaten opponent, Tommy Peacock, at a sold-out Oldham Sports Centre eight or nine weeks after Denton. Tommy had won nine of ten fights and had drawn the other. The Central Area crown was vacant but after my eleventh win I had a belt around my waist. I had sparred with Tommy in the amateurs when he was an England Senior representative and I was boxing for Young England. And there was one squad, at Crystal Palace, where we had trained and sparred together. You wouldn't have thought then that a few years on we would fight each other.

Gomez and Farnell scored quick wins and I joined them, stopping Tommy in two rounds. Tommy was a nice kid and had a great record, but with the manner in which I won it people started to think, 'Maybe he has a chance of doing something here.' Ian Darke, who was commentating for Sky Sports, said of me, 'I think this one has the chance of going right to the very top.' I had knocked Tommy down with a left hook and when I backed him onto the ropes and finished him with a body punch, again changing angles by stepping around, it was that kind of thing I was becoming known for. I went to the left, bang, hit him with a body shot. Then I came round hit him to the right and hit him with a right to the body, then a right uppercut, left hook, then I'd change the angle again and he didn't have a clue where I was or where I was coming from.

That's what Billy did with me, he made sure I hit the target, moved to the side, hit it again, went up to the head and changed the angle again. Not many kids at the age of twenty could do that. I don't mind admitting that it looked impressive when I fired off body shots, stepped around, threw uppercuts, moved back around and worked the angles. The boxing fans liked it because it's not the sort of thing they saw every day; one writer even said I was 'showing the footwork of a young Roberto Durán'. More people were saying: 'He's got the sort of talent that could go all the way.'

I could feel myself improving with every fight. I'd seen Naseem Hamed in Madison Square Garden, I'd been on some big bills and it was becoming an obsession for me. 'This is what I want,' I'd think. It was just like when I was a kid, I loved to go to the gym every day and train.

The pressure should have been mounting as I progressed; perhaps I should have been more nervous before each contest, but I wasn't. A lot of fighters struggle with pre-fight fear but I found coping with nerves before a fight got better over time, although I never suffered from them badly in the first place. Even if I was a touch jittery, I was always very good at disguising it; I always wore the same expression so people probably couldn't tell if I was nervous, felt fear or whatever. I was never short of self-belief; confident, not arrogant with it, but I had belief in myself. In years gone by, when they said, 'Oh, Ricky, he's not bad but I don't think he's going to be a world champion. He cuts too easily, he's too aggressive, he's quite an exciting fighter but he probably won't do much', I'd think, 'You what?' That was a driving force for me, my motivation. Even when there was no one out there who believed in me, apart from Billy, I always had massive self-belief. We just thought people had to be seeing something different, that nobody could see what we saw.

I boxed at the Royal Albert Hall in London about six weeks after beating Peacock. Marco Antonio Barrera was on the show, looking every inch a future legend by defeating Paul Lloyd in a round – I admired him enormously. I stopped Brian Coleman, of Birmingham – also with a shot to the body in two rounds. Afterwards, I worked Ensley's corner as he topped the bill with a second win over Nicky Thurbin.

It was time to step up once more and I was matched with a left-hander, Dillon Carew, for the vacant WBO Inter-Continental light-welterweight title in Halifax on a show that saw me share top billing for the first time with the two other up-and-comers from Manchester, Anthony Farnell and Michael Gomez. Me, 'Arnie' and Gomez were all coming up at the same time and we were all mates. There was a nice rivalry between us because you had these three rising kids from Manchester and people were asking who was the best out of the three and almost everyone had different answers. 'Who's going to get to the top first?' was a frequently asked question. We weren't bothered, but that is what the public and fans were asking. We're still friends to this day, too, and 'Arnie' Farnell is now a quality trainer who brings his fighters to my gym to work with my boxers while Michael's career burned brightly and I still see him at shows once in a while.

Anyway, Carew came in as a replacement for Mexico's Rodolfo Gomez and he was a better fighter. He was Guyanese but based in New York and a natural at the weight, whereas Gomez, a former super-featherweight, was smaller. Carew had gone twelve rounds on two occasions, too, but I'd never been beyond six rounds. It would be my first international belt so it would bring me into a slightly different level. In the build-up, *Boxing News* optimistically called me 'the new Roberto Durán'.

After five rounds, referee Roy Francis stopped my opponent on his feet. He had been on the deck once and bled from the nose, although he'd given it a good go. It didn't make anyone's hair stand on end, it wasn't one of my best nights, just a steady, workmanlike performance against a tricky southpaw, and the victory got me another title.

I was 13–0 with ten early wins going into a fight with Mexican David Ojeda in Doncaster, but at short notice I ended up facing Mark Ramsey once again instead, and I didn't look good. In fact, I got booed for the first time, as I failed to meet the growing expectations around me.

Despite their different names, Ramsey was Paul Denton's brother. 'I don't know what it is with these Ramsey brothers but they must have heads like rocks,' I told the press. 'People expect me to look a million dollars every time,' I continued. 'You can't. He was switching a lot and caught me with a few punches.' It was a bit of a nightmare, really. I was due to fight Ojeda, who had a decent record but we didn't know much about him. Me and Billy decided not to take the chance at such an early stage so another opponent was drafted in with about a day's notice, and in some ways I struggled to get motivated for it. Trainer Nobby Nobbs was the go-to man in British boxing, if you needed an opponent at twenty-four hours' notice then you called Nobby. He provided opponents to save shows up and down the country when someone pulled out or couldn't make it for whatever reason, as he always had a fighter willing to step in. So I arrived at the venue in Doncaster and I saw Nobby sat at the back of the room with Paul Denton and I went to Billy, as I looked round for Mark Ramsey, who I couldn't see any sign of, and I said, 'Where's fucking Ramsey, I'm fighting him, aren't I?' Then I said to Billy, 'Billy, Paul Denton is sat there with Nobby. Hang on, wasn't Denton called Ramsey once? Am I fighting him? Or am I fighting Mark Ramsey?'

'I'll go and have a look for Ramsey,' Billy said.

He couldn't see him anywhere. So Billy went straight to Nobby and said, 'We're fighting Mark Ramsey, aren't we? I can't see him anywhere. Is he here? We've seen Paul Denton. Which one are we fighting?'

'Billy,' said Nobby. 'I don't have a clue. I have a red phone and a blue phone at home and the blue phone rang.'

So it wasn't long before the fight and I was thinking, 'Who am I fighting here?'

I got into the ring, and it was Mark Ramsey. I got cut from a clash of heads and I never got going. The crowd started booing and it wound me up. Actually I was furious. All I wanted to do was please the fans, and I was trying to build my reputation so there's nothing worse than stinking the place out. In my forty-eight-fight career I think that was probably my worst performance. I was sick with it. I hadn't been properly motivated, didn't know who I was fighting, then I got cut. Mark was a southpaw, a switcher and someone who could fiddle his way through fights, and, although I won clearly enough, it was the first and only time I got booed and I deserved it. I had been built up to be exciting every fight and I bet the people of Doncaster thought, 'What the hell have they been watching, to say that?'

It was that bad. But it's part of the game. You get fights that don't happen. You get fights at short notice or your opponent changes and you still have to go in there and do the job, and that night I didn't live up to the hype. You love to get the pats on the back when you perform well, but you have to be man enough to take the knocks when you're shit. And that's one night I can honestly say I deserved to take them.

The cut kept me out almost three months. When I returned I was back on the top of the bill with Farnell again, defending our WBO Inter-Continental titles. I always had a good following but at the time I think Gomez and Farnell, always good ticket-sellers, might have sold a few more tickets than me here and there, while I was starting to get a bit of a reputation for enjoying myself.

I was around twenty or twenty-one when me and Billy started socializing. When I was doing the four-or six-rounders, and sometimes I'd have up to seven fights a year, I was in the gym every day so there wasn't much time to get out. Then, when I got up to championship level, as Inter-Continental champion and further up, when I started doing twelve rounds and having about four fights a year, you spend days in training camps rather than every day in the gym.

As I got older, me and Billy got closer and closer; we didn't go out drinking from day one, but by the time I started fighting for titles we were bestest mates. I think a few of the fighters might have been jealous of the relationship me and Billy had, but we suddenly found there was more time to let our hair down. We weren't in the pub together every night but after a fight we would go out and celebrate. They were good times and Billy really got to know me. I can be a very stubborn person too, mind. I suppose I just love an argument and it takes me a time to admit if I'm wrong. If someone turns round and tells me I can't do something I will try to do it. Even when it comes to things like football and City games, I'll argue and argue. One thing with me, you'll always get an honest answer. If I'm wrong, I might not admit it at first, but eventually I can say, 'I got it wrong.' But I love being right.

It means I can be a hard person to work with and, if Billy had turned round and said not to go out, not to drink and just train every minute, it wouldn't have worked. Billy had to learn to deal with me – not just as a trainer but as a person. I recall him saying, 'I don't think you're a sergeant major-type, Ricky. If I told you not to go out for a pint you'd probably tell me to fuck off.'

'Yeah, I probably would.'

'All I will say to you,' Billy replied, 'is you can go out, have a drink and I will come out with you and you can put a bit of weight on. As long as twelve weeks before that fight you come to the gym, get your weight down, do everything right and don't touch a drop. You've got to do your weight, your road-work, your sparring and dedicate yourself to this. If I find you're misbehaving in that twelve-week period, I will know when you come in that gym because you will be blowing out of your arse. You will be overweight and the minute that happens you won't fight. I will pull you out of every fight. As long as you don't let me down, I won't have to do that.'

That became the way we worked. He'd phone me up on the Friday before we'd start our twelve weeks and say, 'Are you out tomorrow?' I'd say, 'Yeah, I'm out tomorrow. Saturday night.' He'd remind me, 'That's your last one, you know that, you little bastard? Gym, half twelve, Monday. That's it. Twelve weeks. On your diet, on your roadwork. Don't let me down.'

I never did. I wouldn't cut any corners, not one.

I had just turned twenty-one when I met London's Bernard Paul, a former Commonwealth champion who had won twenty-one fights, lost eight and drawn four, at the Bowlers Arena in Manchester. Before you fight for a major title you tend to meet former champions, who might be on the way down. Paul was a big puncher and I boxed a great fight against him. He would fly off his stool like a greyhound, a hundred miles an hour throwing dozens of shots, but I had a decent boxing brain that I was never really given credit for and I certainly wasn't at the time: 'Just tuck up. Catch the shots, slip them, cover up. Let the storm blow itself out. He's not going to keep this up for twelve rounds.'

In about round three I started to put my foot on the gas and began to hurt him with shots to the body and punches to the head. Round four, I began to find a few more openings and then – out of nowhere – he quit on his stool with a bad hand. I couldn't believe it and felt cheated out of finishing the fight off in style. 'You flew off your stool at a hundred miles an hour and now I'm about to have a go back that's it?' I felt like he'd been told to give it his all for four rounds and if he didn't get me he would be pulled out when I started to turn the tables! In that fourth round he was still lobbing punches like he was trying to decapitate me, when, all of a sudden, he had this bad hand. Mind you, I have a hard head and he hit it enough so maybe he did damage his hand.

The year ended better than the previous one had with another win at Everton, over former British champion Mark Winters. He was a decent boxer but he'd not had that many fights – winning thirteen of sixteen – and I beat him with body shots. Having stopped two former champions I felt it proved I was probably ready for a title shot, or I was getting close to one.

The first six months of 2000 sped by and I kept busy with stoppage wins over Leoncio Garces, from Mexico, Pedro Alonso Teran and Ambioris Figuero. Garces was beaten in three on the bill that was headlined by Mike Tyson, whose whirlwind visit of Britain ended with him destroying Julius Francis in two rounds in front of 20,000 fans at the MEN Arena in Manchester. Teran, also a Mexican, and Figuero, from the

Dominican Republic, were dispatched in four rounds on smaller shows in Liverpool and Warrington respectively.

For my twentieth fight I had my third contest in America, this time in Detroit, and I felt like I was on the cusp of big fights.

I had plenty on my mind, though. I had met a girl called Claire and we went out for a while. She was expecting our baby and I was only twenty-two. Everyone knew I wasn't myself but I didn't tell anyone what she and I knew, not even my mum and dad. I just thought we had to get Detroit out of the way and then I could get home and we could work out what we would do.

We got out there early and me, my dad, Billy and our cutsman Mick Williamson went to the famous Kronk Gym. It is well known that it was always hot in there, a real sweatbox, and it is where the great Emanuel Steward groomed so many champions over the years. It was boiling, a hundred and twenty degrees with the heaters firing and the walls sweating, and me, Billy and Mick were probably the only white people in there, maybe even in the neighbourhood. I put my gloves on, with Mick helping me, but by the time he'd finished the sweat was absolutely dripping out of him. 'Facking hell, I've got to get out of here,' he said, in his broad cockney accent.

It was absolutely sweltering so I took my shirt off to hit the bag and warm up. I always grunted when I punched and, looking dead young and pale, I think some of the fighters there were quietly taking the piss out of me. Then Billy and I got in the ring on the bodybelt and it was bang, bang, bang, bang, step round, bang, bang, bang, bang. It changed their perceptions because afterwards all of the other fighters came up to me, asking me my name and what my record was. It had gone from 'Who's this little, pale-faced white kid grunting like an idiot?' to all of a sudden thinking 'Fucking hell. That's not bad, is it?' That was quite pleasing.

But again it almost went horribly wrong thanks to that skin around my eyes. There was another bad cut, one of the worst I had, and as a consequence it was one of very few fights where I thought I'd blown it. I was fighting Gilbert Quiros, a big puncher from Costa Rica. His nickname was 'The Animal', and that was a bit of a giveaway about what I was dealing with. 'Not bad,' they said about him. 'How tall?' I asked. 'Oh, he's between five-seven and six foot,' they said. 'Well, that's almost fucking everyone at our weight, isn't it?' I replied. At the weigh-in, me and Billy had no idea who we were looking for, but after peering about a bit we got some sense out of someone who said this Quiros was a bit taller than me so we knew we were looking around for someone who might have been about five-nine. Lads were waiting to get weighed and I said to Billy, 'I think that's him.'

'Do you reckon?' Billy answered.

'I do. Bit big, isn't he?'

Billy was bullish, in his fashion. 'I'm going to fucking ask him.' He strode over. 'Who are you fighting?' The boxer looked unsure; who was this guy? He said he didn't know and wasn't sure. 'You're fighting Richard Hatton, aren't you?' The boxer tried to say he wasn't and started scrambling for an answer. Bill came back over: 'Yeah, I think it's him.' The next minute, they weighed the guy in and he was fighting someone else. We'd got it completely wrong.

It turned out Quiros was about six foot, a big right-hand puncher and the first shot he threw was straight on my eye. Bang. He cut me and not only was it sliced open but my eye closed. He won the first round by an absolute street. I was the Inter-Continental champion and when I went back to the corner the officials said, 'Ricky, because you're the champion we will give you one more round but we can't let you fight with that for much longer.' I couldn't see out of that eye, plonked myself on my stool and started to feel sorry for myself.

'It's over,' I thought. 'It's all over.' Billy, like every good coach, had other ideas and knew exactly what to say. 'Come on, you've fucking spewed it, you. Haven't you?' he shouted. 'All this talk? World champion? Fucking hell, I've seen another side to you tonight. You've fucking given in, haven't you?'

'No, no, I haven't,' I protested.

'World champion?' he went on. 'You're going fucking nowhere, son.'

'Pass me that fucking gumshield and I'll show you exactly where I'm fucking going.' With my eye closing and still bleeding, I came out, bombing away. I couldn't see a great deal but managed to catch Quiros with a body shot, caught him a couple more times and, although I couldn't really see where I was throwing punches, I knew my way around a boxing ring. I got him on the ropes, pulled his head slightly to the side and felt for his body. I thought, 'It's round about there, isn't it?' as I blindly searched out the perfect spot. I was like a surgeon who's performed the same operation many times but doing it without being able to fully see where to make the incision. I threw the punch into his side and Quiros went down like a tree. I knew the minute he hit the deck he wasn't getting up, and Billy jumped between the ropes and hugged me.

'Don't ever tell me that I'd quit, you fucker,' I snapped. I was still fuming over what he'd shouted, it had pumped me up so much.

'All right,' he said, wanting me to calm down; but he'd said what he had needed to at the time. It was all psychology; Billy was clever and he could read me like a book.

The cut kept me out of the ring for a little more than three months but when I returned, against decent Italian Giuseppe Lauri, at the York Hall in Bethnal Green in London's East End, I was not on my own. This time, my brother Matthew made his debut on the bill.

I had turned pro at eighteen and Matthew was carpet-fitting for my dad. He saw me going to the gym every day, chucking my bag in the boot, driving off and training and doing something that I loved. He was on his hands and knees doing the carpets every day and he couldn't stand it. He said, 'I'm going to turn pro. I'll give it a go.' That's what he said, and it's incredible what he went on to achieve given his outlook at the time.

I had another new supporter, too. Although Claire and I didn't stay together, she gave birth to our son, Campbell, who is the perfect boy and who I adore.

There was an added air of responsibility when I was defending my WBO Inter-Continental title and challenging for the WBA equivalent against Lauri. Man City played Spurs at White Hart Lane in North London that day and, although York Hall has been packed out on many occasions, it was bursting at the seams that night. 'Manchester, na na na,' they sang.

I was still learning in the ring against Lauri, and outside the ropes as well. It was one of the few times I failed the scales; for all of the times I have heard people say 'Ricky Hatton has trouble with his weight', I can count on two or three fingers the number of times I didn't make it. This was one of them. I just left it a little bit too late – well, I left it to the last minute, if I'm honest. I had to go for a run and have a hot bath, but by struggling a bit more than usual, I overcompensated with my eating. Whereas I would normally get in the ring at eleven stone or eleven-one, that night I got in the ring weighing about eleven-five. That might not sound like a significant amount – I'm not superstitious either – but I could feel it and definitely noticed the difference.

I couldn't get out of the blocks as quickly and my re-actions seemed that bit slower, but that's what you learn as you go through championship fights. You learn as you go on. In that condition and feeling that way, I had to learn when to go hard and when to take my foot off the gas. Consequently he caught me with a few more shots than I'd have liked but I still managed to get to the Italian in five rounds, and to beat another international champion like that was good form. I now knew that my best weight on fight night was eleven stone.

The night was tarnished when there was a bit of trouble after the bout. Of all the fights in my career over the years, and with the number of fans that were eventually following me, there was very rarely any kind of trouble. The crowds were growing. I had fought in the USA, in Germany and up and down the country, and I was on the cusp of a British title shot. People were now sitting up and taking notice, and I wasn't doing badly for a lad who never took an exam and left Hattersley High School without a qualification.

I'd be mortified if my son, Campbell, was the same though. How I am with him is how I am with the young fighters I train now. You can't always put an old head on young shoulders – eventually they will always do what they want – but when I'm in the gym, there's so much I can pass on but, as much as I'm aware of that, I can also share what I did wrong. I instruct young fighters to slip the shots, catch the shots on their gloves, not to lead with a body shot. Jab first, move their head in case the counter comes in – stuff that I didn't take much notice of when I was fighting. If any of my lads have a few weeks off and they come back in, I say 'Jump on the scales, let's see where you are', when I wouldn't go anywhere near them in between my fights. Then, if they say they haven't got a fight lined up and don't need to be on the weight, I say, 'I don't care, I don't want you too far above. I want three pounds off by next week.'

I'm like that with Campbell outside the ring. Campbell's done some football, some rugby, some cricket, but the boxing is what he's stuck with and I can really see myself in him. He will say, 'Dad, can we do the pads, can we do this or that,' and I reply, 'No, you must do your homework first.'

'Oh, but, Dad . . . I'll do my homework after.'

'No you won't. You'll do your homework first, then we'll do the pads.'

Homework? For me, I was always in detention for never doing any homework. I still see some of my old teachers once in a while today, whether it's at a City game or a local restaurant and they always remind me that I was no trouble but a right lazy bastard. I was only interested in boxing; I'd done so well as an amateur, winning several schoolboy titles, and when you're boxing at that level they don't announce you by your club, they announce you by your school. So I was Richard Hatton, from Hattersley High School, and my school was getting a mention in the local paper. The head teacher at Hattersley, Mr Leyland, was really into the boxing, and although he never watched my fights he used to put my certificates in the hall when I won the schoolboy championships. He would mention me in assembly if I'd won anything. I've since done some motivational speeches at local schools because my old school has since been knocked down.

I want Campbell to really knuckle down; his test and exam results at school have been improving all the time, the teachers are raving about him and it makes me feel dead proud. He's got other interests away from school but just in case he doesn't become a boxer or the next Noel Gallagher, he's not forgetting his schoolwork. Jobs are hard to come by these days so you need your education behind you. You don't want your children to make the same mistakes you did, and because I made so many mistakes it's easy for me to make sure he doesn't. Campbell is a great kid and well behaved, but what you do in school sets the tone for what you're going to do in the rest of your life.

CHAPTER 4

The Title Charge

There was a roar around Wembley Arena. A sense of anticipation that told me I was in deep trouble as the warm blood began to spill into my left eye. We were just ten seconds into the bout.

It's fair to say the battle with Jon Thaxton at the Wembley Arena made me the fighter I became. Jon had just clipped me with a little right hook and the next minute my eye was pouring with blood. I couldn't have got off to a worse start. I thought I was going to beat Jon, but stop him? Maybe not. Thaxton, who came from Norwich, was always in shape and as tough as nails, as hard as they come. This was supposed to be my big night, my coming-of-age night, and the looks on the faces of people at ringside suggested to me my big night wouldn't last much longer. The script was nearly torn up as badly as my left eye, which Thaxton had split with almost the first punch he threw. It was a massive cut, one that would later require plastic surgery, and we were only about fifteen seconds into a twelve-round fight – my first twelve-round fight at that.

When you get cut in the first round of a twelve-round title fight you think, 'Fucking hell.' I went back to the corner and said, 'How is it, Mick?'

'Have you been cut before?' he asked, knowing full well the answer and doing his bit of in-ring psychology.

'Yeah,' I said.

'You knew you were going to get cut again, so stop whinging about it and get on with the fighting. Concentrate on the fight.' Well, that told me.

I carried on, typically a bit reckless, and the blood was flowing. Mick was able to stop it for a while until it started again in about round seven. Mick was brilliant. An experienced referee would always be more understanding if you were badly cut but had him in the corner, because they knew all about what 'Mick the Rub' could do between rounds.

I was hitting Thaxton with some almighty shots, and the amount of punishment he took was horrendous. I'm convinced that every time he sat on his stool he was tempted to think, 'Bloody hell, I've had enough here.' Then he'd peer up, see my face covered in blood and it would give him a second wind. He'd think, 'That doesn't look too clever, does it? I'll give it another round.' I was watching him between rounds, thinking, 'Jon, will you just fuck off?'

He wasn't going anywhere, though. In some rounds, when the cut started to pour, I was worried but Mick was doing such a great job; it was only in the last three rounds that it really started opening again. Paul Thomas was the referee and I thought if he'd stopped it so late, with me well on top, it would have been harsh on me.

It was a good fight with Jon. A really good fight and an acid test for me; it taught me a lot about how far I could go. It ticked a lot of boxes, answering some of the many questions the critics always seemed to have: 'Has he got the heart for a tough fight?' they asked. 'Is he still going to have it when he goes in the trenches? Has he got the ability to show he can box a bit because he's knocking everyone out with body shots? Can he box, get out of trouble and come back if he needs to? Has he got the will?'

Before Thaxton, the most I had ever boxed was six rounds. Once I'd done six, I instantly asked myself, 'Can I do twelve?' Until I did it the first time I never knew for sure that I could last. Then, the minute I put my first twelve rounds in the bag, I knew it was there, that I could last the course. It gave me more confidence, as I was no longer stepping into the unknown. The training I did with Billy was always full-on, but until I actually got that first twelve rounds under my belt, I just didn't know for sure. And it's not as if people didn't ask the question of me. I would often hear, 'Oh he's past six rounds. Is his stamina going to be all right?' But I was like a train.

The Thaxton fight was a hundred miles an hour, fought at a searing pace, but I showed boxing ability, heart, how to tough it out and that I had a sound chin. Afterwards people weren't just saying I could go twelve rounds, they were talking about the engine I had because it was fought at such a terrific pace. If there was ever a sign that you've got what it takes to go all the way, then perhaps winning a contest like that said more than anyone ever could. People realized that if I carried on developing, I had all of the attributes to maybe get to a high level and achieve what past winners of the British title had. And although it was a very physical fight, there was a misconception that whenever I went into the ring there would be a war, and I reckon that is probably how people thought I sparred and what I prepared for. But it wasn't.

With Billy, training was always very physical but sparring was often tactical. It wasn't about having wars. A lot of people do touch sparring, and technique sparring, and I'm not a fan of that either. Don't get me wrong, I don't believe in real battles in the gym, just like Billy doesn't, but it's got to be realistic: you've got to learn to get cracked on the chin, you've got to learn to get hurt in the breadbasket and in the ribs, you've got to get your body hardened to what happens in the ring. But if you go to war day after day, and your body is taking a pounding in the gym, it's not going to benefit you in the fight. It's got to be realistic without putting miles on the clock; although there were times it could get out of hand.

There was a Belgian kid who I ended up knocking out in sparring. He came out in the first round and went for me – bang, bang, bang, bang. I was covering up, thinking, 'Fucking hell, he's gonna fucking kill me here.' Talk about putting all your eggs in one basket. We had a right ding-dong of a spar for about three rounds. It was like Tommy Hearns against Marvin Hagler. Billy was shouting, 'Whoa, whoa!' and I thought I had to open up on the lad because of the punches he was throwing. I got him on the ropes, threw a right hand that hit him on the chin and knocked him out on the floor. I felt sorry for him after but he was a good spar.

There was another time when emotions ran high. I was sparring with Matthew; we didn't just play football and do almost everything together, we also sparred with each other – he had a very good, tidy defence. We never had many arguments but I remember one. We were sparring as professionals – when I was a champion and Matthew was an up-and-coming professional – and when I got him on the ropes he turned his back on me. I said, 'What are you doing?' and Billy said, 'What's going on here?'

'He's turning his back, Bill,' I replied. Matthew said, 'No, no I'm not.'

I shot back: 'You're turning your back, you dickhead.' We had a row in the middle of the spar. 'You can't turn your back, you've got to face me.' He kept doing it so I hit him and I said, 'Do that one more time and I'll hit you in the kidneys.'

He did it again, so I hit him in the kidneys. He tore his gloves off and chased me around the gym trying to knock me out – Billy ended up having to pull us apart. We still sparred over the years; it was just one of those things that day. In a hard environment like that, when you have a fight coming up (as we often both did back then), it can get heated and charged.

Generally speaking, Billy and I would do twelve rounds of work in the gym every day, so we were getting the rounds in, but sometimes all we'd do is eight rounds of sparring in a session for a title fight. We'd just make up the twelve rounds by doing four on the bodybelt, or if it had been six rounds of sparring, then six on the bodybelt. I always got twelve rounds out. If my spars had been a bit physical, more frantic than Billy would have liked, he'd give me the next day off sparring and we'd work on the bodybelt and the pads so we still did the twelve.

Canada's Tony Pep had visited Britain before and beaten a few of our lads as the Commonwealth champion. He had not lost since he had boxed a talented American called Floyd Mayweather Jr (Mayweather had outpointed him over ten rounds in Atlantic City three years earlier), winning three times and drawing once. We met at the Wembley Conference Centre in London for the vacant WBU light-welterweight title – a tip-of-the-iceberg belt on the world scene, but it was a significant step up for me from most of the lads I'd fought.

Pep was a lanky operator who knew his way around the ring. I was a rookie, had won my twenty-two previous fights, felt unstoppable, and with thirty seconds left in round four I had a new title to my name.

We'd fought for the vacant belt because the previous champion, West Ham's Jason Rowland, had to relinquish the title. Rowland, a battle-hardened thirty-two-year-old, ten years older than me, bred Staffordshire bull terriers and when two of his dogs were having a scrap, he tried to break them up and ended up losing the top of one of his fingers. They couldn't save it and the time he spent out of the ring caused him to lose his title – he vacated it so I could fight Tony Pep. There was one condition:

Jason had to be my first defence, and 5,000 fans packed into the Velodrome in Manchester for this big domestic fight.

I never had any bad blood with Jason. He was a really nice guy, a former WBU champion and he won the title on the same bill when I fought Thaxton. Jason's fight with Thaxton was stopped on cuts, but pretty much from the start I was on top against him, hurting Jason early, and it was exciting. I was using my left hooks and body shots, and he was counted out as he tried to get up from the second knockdown in round four.

It doesn't matter what title you win – whether it's a WBU title, an Inter-Continental title or a major world title – there is always a little bit inside you that feels that you haven't won it properly until you beat the fella who held it initially; by beating Jason I felt like it was my property now.

By the time I faced the man they called the 'Macho Midget', John Bailey, the crowds had begun to swell and there must have been 6,000 or 7,000 fans in the MEN Arena. He came over from West Virginia and was as tough as they come, not really a big name but he was an American, so there was a chance it could help break me into the market in the USA on a small scale.

I knocked him down four times with a variety of shots, a left to the body, a right to the body, a head shot and so on. That was really the start of the MEN adventure for me and after that you could see with each fight, in my hometown in the same venue, the crowds growing from 7,000 to 10,000, then 12,000, then 14,000 and before you knew it the place was sold out.

Just six weeks later I was back there. I'm not going to lie, veteran American Freddie Pendleton had seen better days when we met in the ring (he'd turned pro in 1982 but had fought some big guns, like Félix Trinidad and Vince Phillips) but – having said that – I was the novice coming up, so it was still a dangerous assignment. One thing you don't lose is your punch; another thing a fighter knows after being around the block is how to look after themselves. They can quieten a crowd by staying safe, working for the last thirty seconds of each round, just trying to nick it on the scorecards, and they can capitalize on the slightest mistakes younger, inexperienced fighters need to make in the ring in order to learn from them. Boxers like Pendleton have seen every inch of the canvas, and so to get to him as quickly as I did, and find his body and start hurting him, showed real progress. If you're the wrong side of the age barrier, which he was, you don't get found out in two rounds. For me to find the right shots that early and do the damage I did against someone so experienced meant it was a big, big fight for me. I was looking for the body, looking, looking and looking. When the chance came I threw and the shot nearly missed but it actually sickened him. It did some real damage because he rolled over about three times and made it look theatrical. Non-boxing fans might have gone, 'Hey, what's all that about?' But if you know your boxing, you'd have gone, 'Ouch. That's going to hurt.' Freddie never fought again.

It was not the fact I had defeated him, because he was beatable to me, so much as the manner in which I did it. You might get to an ageing fighter around the sixth, seventh, eighth or ninth, but not in two rounds. Even if he had seen better days, at the age of thirty-eight, you'd think he'd know enough to get through those early sessions.

The Pendleton fight was my first on ShoBox, a programme on the American network Showtime that showed fighters coming up. I started to get introduced to the fans in the USA. The higher you go up in levels, the more noticed you get – and the more advanced warning your opponents get. It's not like you're fighting a six-rounder, when you find out who you're fighting the week before; you get in there and just have to get on with it, deal with who you're facing; when you get to championship level you have plenty of weeks in advance to study your opponent. That meant fighters could study me, too; see I worked the body, that I had a good left downstairs, and that I liked to change angles. I'm sure they were doing their homework on me. The thing was – I was still able to get my punches in.

I had started to get a fanbase outside my hometown, too, and it was no longer just a case of flogging tickets to my mates. I was venturing further afield and it didn't matter if you were from Manchester, Birmingham, London or wherever, people were saying, 'I want to go and see this Ricky Hatton. The body puncher. He's exciting.' I always made a point of spending time with fans and even then, as British and WBU champion, I was doing sportsmen's dinners, talking about my career and doing a stand-up comedy routine. It is something you normally do when you retire, when you talk about your achievements, so I was really the only active fighter doing it while I was still boxing. I remember, later on at one of the smaller venues, some people saying, 'What are you doing coming here, you? You're a world champion. You're obviously well paid for fighting.' But I just liked going out, meeting the fans and talking about my career; I think it stood me in good stead with the public functions I took part in later on.

I enjoyed it and I was often joined on the road by Paul Speak. At Billy's old gym, when I was an amateur, Paul, a local police officer, would watch the pros at work. He'd been stabbed during the Toxteth riots and was always popping in, as Salford was his patch. One day, when I was in the World Juniors in Cuba, he asked where I was and was apparently impressed when he was told I was in Cuba. When I came back, we started talking more regularly and became friends. He's been at almost every fight of mine since; after he retired from the police, he started working for me as my agent. He's been in the camp a long time and had to put up with all sorts from me. We've been together in one way or another for more than fifteen years.

He never got involved with the boxing, but there's certain people you need to have around you and he became one for me. On fight week you need to go here, be there, you've got to have a press conference, pick this and that up and Speaky has been the one who has taken the weight off my shoulders when anything needed doing, and we've got closer and closer over the years. He is probably not well liked in some quarters, only because on the week of the fight if I needed to concentrate I would send him instead of doing it myself, so he's the one that cops for it, whatever I do. If I'm training, sparring, running and something came up or I had to ring someone I didn't always have the time to do it. So Paul did and he was seen as the bad guy, which he wasn't; he's become a very close friend and there's nothing he wouldn't do for me. He's one of life's nice guys, and he's not often seen in that light but he always will be in my eyes.

Generally I tried my after-dinner and stand-up material and jokes on my mates, but I had learned a lot of them from people in the pub when I was younger. I used to walk back from school at about half past three and all the regulars would be in the pub; I'd have a game of darts or a game of pool with them – in the pubs you meet so many characters who were always telling stories and jokes, and I often think that's where I got my sense of humour. There are quite a few jokes that have stayed with me, and a few that are boxing related, too. I've always been a Mike Tyson fan, and later – after we'd boxed on the same bill in Manchester – he would call me to congratulate me on some of my biggest wins. And I'd say to the crowd during my after-dinners, 'Imagine coming home to find Tyson, the Baddest Man on the Planet, in bed with your missus. You'd fucking tuck him in, wouldn't you? Then you'd apologize as you quietly left the room.'

I was never embarrassed. I loved the hecklers and I always had a few comebacks at the ready, because I have been on the receiving end. 'If I wanted to listen to an arsehole, I'd fart,' I'd reply. Or, 'There you go, keep shouting so a doorman can see where you're sat.'

One night, a woman was giving me grief from the back of

the venue and so I tried to get her to make a fool of herself. 'There are some really sexy ladies in here tonight,' I said.

Sure enough, she bellowed, 'Wahay.'

'Not you, love,' I said dryly.

The crowd erupted and I didn't hear from her again.

One day, me and Paul were driving to a show where I was going to do my after-dinner speaking and, before we got to the venue, I said, 'Here, Paul, just pull in to this pub so I can have a pee.' So I popped in. Paul was in the car and waited patiently. A couple of minutes turned to five. Perhaps he thought I needed something a bit more serious than a pee and five minutes turned to ten. When ten turned into twenty minutes and then thirty, Paul became concerned and came in after me.

There I was, at the bar, not drinking but cracking jokes and talking about my fights with two dozen locals. That has happened a couple of times over the years, and, while other people might have come and gone, Paul's been brilliant for me – he's given me stability and helped me in every way he can.

When I fought Australia's Justin Rowsell, *Boxing News* thought it was the first time the Wembley Conference Centre had been full for boxing since Lloyd Honeyghan had fought there about ten years earlier. Rowsell was a good amateur and an okay fighter; some said he should have got his opportunity at a title sooner than he actually did. And although they didn't say it at the time, when he did get it he was probably slightly past his best. Maybe I'm doing myself a disservice by saying that, because he was experienced and he was good, but I found him from the opening bell, just like I did Pendleton. A left hook knocked Rowsell out of the ring near the end of the first and my performance was again exciting. I was switching angles and mixing up my attack. I stopped him early in the second round after putting him down again.

What started happening around that time was, whenever I put an opponent up against the ropes, I could hear the crowd take a sharp intake of breath, producing a quiet roar. It's akin to Lionel Messi getting the ball for Barcelona and how it was at Maine Road all those years ago when I was on the terraces and Georgi Kinkladze picked up the ball and went on one of his mazy runs. There was an air of anticipation. 'Ohhhh,' the crowd'd say. The minute I started slipping and my opponents' backs would touch the ropes, the fans buzzed as they waited for me to work the body. I was firing in these rib-benders and getting so much leverage into each shot, and that's something I noticed growing more and more each fight. It was as if people were saying, 'Wait until he gets this fucker on the ropes.' It was my calling card, almost like coining a catchphrase.

I'd stopped five consecutive opponents since the Thaxton bloodbath and I could hear people whispering that they wanted me to face sterner opposition, and tough Russian Mikhail Krivolapov was a live opponent. He was highly ranked in the world ratings and particularly by the WBC. You will always get critics in whatever sport you take part in as you get successful – it's just the way it is. Some had said Pep was a blown-up light-weight, that Pendleton was over the hill . . . they could always say something, but that didn't happen this time. Krivolapov was a world-class fighter, young in age and with the same ambition as me, so you couldn't fault him.

He was very good and caused me a fair few problems. I hit him and hurt him pretty much from the start, but he was game, sucked it up and fought through it. A couple of times I caught him cleanly and he would come firing back. Sometimes I would hit someone and I could tell how much the shot had taken out of them. If I'd caught them in the head, I knew when they would be foggy and how unclear they would be. When I caught them downstairs I could tell how long it might be before they got their breath back. With Krivolapov, he was digging deep and trying to fight back the whole way through, giving everything he had. He was a good, skilful fighter; not a murderous puncher but when I stopped him in nine rounds in my first fight of 2002 he was number four or five with the WBC.

On that same bill, Matthew outpointed Paul Denton – the man who had cut me early in my career – in a six-rounder to win his tenth fight.

Now I was ranked by several of the world's governing bodies, but in February 2002 the best light-welterweight in the world, Australia's Kostya Tszyu, said he had no interest in fighting me. When you're number one in the division you're not thinking about people who are a year or two away from fighting you, the young guns coming up – you look higher up the food chain. He was looking towards bigger fights and paydays, unification contests – he probably had no desire to fight the eighth- or ninth-ranked fighter. It was not a fear factor; Tszyu had no reason to fear me. That is just boxing and how it's structured; it was still a proving ground for me, even though I thought I was ready for Tszyu back then and was chomping at the bit to get at him.

There were still things I needed to experience and go through before I was ready for the very best, and a valuable lesson was taught to me by Irishman Eamonn Magee. I can safely say I didn't like him one bit and it was the first time I experienced 'banter' and mind games in my career, as he tried to get under my skin and wind me up. I'm not scared to admit I fell for it hook, line and sinker. I'd seen him fight Shea Neary – his best win – and it was nip and tuck. He'd also stunk the place out once or twice since, and watching the tapes, I thought, 'Who is this cocky shit? I don't see anything to be fucking scared of here.' To me he was very slow, sometimes his work rate was not very good and he didn't exactly make you sit on the edge of your seat. But he was full of it: 'You're just a kid!' he shouted. 'I'm going to take you to school. You've not fought a man like me. I've had tougher sparring partners than you,' and it was the way he said it, the way he talked, in that real nasty, spiteful way.

But he was a very dangerous fighter, as I would find out.

I believed I was going to destroy him and in the first round I legged it off my stool at a noisy, vibrant MEN to do just that. He was a southpaw, very sharp, could hit hard and was a counterpuncher. My style was made for him in many ways, with me charging forwards like I did. He'd feint, I'd lead and he would counterpunch. I made the worst start possible. He put me over with a right hand in the first round and it was the first time I had been put down in my career. It wasn't a bad knockdown, I had been caught square with my feet together, but I should have known better and I was more embarrassed than anything else.

Then he started talking to me in the ring. That was another first. 'Did you like that? Did you? Nice shot, wasn't it? Come on, Ricky.' It infuriated me even more and, as we started round two, I thought, 'Come on, fucking do it again.' I was raging and dared him to try it – and sure enough I fell into the same trap. Instead of it being the wake-up call – 'Hey up, slow down here, Rick. You got a little bit giddy, you jumped off your stool too quickly, just take your time and don't get caught again' – I went even faster. I played into his hands and then: bang. He cracked me with one in the second round, a short hook, and that one did shake me. My legs went and I had to smother him and survive the moment.

I sulked back to my corner where Billy greeted me, saying, 'You're blowing it. What are you doing? You're just swinging at everything and he's waiting for you on the ropes. What are you doing? You're not just going to get beat here, you're going to fucking get knocked out unless you change your thinking. Don't go in on straight lines, go in off the sides, use angles, feint. Let him lead first. You're doing all of the leading and he's doing all of the countering. Go in, feint and when he leads, catch him with a few shots.'

That's what I did and, for someone who was known as a slugger, I became a boxer. By the end I was beating Magee at

Top The first of many animals I'd go on to fight in my career. I think this was taken during one of our family holidays to Blackpool. We had a lot of happy times there and I loved it at the Pleasure Beach.

Middle After watching *Rocky IV*, I copied those blond spikes of Ivan Drago. This was my first schoolboy fight at the Assembly Rooms in Derby, Class A. I would have been thirteen, weighed 42kgs and was boxing Dale Youth's Michael Beary.

Bottom Matthew followed me to the gym and into the pro ranks, becoming a European champion and fighting for a world title. This was taken on the steps of the Mottram & Hattersley ABC when we were about to box on the same bill.

Top I won the ABAs at eighteen. This was against Darlington ABC's Michael Hall, who had won it the previous year. I was going to pull out of the final because I thought I'd fractured my wrist in an earlier fight.

Middle On the way to the ABA finals, boxing through the East Lancashire and Cheshire Division against Jamie Spence. You can see from this bloodbath that I enjoyed a good fight back then. Nothing changed.

Bottom Flanked by Ensley Bingham and Carl Thompson, gym mates at the Phoenix Camp, when the Salford gym closed and we trained out of the Mottram & Hattersley ABC. Bingham was still fighting, Carl was world champion and I was in awe of training alongside fighters like them.

Right Training with Billy near his gym in Salford. This is one of the first pictures taken of us together, right at the start of our journey.

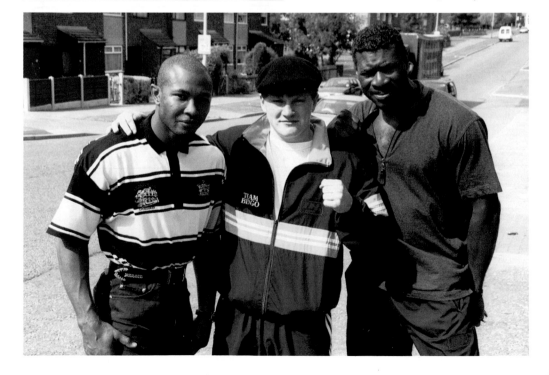

Top I was always known as a body puncher, but Billy fine-tuned it during many sessions at the Betta Bodies gym in Denton, Manchester.

Middle Me and Jon Thaxton knocked ten bells out of each other, but it was the fight that made people sit up and think maybe I could go further in the sport.

Bottom A nice, normal cup of tea round Bernard Manning's house. I had this picture done for my games room. Later, on the after-dinner circuit, we were billed as Manchester Legends. I knew him as a close family friend who raised millions for charity.

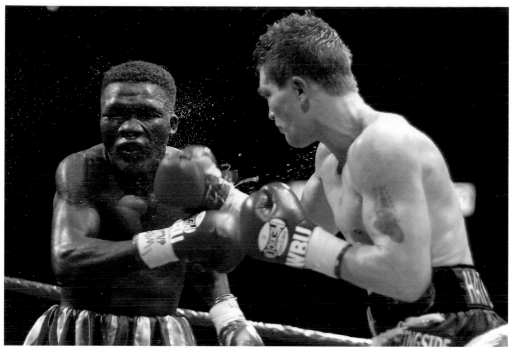

Ben Tackie was the toughest guy I boxed. He wasn't the
best, but he was so durable and my punches just bounced off
him. He took shots like this one and nothing happened.

Eamonn Magee gave me the best learning fight of my career. He knocked me on my
arse and I had to compose myself after a period where I'd been flattening everyone.
He also taught me some invaluable lessons outside the ring, and became an unlikely ally.

Top I remember this like yesterday: me, Kostya Tszyu and promoter Frank Warren. You can see the confidence in me, even though I was finally stood there with the great man.

Middle We're swapping punches and although Tszyu was supposed to flatten me with his right, here's me holding my own and landing mine.

Bottom You hit me with three, Kostya, so here's one back. I catch Tszyu low in the ninth, but he'd nailed me downstairs before then.

I was shattered, trying to summon one last bit of energy before the
final round, when Billy said it was all over. We'd done it together.
We knew we would, but I'm sure no one believed us.

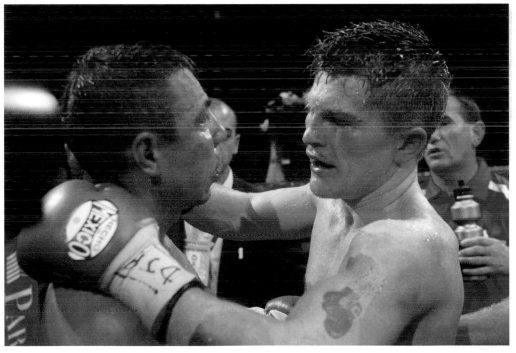

I think the fight will always be remembered for the respect we showed
before and after. We were both very complimentary to each other
when we took the microphone and addressed the crowd.

Left The Las Vegas logo, stitched onto the back of my gown. Las Vegas became my second home.

Below The fans make their presence felt in Las Vegas before the Castillo weigh-in. Little did we know that the crowds would get bigger and bigger. My fanbase was my proudest achievement.

Right Tom Jones and David Beckham watch me warm up in the changing rooms in Vegas, not bad for a kid off the council estate. Tom sang the national anthem for me twice, and I lost both times. Don't call me, Tom, I'll call you.

his own game. I would sit on the ropes or in a corner and I'd feint, he'd throw a big shot and I would pepper him with three or four shots, lean away and in the end I won by two or three rounds. There were no doubts about the verdict – it was a unanimous decision – but he taught me a valuable lesson: not to bite, not to believe my own hype, and that was the first time I'd had to put up with that sort of bullshit. It would stand me in good stead for some of my later fights. Imagine if the Floyd Mayweather fight was the first time I'd had to deal with something like that?

Someone else was running his mouth about me at the same time, too, and that was Sheffield's Junior Witter, my leading domestic rival. If I had fought him I would have come out and done the same thing as I'd done with Magee, been careless and charged out of my corner, so it was important to have learned that lesson. For a long period it never seemed as though Witter's name was far from mine; after the Thaxton fight we had it out during my ringside interview with Sky Sports. I think if Junior had a quiet moment now, and his team and his trainers, the Ingles – they don't have to admit it to me – but I think it was a move that they would all regret.

I'd just been in a Fight of the Year-type fight with Jon Thaxton, filled with blood and thunder – and there was still blood all over the place – and I was the victor, but even in defeat Jon was a winner, he'd given so much. It was that kind of fight. Then, all of a sudden, as I was being congratulated for winning the British title and sitting on the ring apron with a very generous and sporting Thaxton, Witter stuck his head in, acting like a dickhead. 'I'll take that belt off you, I'll destroy you.' It was one thing disrespecting me after doing twelve rounds and winning the Lonsdale Belt in a really hard fight when I was tired and knackered, but not only did I think they were disrespecting me but he was disrespecting his gym mate, Jon, and I was disappointed that his trainers had gone from Jon and on to supporting Junior in a finger-click. I know this is the hurt business – sometimes with business being the main word – but it was as if they were saying, 'Right, Jon, you've had your turn. Junior, get in here. Start winding him up.' I felt it was bad taste all round.

I said to Frank Warren, who promoted both of us, 'I'd love to fight that tosser,' and he said we would leave it for a while, he'd build us up as stars and we would fight for more money further down the line.

After the Thaxton fight, I went and boxed for the WBU title, had all of those defences and went to the MEN Arena and I was boxing in front of 10,000, 12,000, 14,000. Then I went to one of Matthew's fights and Junior was on the bill, boxing Alan Temple; I had another fight coming up in the MEN and Junior was fighting a six-rounder. But he just didn't have a following.

I did an interview in the ring after he fought Temple and he was saying how he'd beat me. 'How do you come to the conclusion you'd destroy me? Certainly not after that, mate,' I said. We then got in the ring to do some pictures and I started taking the piss out of Junior a bit, mocking him by back-pedalling, shuffling with my feet and switch-hitting, giving it all that – which was quite fun.

For me, Junior didn't have the greatest style in the world and he hardly seemed to sell any tickets. I reckon five Frank Warrens couldn't have promoted Junior Witter. How the hell can you build him? If it wasn't for me, I don't think you would have heard of him. That might be hypercritical when you think he won almost every title in boxing, WBC, European, Commonwealth and British, so he was no mug, but if it wasn't for me – even after a career he can be proud of, and I'm giving him credit there – I still don't think anyone would have heard of him. There was a period later on when we were world champions at the same time and we were on *BBC Sports Personality of the Year* together. There was a whole clutch of us who were world champions including, I think, Enzo Maccarinelli, David Haye, Joe Calzaghe and one or two others, and we would enter the studio from all four aisles of the venue. Junior said to me, before we came out from behind the screens, 'One day . . .'

'One day, what?' I said.

'You know.'

I thought, 'I've had enough of this dickhead, here.' It started getting boring. As far as I was concerned he wasn't fighting anyone, he had hardly beaten anyone of note. All he was doing was slagging me off repeatedly and I just felt I didn't want to fight him. I certainly didn't need to and I had contests against bigger names and better fighters than him. I didn't need to prove anything to him, myself or anyone else so it just sort of fizzled out, really.

I don't regret it not happening, either. I'd like to have fought him at the time but as I go into promoting now I realize it is all about timing. With our styles it would have been a tough fight. He switches from left- to right-handed, likes to counterpunch and it would have been very, very difficult, but with how it all panned out in the end there would have been no gain for me. It wasn't worth it. If the truth be known, when I got close to him in the ring I think I would have battered him. I believe with all my heart I would have destroyed him. But, it was all about timing. And Frank Warren was very good at that: timing it just right.

Now, bygones are bygones and I can't help but admire Junior for winning the titles he did, but he showed a lot of dis- respect. In the end, I just became sarcastic in my responses in anything to do with Junior Witter. I said, 'If he was fighting in my back garden, I'd draw the fucking curtains' – stuff like that.

It would have been massive, I know that. I'd like to think I was fighting some of the best contenders and earning my way up the rankings, but at the time if someone said, 'Oh, he's got the Ricky Hatton fight, what did he get that for?' you would have been at a loss to explain it. Fights can be made now if you kick off at a press conference or if there's bad blood, but that was never my philosophy. You had to earn your chances in my book. All of that time I wanted to fight him. I said to Frank Warren, 'Can't we put something in the contract so if I have the choice I can fight him?' I can't remember if we did or not, but I never fought Junior and I don't feel as though I missed out on anything.

CHAPTER 5

The WBU Reign

Darkie Smith lost the plot. He flew into the ring and pushed the referee, Mickey Vann, yelling, 'He fucking nutted him.' That was not exactly the case but Darkie was clearly upset about how his fighter, his son Stephen, was doing in there.

It was a chaotic night and one of the more shambolic episodes in British boxing history as it's not every day a trainer leaps into the ring and puts his hands on an official.

I thought I was on a bit of a hiding to nothing when I was booked to box Stephen Smith. He wasn't big enough, he was a decent fighter at lightweight, a nice southpaw but not a big puncher – so, apart from good boxing ability and being a left-hander, he was really made for me. The style I would have trouble with was always going to be someone with the fire-power to stop me in my tracks and keep me off. He'd only lost one of thirty-one fights but didn't have those attributes. I was hurting him early in the first round and I think he knew he couldn't hold me off. We threw right hands at the same time and mine landed first, and perfectly – just how you'd want it to.

It went right through the target and he went down, got up and looked over to his dad in the corner.

Let's say this about Stephen's expression: he wouldn't have made a good poker player. I could see he knew he was up against it and realized the job in front of him was a big one. He saw the first round out but I was on top again in the second, bulling him around. I got him on the ropes, the crowd moved forward on their seats, and I did something I had always done through my career. I threw a shot but after it missed, I stayed close to him on the inside. Even if I missed I would sometimes stay in there, because if you stay on their chest they can't get leverage into their punches – you don't leave yourself open and you have your chin behind your shoulder. Anyway, as I tried to stay close to him I came back with my elbow which hit him right in the eye and he started bleeding. It wasn't deliberate but the momentum carried me into him.

He got up and said, 'That was his fucking elbow' to the referee.

Then Darkie shot into the ring. 'Hey, referee, he fucking nutted him.' I knew what I had done, I had elbowed Stephen and it was an accident. But Darkie screamed, 'He's nutted him, he's nutted him.' As soon as someone enters the ring, let alone puts his hand on the official, he gets his fighter disqualified. Those are the rules in black and white. 'He doesn't even know what's gone on,' I thought. In my honest opinion, I thought he saw the opportunity to get his son out of there but maybe he really did think I had nutted his son and was so furious he jumped in. Whatever the reality, I know that's not the way Stevie would have liked the fight to have finished, but by getting the contest halted – deliberately or not – I think Darkie had saved his son from getting a longer beating.

I never saw Darkie again but I've seen Stephen once in a while, and one time I saw him in a gym and he wanted me to sign some gloves for his lad, who was apparently a big fan of mine. I'd come out on top against his dad but his son still wanted me to sign them. Stephen is a nice guy.

It was not a particularly satisfactory evening and probably one of the few nights where my fans didn't go home happy. Barely thirty seconds had passed in round two before Darkie flipped, but I'd done all I could do and the crowd at the MEN apparently understood that – it seemed I could do little wrong in their eyes.

I think another of the reasons I got the fanbase I did was because I boxed a lot of domestic fighters. British boxing fans have always enjoyed their big British title nights. Sure, I didn't fight Witter but I boxed Rowland, Thaxton, Magee and Stephen Smith and that helped, as those fighters had their own followings. It's not like some young boxers who have to fight a series of Mexican road-sweepers or Latvian liabilities.

By now me and Billy had started working with Kerry Kayes, who was overseeing my strength and conditioning. He paid close attention to what I was and wasn't eating and drinking in training camp. He was a former British bodybuilding champion and owned both the Betta Bodies gym in Denton and the CNP nutritional empire, and, after Billy's old gym

closed, and we'd spent some time at my old amateur club training for fights, we moved into a boxing gym that you could get
to by walking through the Betta Bodies.

Kerry immediately made a massive difference to me. Boxing
has come a long way in a short space of time; it was not long
ago that things were like they were in the *Rocky* movies, with
fighters chasing chickens around a coup and drinking raw eggs.
Those days are gone but for a long time boxing was slow to
embrace sports science; nowadays everyone has a strength
trainer or nutritionist because it's so important.

My fighting would be in close quarters; I was up close to
my opponent and there would be a lot of pushing, shoving,
mauling, stepping to the side and being explosive – with explosive movements – and I used every part of my body to
punch. If I threw a punch everything went behind it; if I threw
a left hook my shoulder went behind it, my head, my arse, my
hips . . . and that was down to Kerry, not just the nutrition and
making weight but the strength work and weight-training we
were doing. I used to lift very, very heavy weights. People used
to say: 'Do light weights with lots of repetitions', but I used to
do heavy weights and not too many reps so when I was punching correctly, and Billy showed me how to punch with leverage,
the weight went on the end of my punch. It was a lovely balance of adding power to my technique.

Kerry enjoyed a joke, too – it was that type of gym. He
likes to tell people how one day he put a wad of Vaseline in my
floppy hat. I constantly needed my wits about me, it was a nut-
house – you had to be more careful about what people would

do to you outside of the ring than inside it. Every time you turned your back you had to look over your shoulder. We were like a family in the gym back then, we all used to go on holiday to Tenerife with each other and we were incredibly close-knit. Any time one of us fought we were all in it together. That gym banter is one of the things pros miss when they are faced with retirement.

Despite the pranks, Kerry is a very intelligent person. Some strength and conditioning coaches and nutritionists try to take over in camp but what they have to realize is their role is second fiddle to the boxing. Some people think their job is more important than it actually is in boxing today, but the most important thing is the boxer, and everything Kerry did with me was on Billy's say-so. 'What you do in the boxing gym is the priority and I will work to support that,' Kerry said, and he'd ask Billy, 'What do you need from Ricky in the boxing gym?' Billy would tell him what he needed and Kerry would then tailor the weights around the boxing.

It doesn't matter how much you lift or bench press because it's all got to be geared around the boxing and that's why we all worked so well together. Kerry got my body and condition right for boxing – which is what we were all there to do. You wouldn't want to be put through the ringer with circuit train-ing and then arrive in the boxing gym and be unable to train properly. What would be the point if you're too fucked and can't hold your arms up as you've been doing too many weights?

I was a bit sceptical about Kerry's idea of nutrition at first, though. He knows I was, too, and I took some persuading. Traditionally, when you're making weight boxers don't want to drink water for some reason, and Kerry used to have me drinking masses and masses of water. He also used to say I had to eat five meals a day and I said, 'How the fuck is that going to work? How am I going to drop three stone eating five times a day?' I needed convincing because when you're making weight it's scary to hear someone say you have to put food in your mouth and drink loads of water. I had trained myself to think, 'Well, I can't eat that and I can't drink that.'

In that respect it took me a while to get my confidence in Kerry but, once I did, there was no turning back. He certainly made me a believer and it got to the stage where, after weeks with hardly sticking my head through the gym door, I would bowl into training on my first day back and ask Kerry to take a picture of me then and one near the end of camp so we could compare before and after shots.

Back then I had three wardrobes. I had clothes with a twenty-eight-inch waist for when I was in shape, thirty-one inches for when I was in training camp, about five or six weeks out and, when I was not training, there was the thirty-six-inch-waist stuff. What I was able to do to my body, and the condition I could get it in from where it was to what it became, was really impressive. Even though I had a real lack of willpower when I left the gym, when I went back and started that twelve-week training camp I had the discipline that would match or exceed any professional fighter. I am a master of it, armed with good nutritional advice and a willpower that you cannot match anywhere, in any sport. It was feast or famine. People used to see me in the ring – having lost all that weight – and almost shake their heads in disbelief thinking, 'How in fucking hell has he lost all that weight? How is he looking so good and how is he able to perform like that?' It was freaky stuff.

Two nights before training camp begins the phone rings. It's Billy. 'Don't forget, back in the gym on Monday.'

'Don't worry, Billy, I will be there. I'm out tonight, recovering tomorrow and then I'm in.' Billy and Kerry are waiting there wondering what they will see when I come through the door. They shake their heads the minute I wobble in. 'Oh Jesus, he's given us a mountain to climb here again,' they say and smile.

The first day back is always hard. 'Come on, Billy, are we doing some pads?' I ask. 'You're going nowhere near the fucking pads, you,' he replies. 'Get on the treadmill. Get on the stepper. Get working out on the bag and start shifting that fucking weight.' I call it the monastery – you can do a training camp in eight or nine weeks, but mine have to be twelve, so I can shed this extra weight. I follow every instruction Billy and Kerry give me, without fail: 'This is what time you get up. This is what time you eat. This is what time you go to the gym. This is what time you sleep. This is what time you run.'

I start off doing the same run, the back roads from Gee Cross where I live to Hattersley estate, near where I grew up – about three or four miles in all – but the minute I get near a hill I have to stop. The roads are quiet, so quiet that I can hear cars coming from some distance. Shit, a car's coming. The minute I hear that I start running again, hill or no hill. I'm not having anyone seeing me walking on a run. Sometimes when I stop and a car might catch me having a break the driver winds his window down and jokes, 'Come on, Ricky, get moving, you fat bastard' and I pick it up again. I trained at twelve or twelve thirty and did my roadwork in the evening. It worked well for me. I could have breakfast, fuel up for the day, train, have an evening meal, go for my run, have a snack and then go to bed.

Later, I might wish I could find a happy medium but here and now I take the supplements and vitamins given to me, eat what I am told and don't go near anything I should not. I live by every rule, I never cave. I never give in to temptation. Twelve weeks. No cracking. Not once. I can pride myself on that. I was a role model with my attitude and character, being down to earth, the perfect role model in that respect. But when you looked at me, I wasn't; I wasn't easy on the eye when I was so heavy and it was not good for kids to see.

Strangely I was quite proud of being called Ricky Fatton. I've never been a vain person and I don't get embarrassed, but it's probably the worst quality I could have. You should really care about your appearance and what you look like. My mentality has changed since then. Young kids seeing me in between fights and out of shape? It wasn't the best, was it? I wouldn't change too much about my life, but one of the things would be the attitude between fights. People would say I had a lack of dedication, but to do what I did and get my body from where it was to what it became on fight night, I think that showed the ultimate dedication. You have to have massive willpower and

I'm proud to say I did; I wish I'd found that middle ground, if I'm honest. For me it was a matter of, 'Oh, I've finished a fight. Time to go and enjoy myself . . .' If I'd just done everything in moderation it would have made my job a damn sight easier. It's not as if Billy, Kerry and Frank didn't tell me that – plenty of people did.

It was funny but even then I was turning round and saying to young pros, 'Don't be like me, you dickhead. Don't put all that weight on. It's the hardest game in the world. Don't make it even harder on yourself.' It was a great team effort, though, and being with Billy and Kerry Kayes was the best time of my career. I owe them both so much.

Joe Hutchinson, a southpaw from Indianapolis, came over in December 2002 and we shared the top of the bill with Joe Calzaghe at Newcastle's Telewest Arena. Hutchinson had gone the distance with Arturo Gatti – a terrific puncher based in Jersey City, New Jersey – in a really good fight, but I caught him with a body shot that practically took him off his feet. He was on his back, rolling over in pain and for someone who had gone the distance with Gatti it again told me that it was not just about who I was beating, but the way I was doing it. I was doing it more impressively than some of my rivals on the world stage and that was the main thing I could take from some of those fights.

In January we carried on something of a tradition, when the whole family would go on an annual cruise, all of us, my mum, my dad, my aunties and uncles. They had been three or four times before I got on board because the idea of a cruise had never really floated my boat; I had visions of older people with nothing to do idling around – but they were brilliant, one of the best holidays you could have. We used to go every January.

In the early days there must have been about eighteen of us in all, local landlords, friends from the pub, along with my family. It was brilliant, and even when the sea was choppy and the weather wasn't the best you always knew you would have a good laugh. A lot of people are put off by cruises, thinking they're just two weeks on a boat, but they were the best holidays. We'd go out shopping, sightseeing or whatever by day, get back on the boat at six o'clock where there would be entertainment, a comedian, a nightclub, a cinema, a casino, three or four bars – then you'd go to bed, get up in the morning and you'd be on a new island. You can't beat them.

On one cruise we went to New Orleans and me and Matthew went to the Mardi Gras with a few of our pals while some of the older people in our party stayed back on the boat. We went into the city and to all the bars; there was something going on in every bar, people passing weed around, women flopping their tits out, everyone having a good time and before we knew it several hours had passed. I looked at my watch and I thought, 'Jesus Christ, we're not going to make the boat.' We jumped in a taxi and the traffic was chock-a-block. We were about fifteen minutes away; the boat was due to leave in ten, so I phoned my dad, still pissed: 'Dad, Dad, Dad. Hold the ship. Hold it. We're on our way.'

When you're ready to pull out of a harbour everyone is on the top deck looking out ready to wave at those watching; and there we were, piling out of the taxi and legging it up the gang-plank – about six or seven of us – and we could just see my dad on the top deck shaking his head, thinking, 'Look at these dick-heads, here.'

A few incidents aside, it was so chilled out; and it was important for me to enjoy the downtime because I knew the fights would get harder and be tougher.

And they don't come much harder or tougher than Vince Phillips. A week before the quality and experienced American came over to fight me at my MEN fortress in April 2003, we weren't sure that he would be fighting. He had some child sup-port problems and Frank settled them so Vince could eventually leave America, but then he had issues with how much he was going to be paid. They kept it from me, it was none of my busi-ness, but Vince was going to walk out of the arena on the night of the fight and my agent, Paul Speak, ran after him and shouted, 'Vince, where are you going?' He was going back and forth with Frank, while Argentina's Aldo Rios was in the chang-ing rooms, warming up just in case.

It was a weird night behind the scenes at the MEN and Vince did eventually make it into the ring.

He was a good fighter, too – he might have been thirty-nine but he was still respected and clearly the best I had fought at the time. He was a former world champion, a big right-hand puncher and because I was so keen to sink in my left hand to the body I was often getting caught by rights over the top, so he was a dangerous opponent for me in particular. Even though he was getting on in years, he was still highly thought of in

America and not only was he the only guy to beat the reigning champion Kostya Tszyu, he had stopped him in ten rounds, having floored him in the seventh. Vince wasn't seen as a knock-over job and he was very well regarded.

The MEN was buzzing, the crowds were still growing.

I started well in the first round. I was having my successes, but he was getting through with his right, which I think scared Frank Warren and Billy Graham to death. His missile-like right hands were whizzing by my head as the fight wore on, with the odd one getting through. I thought I was hurting him but, in the third round, trouble came. He cut me open; Mick Williamson, who had his work cut out that night, would later say it was the worst cut he'd had to deal with in his career at that point – when you think of how many cuts he has treated in several decades in the sport that was some statement. It was a bad 'un. Somehow, Mick, as always, was able to stop the bleeding, but I think it was the first time in the corner I had been able to read signs of stress on his face. 'How is it, Mick?' I asked. 'Don't ask me that fucking question. Get on with it. It's been and gone.' He always seemed to say, 'Get on with it.'

In the fourth round, I was on the ropes and I leapt at Vince with a jab and he hit me with a right uppercut. It was the hardest I'd been hit in my career. I was trying to find the floor with my feet, but it felt like I was stepping through the canvas and falling. My legs had gone limp, but I was somehow still standing. I groggily tried again to find the floor as Vince followed up. He knew he'd hurt me and tried to apply the finishing touches. It was another crisis. I stayed close to him, smothering him, surviving the moment as you're told to do when you get hurt. If he landed one more shot I would have been in a whole lot more trouble, especially if it was that right hand. He couldn't though, and, as he tried to finish me, I think he shot his bolt. Somehow I turned the tables and was all over him and he couldn't find the distance to nail me cleanly. His success might have taken more out of him than it did me.

By the last thirty or forty seconds of the round I was giving it back to him and I guess that would have sickened Vince. He had been a good champion, he was a very experienced fighter and he'd hurt me, but he couldn't quite finish me and then all of a sudden this little shit was coming back at him. It was hard in there, for both of us. And as the fight wore on I was getting stronger, I was getting better, my work rate was increasing and I was finding him more with my punches. Near the end, poor Vince was hobbling about as if he was ice-skating. He never looked like being stopped, even when he ate some proper hay-makers, and he was able to hear the final bell. Despite having me in such trouble there weren't many rounds I actually lost, even though I'd had that crisis point in the fourth. The judges scored well in my favour of 120–108, 120–107 and 119–109.

That was the hardest I had ever been hit and I was 'gone', he just couldn't get that extra one in. It told me everything I needed to know about how tough fighters were going to be at that level – the shots I hit Vince with had knocked out lesser opponents. He was taking them, firing back and it was a real education, showing me exactly how hard the game was going to become.

My cut needed plastic surgery again. I had to have it reopened because I wasn't happy with the job they'd done stitching it and it would take some time to heal. Of course, it didn't get in the way of a good celebration. It all started in the New Inn one Sunday afternoon when I was the WBU champion and someone walked in, one of my friends, with possibly the worst shirt you could ever imagine seeing. Me and my pals have a certain sense of humour: 'Look at you, you scruffy bastard,' we said. 'Winner of the shit shirt competition – by a mile – is you.'

It grew from there. We decided that after every fight we would do a 'Shit Shirt' competition. We would have fifty quid for the first prize, twenty quid for the second, a tenner for the third and we'd get up on the stage and turn it into something of a catwalk. The shirts were vile. They were the most dreadful things you could find from car boot sales, second-hand shops and the markets. They were all colours, too big, too small. Some of them were absolutely horrendous, but the worse they were, the better the competition. It was mad because it grew and grew to the extent that the papers were covering it, not the results but they always knew where I was the day after the fight and the people started coming from all over, London and Birmingham, and they would go to the New Inn knowing I would go there and we'd all be wearing shit shirts for the competition. The car park would be full, the front of the pub was full, the main lounge was packed. There were cockneys, Scousers, Brummies and they'd shout, 'All right, Ricky, what do you think of my shit shirt?' It was just done for me and my pals at first but we started to make a day of it as it got so big, with people like Tommy Docherty and Bernard Manning performing stand-up gigs for us. It became a tradition and it went on for years.

Maybe doing that on your local council estate isn't how every sportsman would celebrate a world title win, but I liked it and people have never seen me as a 'head-up-my-own-arse-big-time-Charlie' character because of it.

Besides, I was still living at home with my mum and dad. One day, when Sky Sports were coming round to interview me at the family home, I was in my slippers and late getting up and they were due round any minute. I thought I'd just nip out and get some sweets before they came and Ed Robinson, one of their reporters, was pulling up as I was leaving in the car. 'Here you are, Ed,' I said, chucking him the keys to the house. 'Do you want anything from the shop?'

'No, I'm okay, thanks, Ricky,' he said.

'Okay. Let yourself in and pop the kettle on. I'll be back in a few minutes.'

I was the WBU champion and still living in the box room in my mum and dad's and it was mad, really. But I've always been a home bird and I was always so close to my mum and dad. People would say, 'Ricky is this down-to-earth lad. He is close to his family.' That's how it was. We were a really close family unit.

I was flying after Phillips and lo and behold, my next opponent was the Argentine Aldo Rios, who had been warming up backstage when I fought Phillips. His first journey wasn't in vain.

For a while I became extremely frustrated with the way things were going. Everyone saw Rios as a backward step while superfights with big names like Tszyu, Gatti and Floyd Mayweather were always being mentioned. I wanted those big nights. There was Rios, Dennis Holbaek Pedersen and Carlos Wilfredo Vilches in three of my next four fights, and I found my performances started regressing. I understood the purpose of the fights, WBU title bouts at the MEN Arena to build my fanbase, and the way my career was handled at the time was one of the reasons why the following was developing so quickly – the fans became used to seeing me on a regular basis. But I'd made about ten defences and I wanted to kick on, go to America and fight the very best, and my performances kept slipping.

Sometimes I was having four or five fights a year, which was perfect. When you go up in quality, you can't do that – partly because you need a rest after hard fights and in part because fights get harder to negotiate – and that was a problem, as I was always at my best when I was kept busy. If I spent too much time sat about I could go stale, but I was busy all of the time as the WBU champion, even if Rios was another hiding-to-nothing job, as he was another lightweight moving up. He was slippery, good defensively and hard to nail cleanly. He was just about clever enough to stick around, and I had started to tell myself I would have to settle for a points decision, but in the end, during the ninth, I got him with a body shot and they pulled him out when his corner retired him.

After the fight the party started almost straight away, and it would continue until twelve weeks before the next fight. Drinking, holidays – I'd be here, there and everywhere, apart from the gym.

I next fought a very seasoned Ghanaian, Ben Tackie. He was more along the lines of what I was after in an opponent. He was thirty and I was keen to show another side to my game. He had fought in America and had been in some hard fights, and, rather than add to that list, me and Billy decided we would try and outbox him. Going into it, I felt it would be the toughest fight of my career and my future was pinned on beating him. I'd seen tapes of Tackie and knew he had a great chin. Anyone who goes the distance with Kostya Tszyu in a main event in Las Vegas must do, and I hit him hard in the first two rounds and promptly surrendered to the fact that I might not knock him out. But, if you spend the entire twelve rounds trying to knock someone out, there is a chance they could get you in the end, whether you leave yourself open for a split second or you run out of steam.

Every time I hit him the shots just bounced off his head. Nothing affected him, even good solid punches. He just kept coming. I landed two good body shots and he gagged a bit, but basically I thought that if I stood there and opted to slug it out with him I would be giving him the only chance he really had.

So I saw it as an opportunity to go the distance, box him, use my jab, try a few new things, work on combinations, step to the side against a better calibre of opponent. As the fight went on I showed I could use my boxing brain by hitting him with a couple of shots, grabbing him, smothering him and restricting his work, frustrate him, move off, hit him with a few more combinations. I not only proved that I could stand there and have it out with him, punch with him, but at times that I could outbox him, jab and move and display my boxing ability.

Against someone like Tackie you can't just jab and move, though, because eventually he will get to you in twelve rounds. Twelve three-minute rounds of doing nothing but jabbing and moving is a long time, so I had to think in the fight and by round six and seven I wasn't sure I could keep up what I was doing with another six rounds left. So as he came in I would let the shots go – 'Bang, bang, bang' – and then I'd grab him. Now and again I would hit him with those shots and roll out to the side, then again some shots with a one-two at the end and I'd grab him so I could nick a breather here or there.

I showed more dimensions in that fight than I had done before. Tszyu and I both emphatically outscored him. No matter how much people want you to succeed, and although some people had started to say: 'He's our next best chance at a world title', you still get the critics, and they had been asking, 'Well, he's all right, but has he got any boxing ability?' I'd ticked those boxes against Tackie, now demonstrating I could fight and win with bad cuts, that I could always make the weight, no matter what I started training camp at, and that I was not just a body puncher.

I nearly boxed Pittsburgh southpaw Paul Spadafora a couple of times but for one reason or another it never came off. I was then due to be matched with Kelson Pinto, unbeaten and a real puncher and it was mentioned that it might be for the WBO title. 'That's more like it,' I thought. 'That's what I want.' He was a dangerous knockout artist. When one journalist told me Pinto was going to fight Junior Witter, before Witter withdrew injured I said, 'After seeing Pinto's compilation tape I've got a good idea of what he's ruptured.' So I got sparring partners in – big, six-foot tall right-hand punchers to mimic Pinto's style, and then, right at the last minute, they said he wasn't coming over. He pulled out, injured or whatever.

I saw Ed Robinson, a boxing reporter for Sky Sports, who was the first person I'd seen since the opponent changed and he told me I was fighting Denmark's Dennis Pedersen. Pedersen was a super-featherweight moving up. He was listed at five-foot eight but seemed about five foot five. My training to prepare me for a puncher at light-welterweight, and a tall one at that, was wasted. I stopped Pedersen in six rounds and it wasn't the worst performance in the world but no one really took any serious notice of it.

Then I fought another Argentine in Carlos Wilfredo Vilches at short notice and struggled to a points win. I had ripped a load of weight off and after four or five rounds I felt I was gone, I was spent. But I sucked it up. Billy said to me in the corner, 'Come on, you knew this was going to happen. We'll get through this.' I was going off the boil, though, and the press were agreeing with me. I went six rounds with a super-featherweight like Pedersen and, with all of the hype that had gone before, some were turning round and saying, 'Well, he's struggling a bit, now. Maybe he's found his level.' I knew I hadn't.

Any boxer, footballer, sportsman or anyone who wants to be the best in the field they're in, they need something to get their juices flowing to perform at their best. Rios, Pedersen and Vilches were run-of-the-mill opponents and I was expected to knock them out and it was as if we'd hit a brick wall. I had plateaued. I was young, ambitious and growing impatient; but Frank was perfect at bringing the right opponents in at the right time, not letting me off the leash before my time was actually ready. I learned a lot promotion-wise from Frank Warren.

My dad was looking after the money I made and I was still paid wages for my fights. He was getting more involved in my career to help with the business side of things and was speaking to Frank on my behalf. We'd felt it was always better that way, so I could concentrate on the training and the boxing, and he would tell me about what he was doing with the money, what accounts he was moving it into and why and what investments he was making on my behalf. I didn't have a lot of luxuries but I 'invested' in one of the original three-wheeler Robin Reliants from *Only Fools and Horses*. I've always been a big fan of the show and back during these WBU days I used to drive it around Hyde, Gee Cross and Hattersley, wearing my big sheepskin coat and my Del Boy hat. Everyone probably thought I'd lost the plot! I like to think I have a good sense of humour; I always like a good practical joke and I've always been game for a laugh and I loved that car. I've still got it but I can't take it out any more, it's too old and I'd probably end up killing myself in it.

I'm not a flash type, but it was one of my few extravagances. I wasn't into the usual stuff that often goes hand in hand with celebrity and fame. I was invited to certain dos, events, openings, red-carpet nights – and you would never see me there. You would see me in the pub playing darts or in the stands watching City, so the car was a real treat for me.

By the time the fight with Michael Stewart came around it was something of a turning point because if I beat him I would become the mandatory contender for Kostya Tszyu, the IBF champion. I know boxing and I thought, 'The minute I get in that mandatory position, nothing else will matter. I will be there.' I was back up for that Stewart fight, really motivated as it was the eliminator for the world title and to face the top man in the division. If I couldn't get up for that, there would have been something wrong with me and I knew Stewart was a decent fighter.

Called 'No Joke', Stewart had fought Sharmba Mitchell on the same night I'd boxed Pedersen, when Mitchell earned his shot at Tszyu. Stewart, from Delaware, was a good fighter; he was a bit of a puncher, he liked to stand and have a fight, which was right up my street, and I delivered, showing my variety. I knocked him down with a left hook to the body, then a double right-hand jab to the chin, and three left hooks eventually finished him in round five and it was as if everyone was saying, 'That's the Ricky Hatton we knew.' It turned out to be the only stoppage loss in a career that spanned sixty fights for Stewart, and I was now in the mandatory spot. 'You know what, this is definitely going to happen,' I said to myself. 'I'm on pole position.'

However, Kostya Tszyu, who had injury issues and still had to face his leading challenger in Sharmba Mitchell, was going to be tied up for a while, so in the meantime I wanted to keep busy. Perhaps it would have been wise not to have fought and not take any chances, but I fought Ray Oliveira – which, when you think the Tszyu fight was already there waiting for me, was a massive gamble. I ran the risk of getting cut, hurt or, worse still, beaten. But if I didn't fight then I would have been on the sidelines for several months and that meant hanging about when I always liked to keep busy – so we signed for Oliveira.

When I look back over my time as the WBU champion, I think that performance was one of my best. He was a very experienced fighter who threw a lot of punches and he knew how to look after himself really well; it was brutal on my part. I systematically took him apart. Round after round I would chip away and in the end he had blood coming out of his ears.

It was the perfect fight to sharpen my tools for Tszyu. I don't think I was ever in any danger of losing, but there was always the feeling that Oliveira, who came from Massachusetts and owned good wins over Vince Phillips and future champion Vivian Harris, would cause me a few problems because of his style. He had a defence where he would cover up in a shell to protect his chin, I was struggling to land anything upstairs so I was throwing jabs, trying to connect with a hook and then using my right and looking to score with right hooks. He protected his face, but the hooks were getting in round the side of his head, just by the ears. The punches thudded in, horrendous-sounding shots like the right hook that dropped him in the opening session. It was a beat-down – round after round I clubbed away around his high guard, until I trapped him in the corner. I was really putting my punches together in round ten. I fired off a screw shot, followed it with a right hand and he went down. He was clutching his ears and was in such pain and agony that he looked at his corner to tell them he couldn't go on, and I could see the blood running down from his ears from where all of those hooks had been landing around the side.

It had been the perfect fight and the perfect performance; he'd defeated world champions in Harris and Phillips, had gone the distance with top fighters like Vernon Forrest, and in fifty-nine fights I was the first man to stop him. My tools couldn't have been any sharper for Kostya Tszyu. I felt I was more than ready.

When I look back on those WBU days, I do so with massive affection. Those fights helped make me the fighter I became, and Frank Warren promoted me perfectly. At the time I thought I was becoming stale and was getting frustrated, but I think the WBU fights built my fanbase. The WBU also took a little bit of the pressure off me because it was not one of the major governing bodies, but that title ultimately got me a fight with Tszyu and it got me ranked. Even though people looked down on the WBU belt, when you think of Ben Tackie and Vince Phillips and Ray Oliveira, they could have fought for any title. They got me where I needed to be and I look back at the WBU fights as where I had my apprenticeship for the world stage. Don't forget, it got me to the number one contender spot to fight Kostya Tszyu and you don't get to be number one contender – to fight the best in the division – if you're fighting a load of muppets. I made the WBU title what it was; that sounds a bit arrogant on my part, and I don't mean for it to sound that way, but a title's only worth the people who are fighting for it. I'd fought movers, stronger opponents, scrappers, southpaws, and I'd showed my ability.

When your big opportunity comes, for me or any fighter, you want to know that you've experienced it all. You want to have been knocked down and know you can get up. You want to have been hurt and know you can hold on and ride out a storm. You want to know that you can fight on, even if you can hardly see through the blood, or that you can fight twelve rounds at a frantic pace. You want to know that, if you're given one more round before they stop the fight, you can turn it around. You want to know that you have boxed at home and abroad, that you've been hit, hurt and shaken and there was nothing you haven't faced, so that whatever happens in that big fight, on your big night, there is nothing that you haven't seen or felt. When I look back at my preparations for fighting the best in the world in Kostya Tszyu, could it have been any better? I couldn't have done any more. When you can say that, you can't have any better preparation. I was ready and I knew it.

CHAPTER 6

Destiny

Billy Graham nicked the gloves after my pro debut. From day one he was saying, 'I think this kid's going to go all the way. He's going to be in the big fights. Not just world title fights but the big fights.' When he saved my gloves, he had done so planning for this moment.

It was about half eight at night the evening before I was going to fight Kostya Tszyu, when a taxi pulled up outside the house. The driver came to the door and presented me with a glass case; inside it were the gloves from my professional debut, and a couple of pictures of the fight against Kid McAuley at the leisure centre in Widnes. There was also a picture of me and Billy from that night and a small engraved plaque, which read: 'Dear Ricky, I always knew this day would come. Love you. Billy.'

It reaffirmed my own belief that this was it. There was no going back, but we were ready for what we were about to face, and we were facing it together.

Although there are four world titles these days with the

WBC, WBA, WBO and IBF, Kostya Tszyu was the number one fighter in the weight class, and many said he was the best fighter in the world. Being a world champion does not necessarily mean you're number one. The aim for me and Billy was not just to be a world champion but to be the best in the division.

Our day of days was almost here. We were always sure it would come – even if that was not a popular assessment elsewhere – as our belief in our own fate and our destiny was unshakeable. Billy and I also had a fair idea over the last couple of years that when my chance did come, it would be against the formidable Australia-based Russian Tszyu.

I had seen Tszyu fight before, when I went to Las Vegas to watch him against top American Zab Judah in November 2001. It was my first trip to Sin City, and I had just defeated veteran American Freddie Pendleton the week earlier, so me and Billy saw it as a scouting mission, and, typically, as a jolly. As a big Elvis fan who enjoyed a night on the tiles once in a while, it's fair to say I liked Las Vegas from the start.

I was ringside at the fight, working as a pundit for Sky Sports. Judah won the first round, but Kostya's one-punch power was incredible and he wiped him out in the second with that right hand. Judah felt he could carry on but his legs had gone, and as he tried to make his point he launched his stool at the referee.

The next morning, after me and Billy had been out all night, of course, we were hung-over and checking out of the MGM Grand when we saw a group in their black Team Kostya tracksuits and T-shirts. I turned to Billy, 'There's Kostya Tszyu, Billy. I should go and congratulate him.' I went over, with the fumes on my breath from the beer the night before, and said, 'Hey, Kostya. Well done last night. Congratulations.' He politely thanked me. I said, 'My name's Ricky Hatton. I've just got into the top ten. I think I will fight you in a couple of years.' Shocked and probably embarrassed, for me as much as himself, he said, 'Ah, all right. Nice one.' He must have thought, 'Who's this fucking drunk?'

But neither of us forgot this encounter; Kostya mentioned it at the press conference when we announced the fight. 'I remember you pulling me to one side in Vegas. You said you would fight me, didn't you?' he said. I didn't think he had taken it seriously but I was made up that he remembered. You can only imagine one of the best fighters in the world being told by a drunk Brit on a jolly in Vegas saying, 'Yeah, I'll fight you in a few years!' Of course you will, mate.

The bookmakers had the same doubts. You could get me at as much as a 5–1 as an underdog. I never gambled on any of my fights but a couple of my friends bet on this one.

A lot of my stories seem to have a pint involved, but I was out with my mates, having a pint, and it was twelve weeks before the fight. I was in Manchester in a place called the Press Club, the last place open where you could get a late drink. It must have been about five in the morning and I put my pint down. 'Right, that's me done for twelve weeks,' I said. 'I'm going home now, fellas.' As I got up to leave, I turned to them and said, 'Listen, I know I'm pissed and I've had a drink, but I told you this last week, I'm going to fucking beat that Tszyu. Five-to-one. Get your money on it.' They looked at me and laughed. I turned round and staggered out. I bet they thought, 'Yeah, yeah. Shut up you drunken fucking idiot.' But I was so sure. It was just how I felt.

Camp was strict; I lived like a monk and I ate, slept and breathed Kostya Tszyu, watching footage of him day in and day out. Of all of the fighters in my weight class at the time, he was the best. He had been inactive because he'd had shoulder surgery and then been out, but he came back and fought the number one contender, Sharmba Mitchell. A lot of people thought Mitchell would beat him, but Tszyu just splattered him. Even though Kostya had been out for twenty-two months, he floored him four times and stopped him in three rounds. He could be devastating.

Critics said there was a gap in class to Tszyu from the opponents I had been fighting, and there was, but it wasn't about who I was beating, it was the manner of the victories that had given me confidence.

I went to the MEN Arena a few days before the fight, as Sky were filming me for a big build-up and they wanted me at the venue. The seats weren't in and I just looked at the size of the place. It was cavernous and hard to believe how alive it would come in just a couple of days' time. It almost took my breath away imagining how it was going to be that Saturday night.

The first time it really hit home about how big the fight was, came when we were at the press conference – there had always been plenty of press covering my fights, but this was different. There were video cameras everywhere, from all over the world, and flash bulbs going off left, right and centre. 'Fuck me,' I thought. 'This is the big time. This is a little bit different to where you've previously been before, Ricky.' People might not have shared my enthusiasm, but this was what I had dreamed of, what I was destined for.

Me and Billy spent so much time formulating the strategy. We knew that Tszyu would be trying to line me up for the right hand; the power in his punch came at the end of the shot, it exploded when his arm was stretched. It wasn't a short right hand; he had to have it extended. I needed to jab and move in on him quickly, so when he did land the right hand – and we knew he would get it on me, based on the philosophy you can't walk in the rain without getting wet he would be so close that it would not allow him the space to extend the arm, and I would be taking the sting out of the punch.

Ours was a dangerous strategy; they were brave tactics. There was a reason he kept knocking people out and it was because they gave ground. In their fights against him, both Judah and Sharmba Mitchell had kept pulling away from him to the point where his right hand was at its most ferocious, and they got their heads taken off. If I jumped on his chest then perhaps he would win some rounds, but if I was walking through his right hand and taking the edge off it, then his confidence would evaporate later on. Risky, yes – but my confidence was unbreakable.

Frank Warren had done the deal to bring the thirty-five-year-old over to Manchester, and because of the demands of US television giant Showtime the fight would start at two in the morning. It was my first fight on SKY Box Office, and I expect it had to be done that way to pay us what we both needed for a contest of that magnitude. I knew Tszyu – who had come over two weeks before fight night with an entourage of twelve to help him finish his fine-tuning – was making far more than me, as the champion and the fighter making the concessions in terms of conceding home advantage and boxing at an unusual time.

To deal with the late start time, I was doing my roadwork at midnight instead of in the morning, but it is hard to be tired when you have that sort of fight in front of you. Nothing could have made me tired or fazed me for facing Kostya Tszyu, not even the police who one night stopped me, thinking the guy running with a hoodie pulled over his head had committed a crime and was legging it from the scene.

I sparred with a couple of Argentinians and they were really good, giving me great work throughout camp. But the confidence within my team was not shared universally. When I beat Magee and the others and I was saying I wanted to fight Tszyu, I don't think anyone took me seriously. People thought I was a good fighter, that I sold loads of tickets and was exciting, but I really don't think people thought I was going to get that far. Yet I knew. I knew I was, I honestly believed I was going to do it. Others, however, thought, 'Yeah, Ricky's okay, he gets cut, but Kostya Tszyu? No. No way.' That gave me incredible motivation. I would always think of people telling me I couldn't do it and I'd run faster, spar harder and train longer.

I was consumed by Kostya Tszyu. If I'd beaten one of the other champions, a Vivian Harris or Sharmba Mitchell, all I would have heard would have been, 'Yeah, but he will never defeat Tszyu.' I wanted to beat the best so no one could say otherwise – I *had* to beat him.

I was the underdog but the fans more than got behind me. All 22,000 tickets sold out in five hours, and on the night it was electric. Even though it was two in the morning, Manchester was watching – the world was paying attention. Everyone was excited but in the same breath they were nervous because of how aggressive I was. With someone like Kostya Tszyu – a puncher with that rocket-launcher right cross – people thought I would be easy to hit and that it could have been a recipe for disaster.

Backstage there was a nervous tingle in the air as my hands were wrapped. Everyone was saying, 'Come on. You can do it, Ricky.' Perhaps they believed it. I don't think all of them did. Then Eamonn Magee barged in as I was getting ready.

When I fought Magee I fucking hated him. The stuff he said, that I was only a little kid, that he'd sparred better people than me, that I was in with a man that time, all that disrespect, and I thought, 'You fucking wanker.' He taught me a lot, but I actually hated him and I'd never really seen him since I'd fought him three years before. All of a sudden he came charging through my changing-room door.

'Don't listen to all these who have written you off,' he said.

'Don't listen to that "You're gonna get beat and knocked out and all this and all that." Tszyu's not fought anyone like you. Let's see how he does with you stuck to him like glue. Let's see how he copes. If he doesn't get you, it's over. Believe it.' He said everything to me that I was thinking, but there weren't many people telling me that. It was exactly what I needed to hear. That dickhead from a couple of years earlier had gone, the real Magee was a lovely guy – hard as nails – but we became pals afterwards, with a friendship that stretched into retirement. He inspired me against Tszyu, that's for sure.

The stage was set. The fans had set it and so, it seemed, had fate. This was my destiny. I listened to Showtime announcer Jimmy Lennon introducing me as I stood behind the curtain and I walked to the ring first. Some people said that because I was fighting at home I should come out second, but I didn't want to, I wanted to be first. I wanted to feel like the challenger. Everyone was writing me off but I was never frightened of a challenge. I'd rather get flattened trying.

Everyone was singing in the arena. *Everyone.* Normally you might get a section of the crowd, but it was the whole lot, it looked like a carnival. The fans were cheering one of their own. With me, it wasn't just a case of them cheering on a British fighter, but it was like they were pulling for a mate because they could always relate to me. I probably knew half the people that were there; either I'd had a pint with them or had a chat with them somewhere.

People always say there was a packed house in the Manchester Arena for boxing when it had not been, but for Tszyu it was rammed. There was not a seat to be had and I'd never known anything like it. I gritted my teeth and thought, 'Don't let everyone say, "I told you so."'

I read everything beforehand; they thought I was going to get a kicking. No one picked me to win. 'You're not going to do it, Ricky.' 'Tszyu to win in three rounds.' 'Tszyu to win in four.' 'Ricky will come marching on and be dead brave but he will walk onto a right hand.' Brilliant. More motivation for me. I had a great relationship with the sporting press and they weren't being nasty, they were only stating their opinion about who was going to win, but they proved to be one of my biggest drivers.

Of course, I was more nervous than normal, but at the same time I was more geed up and excited than I ever had been. All that was going through my mind was that from day one I believed I would be a great world champion and if I didn't achieve that then nothing else would satisfy me. 'This is the day,' I said to myself. 'You've always said you were good enough to be in a fight like this. Don't let your arse cave in now. This is your time.' When I looked at myself and then at my opponents, I knew I could beat them – I would look at what I could do against them, and what I couldn't. Only a handful of people shared my opinion about Tszyu. I believed I was going to murder him but most people thought I would be good for about four rounds. I couldn't have disagreed more. 'Am I missing something?'

When I got into the ring I was so fired up. I was looking into the crowd at every opportunity, thriving on the atmosphere. 'Come on!' I yelled at them. Again and again. 'Fucking come on!' I roared, clenching my fists. I'd look in the crowd's eyes and I could see the passion. It was like they were fighting with me. Me and my crowd; we had that type of relationship. It gave me a massive boost, it was visceral. Tszyu was the favourite but one look at this crowd – and at me for that matter – and you could tell he had a mountain to climb every bit as big as the one I was ready to ascend.

Mindset. That is what it was. Of course conditioning plays a part, too. But I was always in condition. Billy saw to that.

Tszyu – wearing black shorts had his hair tightly cropped with his familiar ponytail dropping down his back – and I came face to face in the ring. I stared at him; he didn't look at me. Nerves? Maybe. Perhaps it was the occasion and the crowd. In his long career he had never faced anything like this. Manchester was united and it wanted him beaten.

I went straight at him, but it wasn't reckless like I was against Magee. I had learned and we had a strategy in place. I was getting early body shots in, smothering Tszyu, keeping him working, staying on his chest, jabbing so he couldn't get set. 'Keep working,' I said. Busy, busy, busy. It was strength-sapping stuff. Yes, Tszyu was strong. I could feel that. But he was not as strong as me. I was pulling him, dragging him, nudging him. That was my plan. I cracked him on the back of the head to unsettle him early on, too. I would go inside and squeeze his arms, hug him and pull him. His arms weren't tired later just from the pace of the fight but from the abuse they were taking. By the end of round one I had done more than some thought I was going to do in the whole fight, and in the corner Billy told me to stay close, and that when I was inside I didn't even have to throw punches, just stop him from punching.

If you look at Tszyu's fights, they were never at the kind of pace I set off on; I wasn't going to give him a moment's rest, I couldn't afford to. He was a murderous puncher and he always had people standing off him, so he wasn't ready for this – he couldn't get his leverage for shots. Some of the punches he landed, like a couple of uppercuts in round two, I felt. But he normally likes to ease himself into a fight and there was no chance of that here. He'd signed up for thirty-six minutes of hell.

I was flying in the second round, so much so that the crowd started chanting 'Easy, easy' by the time the bell came to end the session. 'Fucking hell, steady on,' I thought. It was going well, but there was a long way to go.

Going into the third round, he knew he had to raise his game. He had to hit me with some big punches to try and slow me down. After trying to drop the pace at the start of the fight so he could box in his comfort zone, because of how I was fighting, he had to raise it instead.

I landed a body shot in round three and it knocked the wind out of him as he groaned; I didn't let up. I wasn't sure if I had won the session because he was an accurate puncher and scoring occasionally: 'Did I win that round, Billy?' I asked. 'Doesn't matter,' he said, ice-cool, 'it's served its purpose. He worked his nuts off that round.'

In the fourth Tszyu even threw a six-punch combination. He never did that usually, but it was the only way he could keep me off. Even then he just couldn't get away.

The champion probably banked rounds three, four, five and maybe six – but to do that, Billy was right, Kostya had had to work his bollocks off. He had no respite. I just didn't leave him alone.

Some people were amazed that he was giving ground, but I knew I would be physically stronger than him, I'd had no doubts about that. That's why we were confident sitting on his chest. It was the single punch at distance I had to watch. Tszyu was going backwards and I was dragging him on, squeezing him and he couldn't get his heavy shots off. Then he started to throw a curving right hand to start each round because he never had the space to get his full leverage. Yes, he was making my ears ring still with his power but I was going through them. Make him pay, make him work. Billy and I agreed that if we were going to lose a round, or lose some rounds, we wanted him to work harder than he'd ever worked in his fucking life because you simply can't keep it up for twelve rounds.

'You know what, Ricky,' Billy said before the fifth. 'There are rounds you are going to lose and he is going to bank. He might win a couple but don't get disheartened. Even if you lose four on the bounce, think how hard he is working to bank those rounds.'

There were many who didn't think I would hear the bell for round five but he'd had to work hard to see the fifth commence himself. A twelve-round fight is about knowing when to put your foot on the gas, when to have a rest, when to nick a break. It's a long time. Some people thought there was no method to my madness but there was. It looked reckless, I know, but as I was going in I was half jabbing, half rolling, taking a shot with half a shoulder, half catching his shots. He nailed me clean a couple of times but more often than not they were cuffing shots that I managed to get something on while I suffocated him so he couldn't get the momentum. The right hand he'd flattened Judah and Mitchell with was bouncing off me. The tactics were working perfectly.

I started to bully and maul him, which nobody did because he was this great punching machine. They had too much respect for him. Maybe he expected me to charge out carelessly and his training team probably would have told him I would come marching out like a headless chicken, perhaps overexcited on the big night. 'Don't worry, Kostya,' I reckon they would have said, 'put that right hand down the pipe. It will soon stop him in his tracks.' As the rounds progressed, four, five, six, and I was still there, still coming, still a hundred miles an hour. I can imagine Johnny Lewis in Tszyu's corner thinking, 'Fucking hell, this is not how we saw it.'

While Tszyu took some of those middle rounds, he was grafting his arse off and paying a price. He started cocking his right hand, instead of throwing it straight like he always did, because I was constantly on him so quickly. That took more sting out of it as he became increasingly desperate to land his pet punch and end the fight. Billy was getting mad at me charging out of the corner onto that right hand. 'He's doing it every time!' he shouted. 'Get out of the fucking way.' I was on Tszyu so quickly he'd come out and just go 'Bang'. He'd hit me every time. I would go right through it but Billy kept saying to me, 'Ricky, you know what he's gonna do, why do you keep running into it? You're just that little too eager to get at him.' The only thing I could put it down to was the atmosphere. It was a special concoction of anxiety and excitement in the same breath.

Sometimes Tszyu hit me and my legs went a little bit stiff and I thought, 'Oof, fucking hell.' But all I could think was, 'Don't let it happen, don't let them win. They said you were going to cave in.'

He managed to tag me with a right hand in round five but I took it, dropped my hands, shouted 'Come on' and marched forwards. I wanted to break his heart. When he scored with that right he must have thought, 'Jeez, what have we got here? Fucking lunatic.' He was out of his comfort zone the whole time, and he'd probably never fought at that pace in his whole career. But with how I fight it was just another Saturday night for me.

I bombed out for the sixth and Tszyu started looking to the referee for help. That whirlwind start to the fight had the crowd roaring but the fans had gone a little quieter by now after he had captured those middle rounds. Still, the boxing anoraks would have noticed that Kostya was fighting with his mouth open, gulping for air.

'Great, keep doing what you're doing. Stay on his chest,' said Billy. He was calm in the corner. We knew it was working, while Kostya's team was yelling at each other to get their man water. They could see the energy draining out of him. With the seventh about to get underway I was bouncing up and down. Tszyu trudged out into the battlefield. 'Keep going, keep going,' I said to myself.

He was marking underneath his right eye but he punched me low and I hit the canvas. The timekeeper picked up the count and I thought the worst. It was not a legitimate knockdown, it was a low blow. It wasn't pleasant to take and not far off the Crown Jewels, but a shot on the groin guard – straight and direct – is not the worst thing in the world. If it comes at an angle where it goes across your knackers, it goes without saying it can be a real killer. The referee, Dave Parris, saw that and stopped the count. It was not a knockdown.

Phew. The fans started belting out 'There's only one Ricky Hatton.' Loudly.

I tumbled to the canvas later on in the round as it got messy, and it took an extra effort to get back to my feet, such was the pace of the fight. It was hard, like climbing a small mountain.

Round nine was underway and things were significantly different. He was really struggling. 'Fucking hell. I've got him here,' I thought. Tszyu must have wondered what he had to do to keep me off. I could hear him breathing heavily when we were on the inside. It was laboured and I knew he was struggling. His mouth was open, his jaw was swelling. Knowing that he was finding it so hard gave me an extra spring in my step, I could see him dwindling so I got a second wind. I was letting more shots go, thinking, 'I've got you here, haven't I?' I was sidestepping more, my feet were a bit quicker and Tszyu's tank was running low. I was bullying him. I could smell blood and was nailing him with heavy shots; his face was becoming increasingly battered as I caught him more and more easily.

I knew. You could see the tactics were working and, as I was coming on again, he was almost gone. The crowd was on fire now, their mid-rounds murmuring was long-since gone.

Then, in the ninth, I purposefully smashed him below the belt and Tszyu was in real pain. It was a left hook, not a straight shot, and I reckon it nearly crippled him. He had hit me low several times and I'd finally had enough. He was seriously feeling the pace before then but that punch took a lot out of him. It had to have done. I went back to a corner while the referee assessed Kostya. 'What's going on? What are you doing?' shouted Tszyu's team at me as I looked out to them. Dave Parris came over to me and said, 'Keep the shots up.' I replied, 'Dave, he's already given me four low ones!' I think he knew, too. He could have taken a point off Tszyu for his earlier low blows. People make a bigger deal about mine but he'd had some warnings already.

After round nine I said to Billy, 'He's mine. He's blowing like fuck.' Earlier, I had been landing but you could say the better quality work was from Tszyu, although my work rate was keeping me in it. Now my punches were quality shots and finding the target regularly. It remained edge-of-the-seat stuff, though, because he was still Kostya Tszyu and, with his punching power, one shot and that could have been it.

Round ten started and I was straight after him. If you put yourself in Johnny Lewis's shoes, in Kostya's corner, you would think, 'Jeez, this guy has a second wind here. Kostya is not hitting him or hurting him. My man's breathing heavily in the corner. He's blowing out of his arse and this fella's just getting started again. And he's hurting Kostya now.' Tszyu was bobbing around the ring a bit, he was running on pride and I was all over him. There was no stopping me and the crowd was going potty. Kostya's punches didn't have much on them any more and I was even beating him to the right hand. He couldn't get a foothold. As the tenth round neared the end, and with Tszyu in real trouble, he threw a desperate right hand and left hook. Boom. Boom. They landed all right, but they didn't stop me. 'See,' said Billy, 'this is what we talked about. There's nothing left now. You've got to work your balls off.'

I knew I had him when the eleventh started but I was aware I had to be careful, I just had to keep my foot on the gas. I had to keep punching and punching and as the round neared an end he had one last burst, throwing about six punches, and I think he hanged himself doing that. It took more out of him than it did me. I replied with a body shot and that was his last hurrah. I swarmed him, using every ounce of drive and energy, pounding him around the ring, and when I stormed back to my corner at the end of round – utterly exhausted – I spat my gumshield out on the floor to gulp in as much air as possible. Fucking hell. I thought my lungs were going to explode. 'You've got him, you've got him!' shouted

Billy. I knew it. Everyone did. I had three minutes left to press my advantage.

'Come on, Rick,' I said to myself. 'One last round. Just try and summon one last bit of energy.' I gasped for air and peered around Billy's shoulder. The referee had been to see Tszyu and as Dave Parris turned around, he waved it off. The fight was over. 'Oh Jesus. I've done it. Thank God I haven't got to go back out there,' I thought. For Tszyu to quit on his stool at the end of the eleventh tells you: 'I can't take any more.'

I just hadn't left him alone and was ahead on all three scorecards: Spanish judge Manuel Maritxalar had me one point up, 105–104; Frenchman Alfred Asaro had me up by three, 106–103; and the card of American official Don Ackerman was 107–102.

I dropped to the canvas in tears, Billy jumped on top of me. I can't remember much but I know it was bedlam in there. I stumbled back to my feet on a tide of disbelief and jumped out of the ring to hug my mum and dad and Matthew.

From the first day I'd walked through the gym door at the age of ten it's all I had dreamed of, being the best in the world. Incredible. This was what it had all been about. Somehow I had enough strength once I was back in the ring to leap up and down. I have no idea where that came from, but I asked my fans to stop chanting 'You're not singing any more' at Kostya. He was a proud champion and he had probably thought if he was ever going to get beaten he probably would have been outboxed, not outmanned and finishing on his stool.

Physically, I couldn't have been far behind him, but I had

that burning desire that meant I was not even thinking about it. I probably could have done twenty rounds that night with the determination and motivation I had. And although Kostya lost you can't say it was a bad performance by him. It was an absolute war.

Paul Speak handed me my Ricky Fatton T-shirt and I looked at the press row, where those who had written me off and said I could not lose so much weight and beat Tszyu, were writing tomorrow's headlines. I waved at them.

I went to console Kostya and we spoke to one another for a while. It is a blur now but there was plenty of mutual respect and that never changed, although our paths haven't really crossed in the years since the fight.

I grabbed the microphone. 'Manchester!' I shouted, 'I always said I would be number one . . . You and me, we did it together tonight.' I announced that if I could be half the champion Kostya Tszyu was, I would be very proud. Then Kostya took the microphone. He was emotional and did not commit to fighting again but said he lost to the better fighter. 'There's no shame for me to say this,' he added, 'I'd planned a lot of things for this fight but today he was better than me everywhere. If Ricky needs any help or support from me, I will always be here for him.'

'Blue Moon' started playing and it was time to party. I was the IBF light-welterweight champion of the world and life would never be the same again.

It was chaos in the changing room and even Russell Crowe, a big boxing fan who was there to cheer on his countryman, came in to congratulate me. By the time we finished the press conference it was 4 a.m. and then there was an after-fight party at the Renaissance in Deansgate. The drink flowed freely for several hours. When I left the hotel to get a taxi it was half past nine, ten o'clock in the morning, and there were still people walking up and down the street singing, 'There's only one Ricky Hatton.' You would have thought we'd won the World Cup. People were clambering up lamp posts at ten in the morning.

Kostya was staying at a hotel in Bolton and, because it was such a draining and demanding fight, I said to Paul Speak I wanted to see him before he flew home, I wanted to make sure he was okay. Kostya came down to meet me and his jaw was swollen like a grapefruit, it was horrendous. I probably stunk of booze, like I did when we first met in Las Vegas all those years ago, when I told him that I was a fringe contender who might fight him one day. He was a really nice guy. You don't make fighters like that. Our night in Manchester will link us forever and I'm proud of that.

It's not often fighters like Kostya Tszyu fight in England, boxing a Mancunian in Manchester. It was a big occasion for the country but also for Manchester. The revenue it attracted for bars, restaurants and shopping must have been incredible. Lots of people come up to me, even today, and say, 'Oh, Ricky. The best night I ever had in my life was the night you beat Kostya Tszyu.' 'The best night of *your* life?' I reply. 'What do you think it meant to me?' Kostya Tszyu never fought again and five years later, when he became eligible, he was inducted into the International Boxing Hall of Fame at the first time of asking.

I don't think he ever spoke to his trainer, Johnny Lewis, again, after he pulled him out of the fight. I've watched it back many times and in one network's version of it, where they had microphones in the corner, Johnny was saying, 'No more, Kostya. No more.' Kostya was shaking his head – I don't know if he was saying 'No more' or 'Don't stop it'. There were a couple of Russian guys in his corner and Johnny was saying, 'No, no, no. I'm the chief second. I'm stopping the fight.' I could see people trying to pass Tszyu a drink, saying, 'Come on, Kostya. You're all right. One more round.'

Johnny shouted, 'No!' You could see Johnny loved him; he absolutely loved him. When we were at the weigh-in Johnny made a point of coming up to me and Billy and saying good luck to both of the fighters. 'The most important thing is no one gets hurt,' he said. He loved his fighters. He loved Kostya and a couple of guys there with the spit bucket, who were saying he could go on, wouldn't have known him as well as Johnny Lewis did. It was a gruelling, hard fight. For these people who say Kostya quit on his stool – and he's had a bit of stick for it over the years – I think they're a disgrace because the fight, the pace and the punishment was brutal. You have to take your hat off to him.

After I had retired years later I heard whispers that they wanted a rematch but there was nothing after the fight. I don't think they had a back-up plan on the night. I'm not sure we did. I don't think I did. Me and Billy were just convinced that what we were going to do would work. Boxing, using your jab and trading jabs with him, would have left me in the firing line for that right hand. He was a distance fighter with a jab and a right hand, not an up-close boxer. He was good at fighting on the inside but it was not his A-game.

Victory took me to another level. I've never really been bothered by the fame, but I started going on things like Michael Parkinson's chat show – who I presented with his own long pair of boxing trunks, like mine – and it was all a bit surreal. When they say the Tszyu fight is one of the best wins by a British fighter in a British ring, I have to pinch myself.

A week afterwards – and with my face just coming to the end of the black and blue stage – my cousin Stephen had a birthday party in Manchester and I went with a couple of pals. Matthew was in training, so he wasn't there, but his wife, Jenna, came with a friend of hers, Jennifer, and we got introduced. She and Jenna had been friends for years and although I had heard her name mentioned I never thought anything of it. She actually went to Mottram Primary School like I had and was two years below me.

I took a fancy to Jennifer straight away. She was really pretty, good-looking, had a nice sense of humour and was fun to be with. After the party, Jenna and Jennifer left and we went to another club and they were there, so we got chatting again and then me and my friends went to a different place in Manchester, which was like a members-only place. I was a little bit tipsy and Jenna was already in there, chatting to her friends, but Jennifer had gone home. So I asked Jenna to call her and get her back; Jennifer was already in a taxi but she returned at my request. I thought there was half a chance, then!

Jenna asked me if I liked her and she told me Jennifer liked me, and we ended up going out a couple of times. She knew I was a boxer through Jenna but she wasn't like one of the girls who become all excited and said stuff like, 'Oooo, you're that boxer. Hiya,' where I start wondering what people are after. On one of our first dates we went to the Walkabout in Manchester; she couldn't believe how many people were asking for my autograph. People were asking for pictures and autographs and she said to me, 'What are you again? A world champion? People like you, don't they?' At that time, ninety per cent of the girls that came up to me said, 'Oh, you're Ricky Hatton. That boxer off the telly.' After a while, you see people coming a mile away. She didn't even know me or how successful I was, and that was half the attraction.

After a couple of weeks Jen came over to my house one day. She was in the living room while I put the kettle on, and there was a photo of me out of training with Campbell above the fireplace. It was taken in between fights a year or so earlier and I looked like a beached whale but, with this not being long after the Tszyu fight, the person in front of Jennifer was as solid as a rock. So when I came in she was looking at the picture and she said, 'Who's that?'

'Who's that, you cheeky cow? That's me and my son, Campbell.'

She said, 'You're joking, what weight were you then?'

To which I replied, 'If you play your cards right and we're

still together in a few weeks that's what you've got to put up with.' I saw an opportunity and asked, 'Do you still like me?' She politely said she did. I took her to Marbella after five or six weeks; she was nervous about it because we hadn't been together long, but we got on brilliantly and had a right laugh. We were on the same wavelength and just laughed and laughed.

I'd won the fight of my life and met the girl of my dreams. Not a bad few weeks, eh?

CHAPTER 7

Made in America

The cuts were really bad. It was two headbutts that did them – one over each eye – and WBA light-welterweight champion Carlos Maussa, a right pain in the arse, had a really disjointed style. I thought that referee Mickey Vann would step in and stop it at any second. This wasn't really the follow-up performance to Kostya Tszyu I'd hoped for.

Sometimes when you study your opponent you can read him in the ring. If he moves to the left, you know to bring your right elbow in or get your right hand up because you know a left hook is coming. Then, if he dips to the right, you know a right cross is coming. With Maussa you could forget that – he would dip to the left and throw a right hook, there was no manual or handbook to go with him. He was so difficult to read, very disorganized and so free with his head, and when you're aggressive like me inevitably you clash heads. I walked onto his head a couple of times and he gave me two horrendous cuts for my troubles. As if it was not a tough enough job as it was for Mick Williamson . . .

141

The cuts had me scared me to death. It was the first time I'd had two. Sure, I'd had plenty before but never two bad ones like that, and as the referee assessed me it made me a bit panicky. The thing was, I was winning a hard fight handily. I just couldn't quite catch him flush because he was tall, rangy and he kept switching stances – with me being short there was always going to be trouble with the reach. It was frustrating not being able to hurt him, but I was slowing him down as the fight progressed, although not getting through as much as I would like to.

I had been ringside to see him upset Vivian Harris, who I had been scouting, to win the WBA title on the Floyd Mayweather–Arturo Gatti card in Atlantic City in the summer, so I knew he was dangerous. This was his first defence and none of what that gangly fucker did was conventional. I don't think even he knew what he was doing half the time, so there was no point me trying to second-guess him.

Then, in the ninth round, I suppose I got that frustrated that I had not been able to nail him flush that I took a run-up as if to say 'Fuck it' and I flew at him with a left hook, and it was probably the hardest punch I ever threw. It's a wonder he's still not there now. I nailed him with a couple of right crosses. A right-hand lead landed, then another and then I gestured with the right hand and leapt in with the left hook, and he slumped to his knees.

I thought he was badly hurt straight away. I had been getting closer for the last couple of rounds and was starting to pick him off a bit more and, as I thought there was less chance of me getting stopped due to the cuts because they weren't getting any worse, I started to relax a bit more and I found the punches and measured him. He was as tough as they come and it would have taken something like that to stop him, and all credit to him. Not long after he hit the floor he put his hand on the second rope and I thought, 'Fucking hell, he's getting up. That's it. If he gets up after that, I'm getting out!' Thankfully he didn't.

That shot was all about the technique. When the time was right, I knew when to put everything behind a punch and it ended well – even though everything had come too close to backfiring for my liking.

It was my first fight having parted company with Frank Warren and there was a lot of pressure on. I'd had a rough patch, I had two cuts, there was a fella who was awkward, switching, pulling away and rangy, and who was going to be tough to knock out anyway.

I was upset about what was going on with Frank, although I tried to put that behind me by making light of it and coming to the ring to the old song, 'Gonna Get Along Without Ya Now'. I was gutted that my split with him prompted a legal reaction and I made a statement with the song. When those cuts came it was right about that time when I thought, 'Jesus Christ, you're going to look a right dickhead if you don't pull this off. I've made that statement and it's all going wrong here. Two cuts. A right handful in front of me.' So when I landed that punch you can only imagine the relief.

I had no problem getting motivated in camp, even coming

off the immense high of beating Tszyu. The dispute with Warren fuelled me big time and, as well as I was doing in my career, there were always critics, and there were still plenty out there. Having beaten Tszyu for the IBF title, I was now taking on Maussa for his WBA belt as I tried to unify the division. 'Oh, he's beaten Tszyu? That was a fluke.' 'He's a one-hit wonder.' There was no lack of motivation – I found that something extra to push myself through everything again. I'd fought so hard against Tszyu for the belts I wasn't prepared to hand them over at the first time of asking.

Life changed after the Tszyu fight, as I knew it would. Back then there had been time to go to Thailand on Manchester City's pre-season tour, which, for want of a better expression, was a disaster. Stuart Pearce was the manager of City at the time – for the Maussa fight he actually carried my belt into the ring, and I was really pally with him. We got on very well; you wouldn't believe that someone who was so aggressive and wore his heart on his sleeve when he played would be so quiet and softly spoken. I suppose I saw some of me in him and maybe he thought the same because I can be softly spoken, enjoy a laugh and a joke but, like 'Psycho' – as they used to call Stuart on the pitch – I could get nasty if I had to. The guys at Sky Sports would say they could see it in the changing rooms before my fights. Something just clicks and I mean business.

I got invited to Stuart's hotel and was having a drink and he was there with Tim Flowers – who was the goalkeeping coach at the time – and Stuart was having an absolute nightmare. Joey Barton had been in trouble when it emerged he'd been in an altercation with an Everton fan. Richard Dunne had tried to break up the melee and kicked a wall in frustration, injuring his foot. Joey was sent home, with a City spokesman left to say: 'Richard Dunne sustained an injury to his foot in his attempts to restrain Joey Barton.' Stuart was up against it. Aside from that, it was brilliant. You'd go to the bars and all the City fans were there with their shirts on and they were singing 'There's only one Ricky Hatton' wherever I went. I loved the trip, and we were in a tournament with Bolton, Everton, City and the Thai team. It was brilliant and a welcome distraction from the Frank Warren claim.

At the time, my dad handled all that stuff so I left it to him. All I knew was, 'Frank's suing me, he's claiming he has a contract . . .' I didn't really know the ins and outs because I left that to my dad. It is understatement to say I never wanted to fall out with Frank. It was not pleasant, I was fond of Frank, I was still appreciative for what he did for me and he's shown time after time that he knows how to bring fighters on and get them the right fights. Promoting is about securing fights at the right time, stepping up at the right time and making the right move at the right time; Frank was exceptional at doing it and I'll forever be grateful for that.

It was my belief that when I beat Kostya Tszyu I would see more '0's on the end of any deal I was going to sign. I wasn't convinced he really wanted me to take the Tszyu fight, though that's only my opinion. When I got to the number one contender spot, I went and watched Man City in Frank's box at

Arsenal and he said that although I was the number one contender there were alternatives, like Vivian Harris and Sharmba Mitchell and that I didn't have to fight Kostya Tszyu; but I said that was the one fight I wanted. I thought that if I signed to fight Kostya then Frank would get me to do an extension of my contract. That's the way it works in the promotional game. 'I've got you this opportunity, so sign for more fights.' I never signed an extension.

I think he thought I was going to get beat, and maybe that's why we didn't do an extension. Before, whenever my contract had twelve months left, he always asked me to extend. That was the first time, in all my years with him, he never got me to do it.

I got the best payday of my career up to that point, but I thought I was worth more than what he offered me to carry on with him. Frank had said he had to pay big money to get Kostya Tszyu over here, that Tszyu had a massive entourage and we had to pay him to have the fight in Manchester and at the time that suited everyone. There's a lot of sense in that, so that's why he could only pay me what he did. 'But when you win,' Frank said, 'that's when things will really take off.' I won but his offer did not match what I thought it would, based on previous conversations. That's when I went speaking to other promoters, and what I was offered by them blew me away.

We spoke to Main Events and Golden Boy in the USA, but I ended up going with Dennis Hobson, a Sheffield promoter who had worked with IBF light-heavyweight champion Clinton Woods. He'd got Clinton some big fights against the likes of Roy Jones and the other leading fighters in his division. Sky Sports also came to me directly, as they knew my contract was up, and said they would pay me a certain amount per fight, and I thought, 'Bloody hell, is that just on Sky?' Not to mention my purses and everything else. We agreed a three-fight deal with Dennis and he paid me more than the others had offered, and the first bout of that deal was against Maussa at the Hallam FM Arena in Sheffield.

Perhaps it would have been back at the MEN Arena in Manchester had Frank not signed an exclusive boxing deal with them so only he could promote fights in that venue.

Bygones are bygones but it was very bitter with me and Frank. I was upset because I didn't think the offer matched what he'd said and I resented him a bit for it. He also claimed that we'd had a verbal agreement. He had a column in the *Sun*, which people told me they called 'The Ricky Hatton article' because he just slagged me off. There was a lot of anger there. We ended up in court. It was a shame what happened because I genuinely got on really, really well with Frank. I was very fond of him, really liked him, but I just felt I was worth more than he was ready to offer.

I can't have any regrets with how things turned out for me; when you look at the purses I ended up getting when I went on alone, I genuinely don't believe I would have got those purses had I been with anyone else. I'm sure I would have had a nice house, perhaps a nice boxing gym and a nice car, but I don't think it would be as nice as what I have got.

Again I was indebted to Mick Williamson against Maussa.

He had become a good friend outside the ring, but on so many occasions he saved my bacon; once in America, then against Jon Thaxton, Vince Phillips and Carlos Maussa. They were all horrendous cuts. Sometimes you hear someone say in the corner when you're watching boxing 'That's a bad cut' but I'd had worse ones shaving. Some of mine were horrific but Mick never used to panic. He'd get straight in there and start putting real pressure on the wound. Some cutsmen just dab at them and I think, 'Jeez, what are you doing?' With the Maussa cuts I went to the hospital to get stitched up and they were going to give me a needle to numb the area. There was an after-fight party at the Hilton in Sheffield and they went to inject me and I said, 'Whoa, whoa, whoa. Will I be able to have a pint after that?'

'Well, not really, no,' they said, shaking their heads.

'Fucking stitch it up,' I said.

My dad doesn't drink and he said, 'All for a drink? You dick-head. Have the needle.' I suppose anyone would have thought the same as him, but I felt I'd earned a drink. I got them to pass me a towel and told Paul Speak to hold me down. I folded the towel up, clamped my teeth down on it and they stitched those two craters up without any painkillers. The party was good, too, and there was a new deal on the table after Maussa, a three-fight package with HBO in the USA, the biggest network for boxing in the world. Showtime had been brilliant for me, but HBO were the biggest spenders, with the deepest pockets, meaning the biggest stars and the largest promotional groups inevitably gravitated towards them.

By beating Maussa I had unified the belts and was recognized by *Ring* magazine as the best light-welterweight in the world. It was clear I was the number one, and I wanted to do what a lot of great fighters have done: try to go through the weights.

People recognized me in America now, too. Kostya Tszyu was a megastar in Australia, had fought in Las Vegas, where he had knocked out Judah and unified the belts, and if you beat someone like that, even if people haven't seen the fight, they're like, 'Jesus Christ, someone beat Tszyu and made him quit on his stool? Oh, that's him.' I was ringside in Atlantic City for some fights at the time and they introduced Mexican legend Julio César Chávez, Oscar De La Hoya . . . and me. It was unbelievable to be mentioned alongside fighters like that.

HBO wanted to showcase me, and my first fight for them was against WBA welterweight world champion Luis Collazo in Boston. HBO selected tough Juan Lazcano first, because I wasn't planning on moving up in weight, but HBO wouldn't accept any of the other fighters, such as my IBF mandatory contender Naoufel Ben Rabah, who we put forward. For a while welterweight champion Carlos Baldomir, a rugged guy from Argentina, was in the running. Seven weeks before the fight, Lazcano pulled out injured and then they chucked in Collazo, who was a little bit unheard of at the time. He was a New York-based Puerto Rican, and I watched the tapes of him and I thought, 'He's not bad. Southpaw, and I've always struggled with southpaws. Pretty good.' He had won the WBA welterweight title from a decent fighter called José Antonio Rivera a year earlier.

He turned out to be a lot better than I thought. Billy Graham advised me against the fight: 'Ricky, I've had a look at this Collazo. Have you seen him?' asked Billy. 'Yeah, yeah. I think I can take him.' Billy still said he didn't like it. I was a five-foot-six-inch light-welterweight. I had no problems doing the weight. Why would I want to move up seven pounds? It's not like the lighter weights, where bantamweight is eight stone six and super-bantam is eight stone ten. I had to move up seven pounds and I didn't really have the height to carry it. So he was a southpaw and I was going straight in for a world title in a higher weight class against a bigger man, in America. 'No, no, no. This is bad,' Billy said. I told him that HBO weren't accepting anyone else, and in the end I just said I wanted to do it and become a two-weight world champion. Maybe I should have had a warm-up at the weight – but you don't really get those luxuries these days. So, somewhat reluctantly, we went with it because it was either all agree on that or get in line and wait for another date.

I always liked to be active and I didn't like the idea of being on the back burner after unifying the titles. The downside, apart from fighting someone with a style I needed like a hole in the head, was that having won the IBF and WBA light-welterweight belts I had to relinquish them to move up in weight and fight for the WBA title.

The story was 'Ricky Hatton comes to America'. It was in Boston. I'd beaten Tszyu, knocked out Maussa and was billed as a new sensation, just like Naz was when I had my second fight on his big Madison Square Garden show nine years earlier. For what the weather was like in Boston, it might as well have been in England, I'd never seen anything like it, severe floods, rivers were flowing down the streets and the rain was non-stop.

I went to a basketball game and a baseball game – neither of which I really understood – but we were cooped up most of the time. Still, training went well. Kerry Kayes assured me the seven extra pounds wouldn't be a problem and I'd always gone to the ring weighing around eleven stone two pounds on fight night anyway having weighed-in at ten stone the day before.

Just days ahead of the fight, we weren't actually even sure whether I would be fighting for the title; in a New York District Court, Souleymane M'baye – a Frenchman promoted by Frank Warren – had challenged the WBA over his position as their number one contender at light-welterweight. He wanted the WBA to refuse to sanction the Collazo fight unless I agreed to return to light-welterweight and fight him before a certain date. The courts denied him that, but they had recognized that the WBA had not treated him fairly and said he would be involved when the vacant light-welterweight title was fought for.

Because I'd surrendered my titles for this, I couldn't afford any slip-ups. If I lost, I would be at the back of the queue for any title fights, so it was a gamble. There was talk of fights with Shane Mosley and Oscar De La Hoya being around the corner. It doesn't get much bigger than that. But Collazo, who had won twenty-six fights and lost just once, said he had been waiting all of his life for an opportunity like this. Raised in

Brooklyn, Collazo said, 'This is the chance to prove to the world that I'm the truth,' he said. He had been a welterweight since the age of fifteen and he was going to make me earn every penny.

There were around 6,000 fans in the TD Banknorth Garden and a good number of Brits making their voices heard. I made the welterweight limit of ten stone seven at the first time of asking, and by fight night I was around four or five pounds heavier than I was when I usually fought – and I felt a little more sluggish because of it.

That said, I started quickly. I went in, turned Collazo so easily and cracked him. I knocked him down in the first ten seconds and thought, 'This is all right, this. That was all a bit easy.' Then he came back at me – he had been unsettled but not hurt. What I noticed was that when we were fighting at close-quarters, at light-welterweight I had been able to nudge people out of the way, push them and manhandle them a bit, and the first time I tried to shove him and throw him he didn't move. It was that extra seven pounds and it was all manufactured weight I'd put on. It's not like I had needed to go up. It was through diet and strength and conditioning with Kerry. I was never a welterweight, I hadn't grown into it, I'd made myself one. When you factor in that I'd struggled with southpaws, thinking back to Jürgen Brähmer in the amateurs and the likes of Eamonn Magee, it began to get difficult. When you go down the middle to fight – and I was so attacking-minded – you're always that nearer to the jab and open for the straight left against left-handed fighters.

The contest went one way and then the other. I was hitting him, banging him and barging him back. I was stronger than him but I could feel the difference having moved up. As the fight wore on, he must have thought 'I'm just as strong as him' and he started planting his feet a little bit more and pushing me back. No fighter had ever done that to me at light-welterweight; even Kostya Tsyzu, who I'd bulldozed. I could tell Collazo started to believe he could have his successes, too.

In the second half, I had no second wind. I just had to grind it out, thinking all the time, 'This fella's not gonna move now.' Previously my opponents would stand there and have a bit of a go. But then, after a bit, they couldn't handle the pace or the strength and started to move. Not Collazo. He stood there and had it out with me. It was a hard fight, a really hard fight. His shots were powerful and hurtful, and he was drilling me with one-twos down the middle. My punches didn't have the same snap in my shots at 147 pounds and I didn't have the same explosive power or strength. Then I started thinking how the last fight was nip and tuck.

More than that, it was absolutely draining. It took everything, and by the last round I was hanging on for dear life and ultimately it was only the early knockdown that won it for me. There's no doubt in my mind I deserved it, but it was only by the narrowest of margins. He thought he'd done enough to win, but it was my heart, work rate and angles that just saw me do enough to win 115–112, 115–112 and 114–113. I didn't even celebrate and could barely lift my arms above my head when Billy raised me onto his shoulders.

Billy was protective of me and blamed my move up on the demands of TV. 'The only reason you move up in weight is if you can't do the weight and that's not the case,' he said. 'But nobody listens to the trainer. Ricky is my friend and I see what he goes through.' My left eye was heavily bruised, my nose was broken and physically it is the worst I've ever been after a fight. Both of us looked dejected, despite the fact I had just become a two-weight world champion.

I changed into a suit for the post-fight press conference, where I told everyone I had noticed a difference in the weight. I searched for the positives straight away. 'If I'm going to stay at welterweight, I have to grow into the weight,' I said, 'but my first fight was against a world champion – and not even Floyd Mayweather did that. I'll get better.'

I'd managed to find a way to win and, after spending some time at the after-fight party at the Hyatt, we ended up raiding the hotel minibars. I wanted to enjoy it but things rapidly went downhill when me and Jen got into the hotel room. The pace of the fight and how gruelling it had been suddenly hit me. It was a long night. I hardly slept and Jennifer kept pleading with me to call the doctor. I plunged the room into darkness and lay on the bed. Jennifer lay next to me and kept asking me to call for help, but I wouldn't. I said I'd be okay, but one minute I was hot, then I was cold, then I was shaking. My face bulged with the swelling. I was like death warmed up, sipping water all night. I couldn't stand light or noise. Even when I closed my eyes, colourful shadows danced around in front of me as I shook more and more violently. It was a horrible feeling and I eventually fell asleep, utterly exhausted.

When I got up in the morning I was okay, although I was still carrying those war wounds to my battered face. Collazo wanted to fight me again but I soon realized welterweight wasn't for me so announced I'd return to light-welterweight and that was that. I think the Americans loved the fight, but HBO might have thought I was not as good as people were making out, yet there was still momentum. It was a good fight for the fans and I'd now won the WBA title at welterweight making me a two-weight champion. I just think it was clear welterweight was not the division for me.

I needed to rest, and a family holiday to Florida with my mum, dad, Jennifer and Campbell was in order. We went there almost straight after the fight and went around the theme parks in Orlando. We went to the Rainforest Cafe in the Animal Kingdom and I had a double rack of ribs and a mountain of chips. My eyes were clearly bigger than my stomach, though there was time to work on that in the coming months, but I was struggling and relieved when they took the plate away. Then they put an enormous gateau, with four or five layers and sparklers coming out of the top (it was meant to look like a volcano), in front of me. 'Congratulations on your fight, Mr Hatton,' they said. 'There's no way I'm going to eat any of this,' I thought, smiling and nodding gratefully. Campbell was only young and he helped me but Jennifer said it would be rude if I didn't eat it. So I was cutting it off, shoving it round the plate and playing with it, and by the time I'd got to the hotel – because I'd just finished my fight and my stomach had shrunk – my belly was almost cake-shaped. I could literally balance a pint on the cake in my tummy.

It was a great holiday. One night, my mum and dad had Campbell, while me and Jen went to Pleasure Island, a place where they have bars, cinemas and nightclubs, and there was an Irish pub there. My eyes lit up, a fluorescent shamrock to me is like the star of Bethlehem. I was so chuffed; they had an Irish band and it was brilliant. We had something to eat – they didn't charge us: 'Mr Hatton, that's on the house.' We went in a few other bars, including a cigar bar as I used to like the odd cigar, and I went to the toilets and came back to find a few guys surrounding Jennifer and one in my chair. 'What's going on here, fellas?' I said.

'Hey, man. It's Ricky Hatton,' they replied.

'Yes, it's Ricky Hatton – and that's my seat, mate.' They couldn't apologize enough.

We went to another bar, and it was a gay club with a rotating dance floor. I went to the bar to get a drink and Jennifer was behind me. Next thing you know, she was moving away from me, thanks to the dance floor, and halfway round the other side of the club and there were a load of guys around me asking me if I was all right and what I was doing. I shouted, 'Jen, Jen. Come back!'

As 2006 ended I'd had just one fight in the calendar year. The court case with Warren was still to run its course; and the WBA gave me 120 days after defeating Collazo to defend against Oktay Urkal, who was a decent German – but that fight meant little to anyone. One thing we did know was that the Americans were pleased enough with the action from the Collazo fight to want us back.

Collazo turned out to be a handful for anyone and someone I did not get much credit for beating because no one had ever really heard of him; but after he fought me he put in a good performance against Shane Mosley and then fought Andre Berto and HBO had him beating Berto. My profile was increasing all the time, and whenever I went back to America I was being recognized more often. Wherever I went it was, 'Ricky, this is such and such from HBO', 'Ricky, this is so and so from the MGM.' It was the stuff dreams are made of. For someone like me, who grew up on a council estate, to have someone like David Beckham texting me and asking me about my next fight, I was really proud. It was getting big.

Seven months after Collazo I was back in business. I was training through Christmas for an IBF light-welterweight title fight with the man they called 'Iron Twin' Juan Urango, who again was not known much outside of boxing's hardcore fans, but it was a fight that would see me as the headline act in Las Vegas for the first time. I actually spent Christmas Day in the gym with Billy and Matthew, who was also fighting on the bill. The co-feature saw the excellent Mexican José Luis Castillo in with Cameroon's dangerman Herman Ngoudjo, and my fight with Urango and Castillo's were seen as semi-finals, with the winners to meet later in the year.

My team and I were walking down The Strip, past Paris and past Caesars, and up in lights there were adverts for Celine

Dion, Tom Jones . . . and then my face popped up, giant-sized. I couldn't believe it – I grabbed my camera as fast as I could and took a picture, I was like a schoolkid. There were problems, however. I was staying in the casinos and anyone who has stayed in the casinos in Vegas knows that they can leave your nose bunged up, courtesy of the air conditioning, and it was terrible – my nose was rock solid. In training I'd said to Billy, 'I feel like shit.' We used to do our traditional fifteen rounds on the bodybelt as our last workout, and we had to cut it down to twelve because I was tired. Billy said, 'You're not going to get any fitter, Ricky. There's no point leaving another three rounds here on the bodybelt and dragging it out.' Mentally, I just thought, 'I've not done my fifteen.' I was back at light-welterweight and should have been more comfortable, but even the change back in my diet and having to drop seven pounds more than I did for Collazo threw me out a bit, too.

The morning before the weigh-in I went down to the area where we were going to take to the scales and I said to the organizers, 'So where are the ropes that corner off the stage?' They said they didn't need it and I went, 'Really? Do you know how many we're bringing?' They assured us they knew what they were doing and we left them to it.

Sure enough, when the fans came they completely took over. Whoosh – the place was under siege. They were climbing up the slot machines, singing, 'There's only one Ricky Hatton', and there were only about five security guards for hundreds upon hundreds of fans. We'd warned them, and it was bedlam.

I had watched Urango, the Colombian Hulk, on video, and he was a strong fighter, unbeaten in eighteen fights with just one draw. When I saw him at the weigh-in he was enormous and I whispered to Billy, 'It's killed him to make the weight. No way is he going to make this.' They said, 'ten stone exactly,' and I thought 'Fucking hell. He's done it.' He was a giant of a man. He had a huge upper body, a big old back. Spindly little legs, though. His top half was massive, and he got me with a body shot in, I think, the sixth round and I really had to hold on. I could have done with being able to breathe through my nose then. In fact he hurt me a few times to the head as well.

Even though I was known as a scrapper, I had a better boxing brain than people thought. Nine times out of ten I liked to have a tear-up but I thought, 'I'm ill, here, so what do I need to do to win this fight? He's built like a brick shithouse, but he's slow.' So it was bang, bang, get three or four shots off and smother him. Then do it again. I could get inside, fire off some shots and then smother him, cover him up. Then he'd come again. I'd pick him off on the way in and grab him once more. It must have pissed him right off.

I got stick afterwards for hitting and holding, but that's where I felt comfortable. I just thought, 'Move, move, move. Don't try to knock him out. Look at the size and strength of him.' The only chance he had was to knock me out and the only way he was going to knock me out was if I stood there and had it out with him. In the end it was a landslide victory, I won 119–109 on all three scorecards, but I was blowing my nose from start to finish and coughing up all kinds of crap in between rounds.

Even though I had boxed okay, my first two fights on HBO were little short of a disaster to be honest. Like Collazo, Urango wasn't a vintage performance and HBO probably thought, 'We've done our money here, you little git.' Of course the performances were not perfect, but the Hatton bandwagon still gathered pace.

I was known more than ever for ballooning up in weight, and fighting less often gave me more opportunity to do that. I used to do it when I was the WBU champion. The most fights I'd had in a twelve month period was five when I was WBU champion and I'd lost two-and-half stone for each fight; I lost more than my body weight in that one year.

Making the weight was easier as I got older. Generally it's harder to lose weight as time goes by, but I got more knowledgeable about what I was eating. Kerry was telling me what and when to eat and saying stuff like, 'Instead of eating all that, cut it in half and have two meals. Have more meals on a regular basis and in the first few weeks in camp spend time on the treadmill dropping weight before you go to the gym.' I made the weight more easily, even though I was still doing damage to my body – taking two-and-a-half stone off every time meant I was still taking short cuts, and sooner or later it would catch up to me.

I feel ashamed to admit it now. That said, when you look at the weight I put on you could tell I was dedicated to getting it off. Being in such bad condition and then looking and performing as I did – you need dedication to do that. You can eat fatty foods, you can drink beer and put weight on if you're delivering papers, if you're decorating a bedroom wall or stacking shelves in the supermarket. But you can't do it when your body pays the bills. You can't do anything that harms your body. You can't do it for ten years, which is how long professional careers can be. The only way you get real wages is if you keep winning, and the only way you keep winning is giving yourself the best chance. It's the hardest game in the world; there's no need to make it even harder or do anything that will damage that engine. But I'd done it for that long and was getting away with it. I thought it would last forever. I honestly did.

After signing up to fight Castillo I was certain I was going to be able to get back on track, but after the tough nights with Maussa, Collazo and Urango there was no reason to think taking on the old Mexican warrior would be anything different. I had not lost in forty-two fights. Castillo was a brilliant lightweight who had twice given Floyd Mayweather all he could handle, and many felt he had actually deserved the decision in their first fight. He'd also defeated some top quality opponents like Julio Díaz, Juan Lazcano and the Cuban Joel Casamayor, and he moved up in weight to beat Ngoudjo in a WBC title eliminator. The fact that he was involved in one of the most thrilling fights of all time, against Diego Corrales, also appealed, as the common thought was that our styles would blend to provide an all-action fight.

I think people were expecting a war of Corrales–Castillo

proportions; I said at the time, 'I didn't think it would be a tickling contest.'

Castillo lurked on the peripheries of some pound-for-pound lists but he had publicly outgrown the lightweight division when he failed the scales ahead of a rematch with Corrales. Diego, a true warrior from Vegas, still took the fight but was chinned in four rounds.

There was a real buzz about our fight at the Thomas & Mack Center in Las Vegas, the most for one of my fights since Kostya Tszyu. I had a couple of special guests walk to the ring with me as Mexican legend Marco Antonio Barrera and Manchester United and England striker Wayne Rooney carried my championship belts. I knew I'd need every bit of help I could get to beat Castillo, who I had the utmost respect for.

Marco and I had become great friends over the years. We had boxed on the same bill in Atlantic City in 1997 – we didn't run into each other then, it was only years later when I was in Vegas that we met. He had been a world champion and finished Britain's Richie Wenton in three rounds on the Naseem Hamed–Wayne McCullough bill. Marco was world class while I was just having my ninth fight; I had been to Las Vegas to watch some of his as a fan. As I walked through one of the casinos, Robert Diaz, the matchmaker for Golden Boy Promotions, came over to me and asked what I was doing in town, and I told him I was visiting to watch Marco fight. He said Marco, who was one of Golden Boy's major names, would love to meet me and I was amazed. Marco ended up inviting me to his suite, where his kids, mum and grandparents were, and he introduced me to everyone and we struck up a really close friendship.

It might have been slightly problematic when I asked him to carry my belt in, and I thought hard about asking him. Castillo was his countryman, and perhaps I shouldn't have put him in an awkward position, but I put him on the spot and asked him anyway. 'I'd love to,' he said.

'Are you sure?' I checked. 'You won't upset Castillo?'

He said, 'Fuck Castillo, you're my brother.'

I think Wayne was really pleased to be asked, too. I'd met him twelve months earlier, and I don't mix with a lot of footballers but with Wayne what you see is what you get with him – he likes a laugh and a joke and we hit it off from the start. So I asked him to carry my belt in, told him that having someone like him carrying it in would inspire me, and he said he'd do it. Yes, he might have been a Manchester United player but he represented my city, and I was proud to have him in my corner.

I rented an apartment just off The Strip and I had fans in my room instead of putting up with the extreme air conditioning in the casino hotels and felt much better for it. I reckoned I was under pressure to perform after the Collazo and Urango fights and, as me and Castillo got stuck into each other from the opening bell, I did just that.

Early in the fight Billy actually told me off in the corner because I'd gone out there with the intention of boxing a bit, settling in to it and it was not long before I deviated from the game plan.

The first time I came together with Castillo and we exchanged, he leaned in to me and I got him, grabbed him and pushed him to the side, hit him with a body shot. He hit me with one and I pushed him back and was quite surprised at how weak he felt. Having fought a welterweight in Collazo and a muscle-bound freak like Urango, in comparison Castillo felt like a rag doll. Billy turned round and said, 'What are you doing? You're going crazy in there.' I said, 'Billy, you don't know what I'm feeling. He's ready for the taking.'

When you get there you can just feel it and you know. I could nudge him and he was on his heels, and I could throw him to the side and bang away with both hands, get into him and beat him to the head and body. When you feel that it's not the time to jab, it's the time to fucking jump on him.

That's why me and Billy had such a great relationship. We would both get tapes of opponents, go away, come back to the gym and talk about it and, before I could say it, he was thinking it and, before he could say it, I was thinking it. It was boxing telepathy.

In my first exchange with Castillo, I thought, 'You ain't gonna last here.' So I did what came naturally and jumped on him. Fighting at close-quarters is in many ways more artful than boxing at distance – the way you use angles, push their hands away to make the gaps, flick their gloves away to get your own shots off, step to the side, turn, pivot, tuck your elbows in. It's poetry. It's violent, but it's poetry. Me and Castillo, with our foreheads pressed up against one another, trading body shots, with the timing and both of us going for it, was like two masters of infighting. Referee Joe Cortez just let us get on with it.

Castillo was getting me with body shots up the middle and I was getting them in the middle and round the side. He was catching me, not hurting me, but he was getting the shots off and scoring here and there. When I went for him with my punches he was pulling his elbows in to his sides, reducing the target area. The only way you can look after your body is with your arms and I was throwing the left hook to the body and he was getting his elbows down, so I realized I had to punch somewhere else first to open him up. If you hit someone in the head their elbows will come up and you can then sweep round the sides.

So I had to get him to the head, then to the body, but it was easier said than done because he'd studied me. I tried a few right hooks to the body, then a few down the middle into the pit of his stomach, but it was hard to get through, past his arms. Castillo was very clever but just then, after about two minutes of round four, I got him in the right position; I could see his elbow had finally left his body open and with my entire body weight I just touched him with a left hook. I heard him gasp for breath and he wheeled away in pain and onto one knee.

You could tell the way he went down – he scurried away spinning around – that it had got him. And I thought, 'He's not getting up here.'

I like to think that body shot would have knocked anyone out. It was the best body shot I've thrown. The minute it landed I thought, 'Oooo, that's the one. That's the spot, that's got him.' And it did. If he hadn't gone down from that I think I would have shit myself. I just got him in the perfect position and it hit the spot. Straight away, as soon as it landed, I knew he was gone.

No one had predicted an ending like that and it was just what I needed to breathe new life into my career. Again, although I was really pleased with the performance, there always seemed to be naysayers – there always have been. 'Well, he struggled with Collazo. Yeah, Urango, no one had ever heard of him. Ah, Castillo's past it.' I thought, 'What more can I do?' Maybe Castillo had seen better years, maybe he hadn't. But to knock out someone as tough as him with a body punch like I did was something else. You always get critics who say he would never have gone down from a body shot like that a few years ago, but why wouldn't he? I broke four of his ribs with one punch – if I broke four of *your* ribs with one punch you'd probably go down.

It disappointed me that people seemed to say he was past his best only after I'd stopped him. When they saw his fights with Diego Corrales and his first fight with Floyd Mayweather, the fans and experts thought we would have a tear-up. People in boxing might have known I'd broken his ribs, and the excellent light-middleweight Winky Wright, who was ringside that night, can be seen applauding the shot as soon as it landed, but I don't think I quite got the respect I deserved for that performance because people started asking questions about whether Castillo was over the hill. Not many people had said that beforehand. Regardless of that, however, it put me in a far better standing with my career, and needless to say the celebrations started almost instantly.

The day after Castillo, me and Jennifer were round the pool by the Mandalay Bay drinking, spending some quality time together, and I'd treated her to a cabana and some champagne. Then, during the day, I said, 'I fancy going to see Tom Jones, love.' We made our way through the casino, a little worse for wear, went to the front desk and tried to order some tickets for the show that night.

'Certainly, Mr Hatton,' they said. 'How much is that?' I asked. 'They're on the house.' Wow, free tickets to a Tom Jones concert. 'And your beer and wine will be paid for all night.' By now the pair of us were steaming.

Tom Jones came on stage and said he'd like to give a mention to another Brit in the audience and he introduced me. The lights then beamed on me. 'Ricky, are you going to join me for a drink afterwards?' Tom said in front of everyone. Me and Jennifer were in a bad way by now.

Later on, Tom took us back into his changing room and he had his own bar there. His agent was there and we were having a drink, with different people coming in for pictures with him, and he asked us if we'd eaten and invited us out for a meal.

Now I can handle my beer but Jennifer can't, and she was struggling. You know when you're thinking, 'We need to get out of here' – that's what I was thinking. Jennifer was talking the biggest load of shit I'd ever heard. At dinner, Tom turned to me and said, 'Would you like a cognac, Ricky?' My knees were knocking as it was – and I didn't even know what cognac was. 'Of course I do,' I said, politely. Then Jennifer said to Tom, 'What does your wife think of all the gallivanting that goes with show business?'

'We're going to have to go now, Tom,' I interrupted, and we bailed out. He was laughing, though. He could see we were in a sorry state.

On a more serious note, people had been talking about the possibility of me fighting Floyd Mayweather long before Castillo, even though I hadn't been over the moon with those fights against Collazo and Urango. I'd won both fights and added a welterweight title, so speculation was increasing. It helped that I had this incredible following – rising from about 4,000 for the Collazo fight in Boston, to about 6,000 in Las Vegas for the Urango fight and then for the Castillo fight around 10,000. It was just growing and growing.

After the Castillo fight, live on HBO, I was asked about Floyd Mayweather. American TV didn't just like the fighter, they liked the story: 'Who's this slugger-scrapper with the massive following?' Floyd had the bling and all that – we were made for each other because we were polar opposites. I jokingly enquired how many rounds Castillo had done with Floyd. They had boxed twenty-four rounds in their two fights, with Mayweather nicking the first by the skin of his teeth. I responded to the interviewer and said in front of millions of people, 'There's a reason all these fans have come over to watch me and that's because I'm all about excitement. You saw more excitement in those four rounds than you've seen in Floyd's whole fucking career.'

That did it. That one line tipped my popularity over the edge in the USA. I'm proud to say I became a big star in America and on HBO, but from where it started off with Collazo it was a bad beginning, with people thinking, 'This kid's not that good.' Then, with three wins and that one line during a post-fight interview, well, that got the interest going all right – and it led to more than 25,000 fans going from England to Las Vegas.

CHAPTER 8

Mayweather

I first laid eyes on the 'Pretty Boy' in 2005 when he fought Arturo Gatti in Atlantic City.

It was only a couple of weeks after I'd beaten Kostya Tszyu, and for a while people had speculated that one day I might face Gatti – a crowd-pleasing puncher who was born in Canada but fought out of New Jersey. So I went to the fight and spent time with Arturo in his hotel beforehand. They were boxing for the WBC light-welterweight belt, and Floyd Mayweather had recently moved up from lightweight. He had won world titles at super-featherweight, lightweight and now, after demolishing Gatti, light-welterweight, killing the idea of me ever fighting Arturo.

Floyd was incredible that night, to be honest; he was something else against Gatti – he just made it look so easy. Gatti was a future Hall of Famer, but Floyd absolutely took him apart with a master-class of spiteful counterpunching. Floyd had something that I had not seen before. It was a mismatch, really, and it looked like Floyd could finish it at any time.

When I beat Tszyu, he was above Mayweather in the pound-for-pound rankings so I thought, 'Okay, so Gatti was just a plodder. With my work rate, and if Kostya Tszyu couldn't keep me off, how could Mayweather?' So it was in my mind that we might fight one day. I knew it was possible. Mayweather called me out after the Gatti battering, saying we should fight at Madison Square Garden, and that I was a dirty fighter.

As a young gun, and having walked through everything Tszyu had given me at the time, nothing frightened me. I just thought, 'All in good time, mate.'

I did not see Floyd Mayweather again until it came time to publicize our fight, set for 8 December 2007, nearly two years later. We did a five-city press tour through Los Angeles, Grand Rapids in Michigan – his hometown – New York, Manchester and London to publicize the event while filming a mini-series, *Hatton Mayweather 24/7*, for HBO, a show that documented the build-up to the fight to create intrigue and awareness for the pay-per-view.

In America, Floyd gave me such a drilling everywhere we went – he gave me so much stick. The Los Angeles press conference was at Disneyland. There was a red carpet and it was in the sunshine, and he was slagging me off, saying, 'Come here, give me some of that face-to-face shit', wanting to square up with me for the cameras and just talking down at me the whole time. I was simply hitting the usual soundbites, like 'Yeah, it'll be a good fight' and all the rest of it. I tried not to sound bothered, but I came out of all of our meetings thinking, 'You wanker.'

One night, I was out for a meal in a restaurant in Los Angeles with my dad, Kerry Kayes, Paul Speak and Billy Graham. We were all sat round the table when Floyd comes in and says, 'Ah, Ricky, you're having something to eat. I'll get this.' He started throwing $100 bills at us, shouting, 'The meal's on me.' I thought, 'You fucking idiot,' until I saw the bills all over the table – 'Hang on, there's $600 there' – so I stuffed it all in my pocket!

He wasn't getting a bite from me but I didn't like him at all. At Grand Rapids, we went to a place where he went to school and there were loads of kids there and every time I came out they booed, and every time Floyd came out they cheered. That was part of it. I just thought, 'You wait until we get to Manchester. You're going to fucking have it, you.'

At Manchester Town Hall I had home advantage for the first time. It was pissing down with rain but they put the big screens up and there were 5,000 fans there, inside and out, singing, 'There's only one Ricky Hatton.'

Floyd could never be accused of not playing up to a crowd and so almost predictably showed up in a Manchester United shirt. I stood behind the curtains with him waiting to go outside, with the biggest security guard I'd ever seen flanking him. Somebody launched a plastic bottle at the stage and the security guard dipped out of the way and the bottle hit Floyd right on the head – some security guard he was.

In the Town Hall we got on the stage and I started saying, 'We've been on this tour for several days. We've been to Los Angeles, Grand Rapids and New York, and I've been away from my little lad Campbell for more than a week. But it's not been too bad because I've spent the time with another fucking eight-year-old, this dickhead here.' The crowd loved it. He might have had the edge in America but at the press conference in Manchester I was relentless with the microphone and I let him have it.

Floyd, in his Manchester United shirt, started dancing to my fans, singing: 'There's only one Ricky Hatton.' He was about to be on *Dancing with the Stars* in the USA and I went on, 'If you dance like that on *Dancing with the Stars*, you're going fucking nowhere, pal.' I bet he couldn't wait to get back home. Over Floyd's shoulder, however, I could see the Sky Sports camera-men shouting, 'Ricky, we're live.' It was only about lunchtime. 'Stop swearing.' Nobody had told me it was live – I had been effing and jeffing, and they had to cut it and start making excuses, saying how heated it was becoming. 'Emotions are running high,' they tried to explain. I was doing my after-dinner speeches and was in full flow. Friends of mine were watching outside on the big screens and they were in stitches.

On the train to London, Oscar De La Hoya and Richard Schaefer told me Floyd was absolutely seething, saying I'd been disrespecting him. Still, it was no more than he'd been doing to me for the last nine days. People would ask me if I was insulted by him filming *Dancing with the Stars* at the same time as he was training but I wasn't. I was still watching City, still playing darts on a Friday night and doing what I wanted to do.

Once we hit America, I stayed in the same apartment we

had for the Castillo fight and training camp went well. I was also given a boost thanks to a phone call.

'Ricky, it's Kostya,' he said, with the familiarity of an old friend.

Kostya Tszyu phoned to wish me luck, even though we had not seen one another since the morning after our fight. 'Believe in yourself, Ricky,' he said. 'I know you've got the heart to do it. Stick to your game plan, no matter how hard it gets.'

That is the only time I've spoken to him since. He offered me help on the night of our fight but our paths hadn't really crossed since. I appreciated the call.

Jen had been working as a schoolteacher, and in that job the staff only have their breaks when the kids are on holiday. She asked for permission to come to Vegas to support me with it being such a high-profile fight against the best boxer in the world. 'I've got to be there, Rick,' she said. 'If something happens I'd never forgive myself.'

It was unfortunate, and I thought it was poor of the school, but Jen ended up retiring from her job because she couldn't be at the fight otherwise. She came out the week of the fight.

By then Las Vegas was buzzing with thousands upon thousands of Brits and the event was billed as 'Undefeated' because Floyd's record stood at 38–0 and mine was 43–0. It was huge. He had defeated Sharmba Mitchell and Judah (like Tszyu had) and the Argentine hardman Carlos Baldomir – all at welterweight. Not only had he grown into the bigger weight, but he had even stepped up to light-middleweight to beat Oscar De La Hoya in the fight that grossed more than any other in boxing history.

The final press conference in Vegas saw us go head-to-head for nearly two minutes and the media shots taken that day clearly did the trick. The day before the fight, fans started queuing at six in the morning for the afternoon weigh-in. It snaked through the casino floor, the beer was flowing and the fans were in fine voice. By the time I got to the scales on the makeshift stage in the Grand Garden Arena, where we would fight in the MGM Grand the next day, I was on fire and more than ready. More than 8,000 fans were there waiting for me – I'd never seen anything like it. They were in half of the arena that had been curtained off, and they were singing, cheering, shouting – it was a huge occasion in its own right.

We both weighed in and I grabbed the microphone. 'Who've you come to see?' I shouted. 'Floyd?'

'No,' they yelled, with the unison of an army battalion.

'Me?'

'Yes,' they screamed.

'Who's taking the belts?' I shouted.

'You,' they yelled back.

'Let's fucking have him.'

Maybe I got caught up in the occasion and the selling of the fight but I wasn't stressed out or worried. Not at all, I was living for it. It was electric in there. The Brits absolutely shouted the house down, singing and chanting, 'You're supposed to be at home', and 'Who are ya?' at Floyd.

I weighed in at ten stone five. Fine. Mayweather, who fired off a pointless throat-slitting gesture in my direction, was bang on the welterweight limit of ten stone seven.

I roared at the fans, threw my T-shirt into the crowd and felt great. Then I went head-to-head with that mouthy dick-head. At every press conference he had been all: 'Yeah, come here, give that face-to-face shit,' and finally, after we weighed in, I motored up to him, got in his face and went, 'Now's the time for the nose-to-nose stuff, you prick.' I got right in his face, pushed forwards and he raised his arms to hold me back. I think he was really taken aback – what with the crowd and me getting right in his face, it worked. There was a little bit of pulling and pushing. Nothing major. But I was fired up.

People thought he'd wound me up and that I'd lost my cool but I hadn't. I came straight off the scales, posed for pictures, went round the curtains and laughed with Billy, 'We've got him riled here.' I was laughing and joking, I didn't lose my cool. I knew what I was doing and I was loving it.

When I got in his face I wanted to show Floyd I didn't give a fuck who he was, I wasn't scared. Everyone thought I'd lost it a bit, but I promise you I hadn't.

The place was alive. Oscar De La Hoya said to me he'd never even seen it like that for his weigh-ins, and he was the biggest draw in boxing for a decade. The casinos were running out of beer, then they were running out of spirits. My fans sang songs up and down The Strip, and in and out of the casinos. The Brits had taken over Las Vegas.

I was the underdog, but there was still a school of thought that I was going to be the stronger man. I'd seen a lot of Floyd's fights and I drew heart from his fights with Castillo, in particular the first one, which I thought he lost. Although the fight was at welterweight, where Floyd had won the WBC title we were fighting for, I was a fully fledged light-welterweight, whereas Floyd had been moving up in weight over the years.

It was always going to be important who the referee was. Would he let me fight up close? What pace would he let us fight at? Would it be one who would let us fight, or was it going to be a referee that was going to break us every five seconds?

'Absolutely fantastic,' I thought, when I heard it was going to be Joe Cortez. 'Great.' It was like 1–0 then – 'Advantage Hatton'. Against Castillo he had let us go toe-to-toe.

The MGM Grand Garden Arena wasn't as big as the MEN, and I'd argue this night was not as big as the Tszyu one for me personally, because that was a Mancunian in Manchester. That was my moment. But this was Mayweather's hometown and beforehand all you could hear was the fans chanting, 'There's only one Ricky Hatton.' I thought, 'Jeez, if that was my hometown and they were singing "there's only one Floyd Mayweather ", I'd be gutted.' The crowd was ramped up, deafening; it was one of boxing's glamour nights, with Denzel Washington, Bruce Willis, Gwen Stefani, Jude Law, David Beckham, Will Ferrell and Kid Rock all ringside. Tom Jones sang the national anthem for me, while R & B artist Tyrese did the honours for America. The crowd booed Tyrese and the American anthem; a few people later told me referee Joe Cortez was holding his heart at the same time as it was being played, shaking his head at the boos and apparently looking disgusted. I don't condone booing a national anthem and never would.

The game plan was to ease into the fight, try to time

Mayweather's speed first and not be too careless because he was a master of defence. But the first thing I noticed was his speed. Against Tszyu I felt that if I stood at a distance he would get me with the big right hand, but here I thought, 'I'm not going to win this fight by outboxing him.' I thought I'd be the stronger man – Floyd isn't a big welterweight, but he looked bigger than me by a fair bit. I was never a welterweight.

Floyd's speed and defence was really outstanding, it nearly took my breath away at times. He hit me with one lead left hook and it was that fast I didn't see it. I thought, 'Jesus Christ! I'm going to ease into the fight here' – and then – 'If I stand-off, he's going to have a field day; he's got the speed, he's got the technique, that's the distance he likes, so you're going to have to do what you do best – get in close and bully him.' That left hook was that fast – bang! 'Fucking hell, I can't stand on the outside here.' So I moved in on him, although I still struggled to get my punches off he was so slippery.

But within seconds Joe Cortez was stepping in – even though I had some early success with my jab. One knocked Mayweather off balance in round one but moments later Cortez was getting stuck in again. And again. And again. Where was the Joe Cortez who'd said 'Break free' and 'Punch your way out' during the Castillo fight? He was ruining my rhythm.

In the early going there were times Floyd and I were both punching and Cortez still told us to break. I landed a left to the body and Cortez was in again. Floyd picked me off with a few shots, but I thought I won the first round.

Yet for me Cortez got worse as it went on, and I was promptly becoming more and more frustrated. Increasingly I lost my shape. My blood comes to the boil in the second round even when I watch it back now. I was catching his shots, getting in close and then we were told to break. Of course it's Floyd Mayweather and he's going to get you with a few punches, but he was holding me sometimes and Cortez was ticking me off. By now, Oscar De La Hoya was on his feet at ringside asking Cortez what he was doing. He was holding his hands up in disbelief.

Mayweather grabbed me at one time when I wanted to punch and we were told to break before I could do any work. I got through with jabs here and there, took a right, but after I'd scored with another lovely jab the referee was straight in there again.

As you can imagine, it's a hard enough task fighting that fucker Mayweather at the best of times – he was holding me constantly before I'd had the chance to throw anything. Cortez called a timeout and warned us both he was going to take a point from each of us, when I felt all he needed to do was sit down, shut up and let us fight.

At ringside people were shrugging their shoulders, wondering what the hell was going on, but I felt I won the second, too. As well as I was doing, though, I couldn't get a rhythm going. Cortez would break my momentum. Seconds after round three started the referee was involved again. Then, after me and Mayweather nailed each other, Cortez intervened once more – I felt he wasn't even giving us time to see if we were going to throw a punch.

'Hatton, Hatton, Hatton' chants echoed around the arena but they sounded understandably frustrated. I got Floyd on the ropes and I felt good with him there but I still couldn't hit him cleanly. His defence was so masterful that if I did get a shot in, and I was landing occasionally, it was never solid. He would get something on it or just get out of the way. He was catching me with the odd clean one, too, but I was still getting jabs in. My work rate was good.

Then he started doing something different, ducking low in a defensive position, falling beneath my waist and that was not legal. He landed some lovely shots, clean punches, and I took a right and then a cut opened above my right eye. Damn. I was doing all right, though, it was a nothing cut. Not when you think of the wounds I'd had before. I was landing shots but could never really hit him full on. He would slip, shoulder-roll or duck.

I can't emphasize it enough: he had a brilliant defence – the odd one would get through but nothing clean, or with any venom that would do Floyd any damage. But because of my work rate there was not much in it by the time the fourth round started.

Cortez was again on my case. 'Ricky, no holding.' 'Ricky, let go.' I couldn't hear Floyd's name but it takes two to tango. He did get a warning for using his elbow to keep me off – and rightly so – but for me Cortez was not picking up on how low Floyd was ducking, and, although I was still having some success, Cortez never seemed to let the fight flow. The crowd was also getting impatient with Cortez. There was a buzz as people talked about what he was doing, but the volume increased when I shipped some flush shots in the fifth.

It was Floyd's best round of the fight up to that point and when he opened up he was something else. It wasn't just the referee who was infuriating me; I was frustrated by how good Mayweather was – the prick.

I walked back to my corner just thinking, 'This fucking referee. I have a difficult enough job as it is and he's not letting me fight.' Whether I was right or wrong that is what I was feeling and it was affecting me. Mayweather was dipping low again, below my waist, and when I didn't nail him cleanly I just had to admire what a master of defence he was. It was so hard to nail him. I still was getting one or two through, but not whacking him cleanly. He was exceptional. It was impressive, to say the least. Again, with no one holding but with us both in close, Cortez bellowed, 'No holding.' Cortez kept pulling me away, and pulling me away, making a difficult job virtually impossible. I couldn't go to the body as much as I wanted because Floyd was so good in defence. Some thought I'd won round five, others thought he was slightly ahead, but I don't think there was masses in it.

But the frustration within me was coming to the boil and from the sixth onwards, the fight just started to drift away from me.

I forced him to the ropes, turned him and threw a right hand in the direction of the back of his head and it missed. It actually connected with the top rope he was sheltering under. Usually, if a referee is going to take a point off you he will delay the action and warn you, one-to-one, formally in front of everyone. Cortez deducted a point from me for a punch that did not even land. Oscar and Bernard Hopkins at ringside were incensed. So were the fans. They sounded disgusted. That is when I really lost it.

When Cortez waved it on I turned my back and gave Floyd a free shot, sticking my arse up into the air. I was fuming. He'd turned his back so I asked Cortez, 'Where do you want me to fucking hit him?'

Then Floyd was using his shoulder here and there, but by that time it really didn't matter as I had played into his hands. I was like a bull in a china shop – reckless. He was elbowing me, ducking low, the referee was straight in and, from the moment that point was taken away from me in the sixth round, that's where the fight slipped.

'The referee's a wanker,' the Brits sang. I couldn't have agreed more. 'Break, break,' was all I could hear. Don't get me wrong, I am not saying Cortez was being dishonest in his refereeing. I did feel though that he was having a bad day at the office and that his calls were wrong, but I am not saying he was trying to cheat me.

I was deviating from the game plan now, and, instead of fighting with a strategic mind, I was trying to take my anger out on Floyd. At the end of the sixth Floyd hit me on the back of the head and Cortez did nothing. Great.

In all of the years I had Mick Williamson in my corner I'd hardly heard him say anything to an official. In between rounds six and seven, with the crowd still singing a less than flattering song about Cortez, Mick turned to him and said, 'Watch his facking elbows.' You'd never hear Mick do that.

According to HBO, I was a point up. That might not have been a common view, although it showed I was in the fight.

You could see Floyd's class when he opened up again in the seventh with quality shots, though. I was working hard but the success was becoming more restricted because I'd lost my rag. He was really finding the gaps in the eighth. He landed a flush right. I didn't lose my legs, he was not a concussive puncher, but he could pick the right shot. That's the difference between the good fighters and the great fighters. I still had some good bursts but the referee was in again, even when there was no holding. The fans, as it was slipping away, still sung their hearts out, every one of them.

When Floyd cracked me with a few more consecutive shots in that eighth that was probably the moment when it dawned on me that night: the fight had gone. My senses were there, my legs were under me and I was firing back, but his punches were having an accumulative effect. It was not the single punch power that bothered me, he was chipping away at me.

Along with me getting frustrated, as the rounds progressed, Floyd started to show what a clever fighter he was. I was throwing punches ten to the dozen but he was throwing the ones that counted. That's a good champion, who knows when to put his foot on the gas and when to try and soak it up a bit. That's why he is what he is. I was losing it bit by bit. He just missed me with a lead left hook as round nine was coming to a close. It didn't miss by much. It was a warning shot. When you think that boxing is all about hitting and not getting hit, Mayweather is everything a fighter should be.

As I sat on the stool before round ten, Cortez said he wasn't going to let me take too much punishment. 'I'm firing back,' I said, not that it had made any difference to him so far. Roger Mayweather, Floyd's uncle and trainer, had been saying to his nephew in the corner, 'He's ready to go now, just put the finishing touches on him', while Oscar De La Hoya stuck his head through the ropes and said to me, 'Ricky, you're five rounds down.' Billy advised, 'Ricky, just jab, move, keep out of the way and keep low. You'll be okay. You'll see the final bell. And I said, 'Billy, I'm five rounds down, I need a knockout.' 'Ricky, don't do this to me,' he said. 'Don't do this to me. Keep out the way and jab and move.' 'Billy, I didn't turn up to go the distance, I turned up to beat him. I'm five rounds down. I need a knockout.' He put my gumshield in and sighed. That was my mentality and it always had been. I didn't turn up to win on points or go the distance. I turned up to impress and win well. 'Okay, Rick. Go for it,' he said.

Back in the midst of the action, Floyd was starting to look for that right hand to the body and the jab up top, while the check hook that had nearly got me a round or two earlier just missed again. He was trying to time me with it. Then, as I came forward trying to jab him, he did just that. He arced the hook perfectly, and it sent me crashing head first into the corner post and onto the canvas. My legs had gone. Totally.

I scrambled back up and tried to fight on but knew it was all over. I'd never give up. You'd have to nail me to the canvas to lose but when I got up my legs had gone and were disobeying me. It was only through discipline and heart that I was able to briefly stand with Floyd one last time, but he managed to bundle me over a second time and Cortez stopped it.

Devastated wasn't the word. I just lay there, on my back, looking up. I wasn't hurt. I was just numb. I had lost for the first time. And I'd been knocked out. It's hard to explain what goes through your mind at a moment like that. Not only was it my first defeat but it was my first stoppage defeat. I was so disappointed. Beyond heartbroken. There was no doubt I had thought I was going to win the fight at the start.

Floyd hit the deck and was praying. He knew he'd had a hard fight. It was a light-welterweight against a welterweight and I was soon up and talking. It wasn't a brutal end. I was just pissed off. More damage was done to my pride than my face by the punches that ended it. There were a lot of tears at ringside; my family and Jennifer were in bits.

The crowd had been amazing and they remained that way. They were brilliant throughout my career, and not even Mayweather could shut them up as they still belted out 'Walking in a Hatton Wonderland'.

'Ricky Hatton is one tough fighter,' Floyd said afterwards in the ring. 'He's still a champion in my eyes. He's one of the toughest competitors I ever faced. He kept coming, took some shots and big body shots but he kept coming.'

Larry Merchant, HBO's veteran broadcaster, then came to me. 'What a fluke that was,' I joked, and the fans laughed with me. Larry asked me a number of questions and I gave several sporting responses. It's actually quite easy when they put a mike under your mouth like that. You've just got to go through the motions and say the right thing.

At the end of the interview I did something I had never done before. I apologized to the fans and everyone I had let down. The million-plus people back home who had paid fifteen pounds to see it live on SKY Box Office in the United Kingdom, staying up until five in the morning to watch, and the thirty-or-so thousand who had invaded Vegas. I apologized to those who had always been with me or recently followed my story. I apologized to everyone. 'I'm sorry everybody. Thank you,' I said.

I got into the changing room and cried my eyes out.

I was never the same man again.

Later that night me, my brother, Matthew – who had won on the undercard – Matthew Macklin, Jennifer and a few of my mates went out for some drinks. Jennifer went off to bed, but I wanted to stay out and drink more. I'd trained so hard and normally when you finish a fight you would sup a load of beer, go around the bars, spend time with the fans and that night they made me dead proud. 'Oh Ricky, you did great. You didn't let us down,' they were all saying. I stayed out late and then went staggering through the bedroom door of the apartment the next morning.

That day, it was *BBC Sports Personality of the Year* back in England. So after drowning my sorrows I came back at half-nine in the morning, bleary-eyed to say the least, and Jennifer was sat at the table putting on her make-up. I muttered, 'What are you doing?' She said, 'It's the Sports Personality of the Year over in the arena in less than an hour because of the time difference.' I protested I couldn't go, but she sorted me out with Red Bulls and coffees and there was me, Joe Calzaghe, Lennox Lewis and a few others, and we were sat in the front row. I was still steaming – it was a nightmare. I came third; perhaps it would have been different had I beaten Mayweather, but Joe Calzaghe, who was out there talking up a fight with Bernard Hopkins, won it courtesy of his unification win over Mikkel Kessler.

It says something about how big my fight with Floyd was that the Spice Girls, who were on their comeback tour, had been scheduled to play at the MGM Grand until Floyd and I took the date. They ended up having to move their gig down The Strip to the Mandalay Bay. David Beckham, husband of Posh Spice, Victoria, had invited me to the show the day after the Mayweather fight, and he let me and Matthew use his box to watch them that night. Me and Matthew piled in there, Jennifer and Jenna were still getting ready, and you can't take the council estate out of the man, can you? I saw a bar in the box and I said, 'Come on, Matthew, there's free beer back here.'

We were stood by the balcony and at the back of the room there were some big, comfy settees, so me and Matthew staggered in, and there was a bloke lying on them with his feet up, and a woman was lying next to him. We hurried past like two naughty schoolkids, barely looking up, and said 'All right?' And they went, 'Oh yeah, how are you doing?'

Matthew took a quick glance at them and said, 'Why don't you relax a little bit and put your fucking feet up?'

Me and Matthew got to the balcony looking over the Mandalay Bay Events Center and I turned round, quickly spun back to check and looked back out. 'Fucking hell,' I said to him. 'That's Tom Cruise and Katie Holmes.'

'Matthew,' I repeated, 'that's Tom Cruise who you just said to take his fucking feet off the table.'

'Is it fuck!' he said, looking back over his shoulder. 'Bloody hell, it is.' So Matthew went back over. 'Mr Cruise, would you like a drink?' Matthew is a cracking lad, but he's got a mouth-and-half on him. The amount of scraps I've had to bail him out of . . . The little shit! Still, we were having a right laugh with them both as the night went on. Katie was asking us to repeat things in our broad Mancunian accents. I'd said to Matthew, 'Someone's done my napper in again,' and she'd ask, 'Napper, what's that? Say that again.'

After the concert we went to the Pure Nightclub in Caesars Palace, and they had reserved us a cabana that looked over the dance floor, which was packed with Brits. The dance floor was on a raised level and behind glass, and the fans saw me and started singing, 'There's only one Ricky Hatton'. The glass was nearly cracking as the number of people coming over increased, and the DJ stopped the music, shouting: 'Step back from the glass. Step back.' Then Mel B, fresh from the Spice Girls gig, came out and started shouting for everyone to step back, too, and all the fans were chanting, 'Who the fucking hell are you?' I was cringing inside but it was hilarious.

I stayed in Vegas until the Tuesday after the fight, and it was surreal because nothing had really sunk in. No sooner had the fight finished I was up and about in Vegas. I was gutted, of course I was. But it was only when I got back to England and I didn't have that beer in my hand – when I sat down, sobered up and got back to reality – that things began to change. You weigh it all up and then Paul Speak would say, 'Ricky, don't forget you've got that sportsman's dinner on Thursday.' 'I'm not going,' I said, 'I don't want to go. I feel a dickhead. I don't want to go.'

I had to face up to losing for the first time as a professional. You'd think that as the days went by it would get easier. But while the cut healed and the bruises faded, the feeling within me stayed the same. In fact it didn't   it got worse. I was embarrassed. I didn't know what to do, or where to go. I ended up drowning my sorrows in the bottom of a pint. After the first few I was up, happy and buoyant, but the more drunk I got, the deeper and deeper I went into myself; then I'd wake up hungover and it was worse. Then I thought, 'Right, I've had a jolly up. Sobered up. Now I'm going to chill out, relax for a few days and get some normality back.' But the worst thing I could do when I was depressed was have a drink. I couldn't use that as an excuse, though, because even when I didn't have a drink I was still down and depressed. I didn't want to do my appearances or go back to the gym; I was absolutely gutted, it was devastating.

So many fighters were just happy to fight Mayweather but I wasn't happy just to fight him, I thought I was going to beat him. I *was* going to beat him. Probably the best compliment Floyd paid me after the fight was when he said, 'You know what, Ricky? Sometimes when I get to rounds six, seven, eight, it's almost like my opponents give in. It's like the fight's running away from them. But you, you flew off the stool in the tenth round.' I haven't seen him since. I didn't really like him, really haven't got much time for him and I haven't got much to say to him. We didn't have any common ground. But as a fan I can sit back and admire his talent, and I feel proud I've shared the ring with him now, on reflection. We were just total opposites.

I think the only person who would beat Floyd is someone who tries to fight him at his own game. When he fights people like me, Miguel Cotto and Gatti, fighters who come to him, we bring the best out of him. He doesn't like chasing the fight, he likes people coming at him. That's what I did and it didn't do me much good.

Nowadays when I go to America, people look at me, astonished, and say, 'You boxed Floyd Mayweather?' When you see what a good champion he's become maybe I see their point, but I didn't for the life of me see it that way. I thought through gritted teeth beforehand, 'I'm going to win. I'm going to kill you' – I genuinely thought I was going to beat him. Now people say, 'Well, you did almost go eleven rounds; he is the best.' But that didn't mean shit to me then. I thought I was going to win, I wasn't just there for the payday. When I got beat, that's when my depression started. When I didn't beat Floyd and people were still trying to tell me I'd done well, it infuriated me: 'Fucking did well? I should have beaten him.'

I just wanted to apologize to everyone over and over again. Beforehand I was fired up, 'I'm going to do this, I'm going to beat him' and then . . . Fucking hell. But it's always meant a lot to me what the fans think and I felt I'd let them down.

I have watched that fight back a hundred times and Joe Cortez still winds me up to the point that I want to jump through the TV screen and headbutt him. I can't figure out why he was like he was that night.

I would never say 'If it wasn't for the referee I would have beaten Floyd.' Not at all. But I certainly feel Cortez didn't help the matter. The top and bottom of it is I was fighting an all-time great; Mayweather was an outstanding fighter. Half the battle was getting to him because he was so good and slippery. The other half was trying to work once I did get in there because that night I felt Cortez wouldn't allow it.

Had I won, I think there would have been a big-money fight with Oscar De La Hoya, but the money from Mayweather ended up being astronomical. It was an extraordinary deal, and revolutionary in some respects, but at the same time it is something that I don't think will happen again. I think everyone was taken aback by how well the fight did on SKY Box Office, and the deal I had with them saw me get a percentage of each pay-per-view sale. More than one million people stayed up to watch that fight in the United Kingdom. Floyd had thought that if he kept most of the US pay-per-view money and I kept the money from the British side that would be fair, but no one anticipated it being as big as it was. It was the best financial move of my career, agreeing to take all of the money from the British TV.

No one saw it coming, despite mine and Floyd's blend in personalities. None of us did. I didn't know, Sky didn't know, I think you can safely say that. No one knew. It took us all by surprise. Financially, life was never going to be the same after that. It also changed the landscape for English fighters on the world scene because their opponents all felt that the UK money should be divided once they could see the appetite for big-time boxing in Britain. It was one of the main issues that had to be ironed out before David Haye fought Wladimir Klitschko for the heavyweight titles years later, because Wladimir knew full well that the fight would do big business in England and he was on terrestrial TV in Germany, so any money he earned would have probably been a set fee, whereas David, on Box Office, would have potentially made far more. They could never have had a deal where David kept the UK TV money and Wladimir kept all of the money from Germany, because David would have taken home the lion's share. In the end they reached an agreement, but it will almost always be a factor now when any British fighter gets a massive fight.

More opportunities came for British boxers, too, as a consequence of the Mayweather bout, because every time a Brit fought in America, the US promoters thought the fight fans would go in their droves – though that has not necessarily remained the case.

The Mayweather fight unquestionably paved the way for mine and my family's financial future, but some people just don't understand that I never turned up for the cash. Of course it helps, I'm not going to be a dickhead and say it doesn't. It was not about the money, though. I never started boxing for the money. It was about the glory and fighting the pound-for-pound best fighter in the world. Floyd, who retired for two years after our fight but returned to dominate the sport, had won six world titles in five different weight classes. I wanted to fight him because he was the best and he certainly was, by a country mile.

Now, after several years, there are pluses I can take from the fight.

One, for me the referee had an off night. Two, I think Mayweather's an all-time great. Three, I was a light-welterweight fighting at welterweight – it wasn't like we were even weights, but when you get the opportunity to fight the number one pound-for-pound fighter in the world, you're not going to turn around and say, 'No, I'm only a light-welter.' I could have stayed in my division but I still dared to move up, even though it hadn't worked out particularly well against Collazo. There was nothing wrong with my heart, it was all about the glory, for me. There were never any talks to get Floyd down to ten stone or fight at catchweight, he doesn't need to – he's Floyd Mayweather.

It was a tough fight and fought at a frantic pace. It was nip and tuck for five rounds. Then, bit by bit, he pulled away. He was very good defensively, his speed was outstanding and although Floyd wasn't a murderous puncher, he ended up knocking me out because he knew the right time and when to punch. It was about timing. He knew when to hold, when to break and knew when the storm had blown itself out.

Well, the storm in the ring had blown itself out.

I was left to contemplate the defeat. My sense of invincibility had now gone, having been an unstoppable force for so long, and I was forced to think about how I had let a nation down, as a fresh storm brewed.

CHAPTER 9

Rebuilding

Defeat was hard for me to deal with but in the ring in Las Vegas that night, after I joked I'd slipped to Larry Merchant, I said I would fight on. That was never in any doubt. I was only twenty-eight, had just lost to the best fighter on the planet but I was still undefeated in my weight class.

Training camp had been okay for Floyd but when I look back, in hindsight, I'd love to have had the Billy Graham of the Kostya Tszyu fight training me. He was having painkilling injections in his hands and elbows and it wasn't the same; but it was business as usual when we started again after Mayweather.

Ever since I was young I had wanted just three things, to be a world champion, support Man City and listen to Oasis. So here I was, not a world champion any longer but I had been, and I wanted to box at Manchester City. I ticked boxes as I went along: I'd boxed in Vegas, Madison Square Garden, in Manchester – and I still wanted to box at Man City.

A few years ago, there had been talk of me and Junior Witter boxing at Maine Road, but now City were playing at the huge City of Manchester Stadium. I'd formed my own promotional group, Hatton Promotions, and we worked with Frank Maloney when I signed to fight Juan Lazcano, back at light-welterweight, at City's ground. It was billed as my 'Homecoming' but I was coming off a defeat, and my return to box in Britain came after four fights in America. It had been three years since I'd fought Maussa in Sheffield.

When we first booked the stadium, guys in the team said to me, 'If you get 35,000 here it will be unbelievable.' That sounded good to me. But then more than 40,000 tickets were sold in six hours, and by the time the fight came, it had been sold out weeks in advance. There were 58,000 fans there.

Despite everything the Mayweather fight had been and its aftermath, it wasn't hard to motivate myself once I eventually got back into the gym. In fact, the first time you come back from a defeat – and a knockout defeat at that – it is a very nervous time. And I did it in front of nearly 60,000 people. I don't do things by halves, do I? The pressure was on.

Some people might say I can't have been that nervous because I wore a fat sumo-suit into the arena, but it's always been about the show for me. It's about making it an occasion for the fans. It was, of course, a nod to the critics who continued to bang on about me putting weight on between fights.

On the undercard, IBF light-welterweight champion Paulie Malignaggi defeated tough Lovemore Ndou in a drab encounter on points that was remembered more for Paulie having to have his dreadlocks cut in between rounds so he could see what he was doing. Even after that he wasn't much better. To compound the misery, Matthew lost that night, too, to Craig Watson in a challenge for the Commonwealth title.

I had been down in the dumps after the Mayweather fight, and I wanted to come back and look impressive. My feelings were that I wasn't a welterweight, as shown to me by Collazo and now Mayweather, and I wanted to move back down to show I was still the best light-welterweight in the world. Lazcano was a good opponent, world-class in my eyes, but he was someone I was supposed to stop and look good against. That's not how it panned out.

I failed to impress and the worrying thing was that Lazcano wasn't really a puncher yet he shook me up twice, in rounds eight and ten, and all sorts of things started running through my mind. 'God, I've been knocked out by Floyd, can I take a punch now?' I started doubting myself. He didn't hurt me to the extent that Vince Phillips did, but he wasn't the puncher Vince was either. My knees dipped a bit, although I knew enough to be able to slip, slide and survive the moment, and when I did get tagged I never really thought I was going to get knocked out. My head was pretty clear, but Lazcano had spent most of his career at lightweight so they were worrying signs for me. The fight raised more questions than answers, but it was answers that I needed.

When the bell sounded at the end of the fight, I felt like I was going to a funeral. The fans seemed happy, but I'm never usually happy with my performance and it's fair to say I wasn't pleased with this. Even after the Kostya Tsyzu fight I'd said to myself, 'Well, I could have done better. I could have done some things differently.' Then people would say, 'Shut up, you dick-head.' But after the Lazcano fight I knew no one would be joking. I had wanted a performance that would make people's hair stand on end, an explosive knockout or a really clear-cut win. I won widely on the scorecards but I wanted people to say, 'Wow, that loss to Floyd hasn't halted Ricky's progress.' But it actually looked like it had. That's exactly how it looked. As a consequence people started to say, 'Maybe he should hang them up.'

Me and Billy thought we were going to bounce back stronger and then all of a sudden there were doubts. I was worried. I think we were all concerned. About the only positive was that I'd boxed at the City of Manchester Stadium with a great atmosphere on a mega occasion.

As the days ticked by after the fight, some members of the team started saying to me, 'You've been beaten by Mayweather, you didn't look the best against Lazcano. If you want to carry on your career, you've got to leave Billy. He's not the same. He needs to have injections in his hands or in his elbows before he does the pads. He's not as quick as he used to be.'

Billy told me not to worry, but it was eating away at me and I started wondering if people had a point. Most fighters would have taken heart from boxing in a stadium like Eastlands, filling it and living a dream. It was a sad time for me, though, as it made me realize that me and Billy had come to an end. Those nagging doubts from the Mayweather fight had stayed with me.

I felt uncertain about what to do, and Billy invited me to a pub for a pint one afternoon. 'Listen, Rick,' he began. 'You're showing signs of wear and tear. You were hurt by Lazcano. Maybe you should contemplate retirement.' Billy was right to ask the question, but when he put it to me I was struggling with my self-esteem. It was a bad time for me. I was twenty-nine years old but I guess Billy was looking at it and judging it by the fights I'd had. There'd been so many hard battles, including a few ding-dongs in my early days, then some tough ones as the WBU champion, then Tszyu and after him there was Maussa, Castillo and the knockout to Mayweather. Maybe Billy was looking at it and saying, 'Ricky has nothing more to do or achieve. Financially he's done really well for himself.' Perhaps that's what Billy was seeing, that there was evidence I was past my best; basically it felt like he was saying, 'You could come back stronger than ever, but what's the point?'

I didn't agree but it got me thinking. 'Before I retire,' I thought, 'I need to know I've given my career my best shot.' I would go in the gym and say, 'What are we doing, Billy? Are we doing eight rounds on the pads?'

He'd reply, 'Yeah, I've had my needle. I should be able to get eight rounds out.'

Should? It's not what I want to hear if I'm training for a world title. It told me. He was having injections in his hands to numb the area and he was saying, 'You're hitting hard, Ricky' – and I was thinking, 'How do you know? How can you tell? You can't feel it.'

There was a coach called Lee Beard who came into the gym and I said, 'Billy, because of your hands and your injuries, why don't you teach Lee how you want the pads doing, how you want the bodybelt done? Why don't you mould him into you? I could do the pads with Lee and you can stand on the outside and advise me.'

He replied, 'No, no one can do it better than me. I'm the man with the bodybelt.'

I would have loved to finish my career with Billy and stayed with him to the end. It wasn't his fault, it was just Father Time – it catches up with all of us.

So, one day, I remember going to the gym and saying, 'Billy, I think we're going to have to part company, mate. It breaks my heart to do this.' I was choking the tears back. I told him that, having been beaten by Mayweather and not looking my best in the Lazcano fight, if I was going to continue with my career I needed to give it the best chance possible and I didn't think that was with him. He said, 'Well, I disagree.'

It was terrible.

Everything in my heart told me I wanted him to say, 'Yeah, you're right, Rick. I can't get through workouts without injections in my hands and elbows. You're probably right. Good luck to you, son.' That's how I wanted it to go.

Instead, it was along the lines of, 'Okay, Rick, if that's what you want to do . . . If that's your decision, that's your fucking decision.'

I saw it going completely differently from how it actually went. The meeting did not end how I wanted it to either: I shook his hand, walked out, got in the car and cried buckets.

Billy loved me, I know that; I heard him say afterwards it

ruined our fairy tale and unfortunately it did. I didn't think he was fair with me. He was falling to bits. Sky filmed a documentary series called *At Home with the Hattons* before the Lazcano fight and it was about my family and how close-knit we all were. During the show, Billy had said, 'Experience-wise I'm at my absolute peak. Physically I'm falling to bits.' When I said I wanted to leave him he sort-of back-pedalled: 'No, no, no. I'm fine, me.' But your hands are only going to be as fast as the fella who's holding the pads for you. Billy was getting older, it's not his fault. When I joined him as a youngster the padwork sounded like machine-gun fire, but at the end he was struggling. To this day, I would say to him, 'You knew you were gone.' If he looked in the mirror and genuinely asked himself the question, I think he'd know it wasn't there any more – you can't be having injections and be thinking you're the same as you were. It just doesn't happen.

One of the saddest parts of my life was falling out with Billy. We had been best mates in the early days, we'd nothing, we'd done runners from hotels, had so many good times, getting pissed up; he wasn't just a coach, he was my best mate.

When I first turned pro there had been Steve Foster, Ensley Bingham, Maurice Core, Peter Judson, Carl Thompson, Paul Burke, Chris Barnet, Andy Holligan. In the gym it was packed and I was surrounded by champions. Then, later on, there was Anthony Farnell, Matthew Macklin, Paul Smith, Stephen Bell and our Matthew. It was brilliant; we had a right laugh in that gym. Along came Kerry Kayes, and there was another trainer – Bobby Rimmer. We would put our food in the fridge there before we trained and once I went to get mine after a workout and Bobby had eaten it, the fat bastard. So I went in the changing rooms, took all his clothes off the pegs, his shoes, bag and everything like that and chucked it in the shower and turned the water on. Then I went downstairs and turned the seats upside-down in his car, put shower gel all over his windows and took all of the water out of his wipers so he couldn't clear it.

But that's what it was like there. You had to be on your guard all the time. They were good days. We were all training, all working hard, but eventually everyone left. Macklin left, Paul Smith left, Stephen Bell left. Even our Matthew left and there was only me and Billy. You'll never convince Billy, but they all left for a reason. He couldn't do what he did years ago and bit by bit they all left. I was the last one. I still would have stayed with him if he was up to the job but I just felt he no longer was.

To get away from everything I went on holiday to Tenerife, and my dad phoned me while I was over there. 'Ricky, Bill's suing you.'

'What? What is he suing me for?' I said, stunned. He was claiming I had not paid him enough for the Mayweather fight.

It is an understatement to say I was disappointed. I felt that I'd always been honest with Billy, always paid him what he'd been entitled to and I was a little bit miffed that when I said I was going to leave he said I hadn't paid him the right amounts after the Mayweather fight. 'Hold on, Billy,' I thought, 'we've had another fight since, the Lazcano fight at Man City. Why did you not mention it then? Why is it now I've left you're suing

me for a fight that was nearly twelve months ago?' But Billy
was also suing with respect to Lazcano. The court case dragged
and dragged.

Once a fighter's purse exceeds £100,000 the trainer's fee
is supposed to be negotiable but I said I would give him ten
per cent all the way through. I have no doubt he was one of
the best-paid trainers the sport has seen. Oscar De La Hoya
sounded shocked when he said, 'You give him ten per cent?'

I said, 'Yeah, I shook his hand and we agreed to it.'

From those early £3,000-per-fight nights to the bouts that
made us millions, I told my dad to pay Billy ten per cent, always.

My dad was handling my finances, as he always had done,
and he used to deal with Billy and I just used to check with my
dad. 'Ten per cent, Dad?'

'Yes, son.'

'And Billy's happy.'

'Yeah.' Billy was always happy I thought. But there was an
issue with what revenue Billy's ten per cent attached to and
what had been agreed.

It was the last thing I ever wanted to go through with him.
I thought the world of him and I know he thought the same of
me. No longer being with Billy left a huge emotional hole, as
well as a vacancy to fill.

Although Paulie Malignaggi had not looked a million
dollars on the undercard of me against Lazcano, our match
was confirmed for November in Las Vegas, and I needed to find
a new trainer. Me and Jennifer went on holiday to Vegas and
Lee Beard, who was training Matthew at the time, said, 'Why

don't you go and see Floyd Mayweather Sr – I've got his number.'

So I visited Floyd in the gym, we spoke and I didn't just see him on the pads – which he was very good on – but his defensive work also caught my eye – the way he taught catching shots, rolling, sliding, rolling and coming back with a counter. My training had always been a hundred miles an hour and I'd never concentrated fully on the punches coming back. I thought maybe he wouldn't change me completely, but I liked it that he was a character, enthusiastic and the stuff he was saying to me hit home so much so that, when I came back to see Jennifer by the pool, I'd been there all day and was late, as usual. She said, 'How long have you been?'

'I think I like him,' I replied.

There was no rhyme or reason behind my going with Floyd; I wanted to add a few new facets to my game. We never talked about me fighting his son again – it was during one of the many periods when Floyd Sr and Floyd Jr were not on speaking terms – but I thought that maybe, having done all that attacking on the bodybelt for so many years, I would focus more on timing, defence, and catching shots with Floyd Sr. So, one fight after losing to Floyd Mayweather as a fighter, I hired his father, who had taught him how to box, as my trainer.

I was looking forward to doing his padwork. It was not as physical as Billy's and seemingly much faster. I don't think Floyd Sr was any better than Billy, but the new change and perspective revitalized me.

Billy had been saying I was showing wear and tear, and

maybe that was the case, but against Malignaggi I felt I could put it right. Perhaps the damage was done. Maybe it was the defeat against Mayweather, maybe it was getting shaken up by Lazcano. Maybe it was the depression. Maybe the damage was done as far as my confidence was concerned, when you think that there had been clear signs of me slipping.

But for Malignaggi, training went absolutely perfectly. Floyd Sr came over to England for a couple of weeks, then we did a few weeks in Vegas – I stayed at the same apartment I had used for the Castillo and Mayweather fights – and it was perfect. A new trainer, a new atmosphere in the camp, it gave me the extra lift. Going into the Malignaggi fight I was sure that the only person who could beat me would be able to punch a bit, stop me in my tracks. You need to be able to stop me, and, as talented and fast as Paulie was, he didn't have the power to hold me off.

I tell fighters who I train now that if you have one of those stocky lads who comes at you then you can run and run all you want but sooner or later you need to plant your feet and crack them. Hard. There was nothing worse for me than me trying to cut the ring off and being drilled down the middle with big shots. I figured Malignaggi, as someone who couldn't punch hard, wasn't capable of that. The thinking was that even though I had been beaten by Mayweather at welterweight, I had to have a fight at light-welterweight to get ranked there again. That was the Lazcano one. Then, as soon as that happened I wanted to fight my nearest rival, and that was Malignaggi. I was considered number one, Malignaggi was number two. I wanted to prove I was still the best, and in order to do that I had to beat him. And when I boxed Lazcano, Malignaggi had fought Ndou on the City of Manchester bill, so it was always likely we would fight providing we both won.

Malignaggi was one of the nicest guys you could ever meet. He had ability and determination. He had a thumping from Miguel Cotto, a bad beating when he got his jaw broken, and he had a thumping from me, but he achieved a lot. There is a lot to admire about him. He can't punch and I think he'd admit that; but to become a world champion in two weight classes you need more abilities than just punching power – it can't just be speed, the same way it can't just be fitness, ability or power. You've got to have more strings to your bow.

One of his other attributes, if you would call it that, was the way he would hype a fight by talking crap to his opponents. But his smack talk didn't get under my skin. I'd already worked with the grandmaster of bullshit in Floyd Mayweather Jr. Even though Paulie came up with some shit, and that's what it was half the time, when you've had to do a 24/7 tour with Floyd Mayweather Jr across two continents, and you have had countless press conferences and the weigh-in to deal with, what Paulie Malignaggi did was very timid. Very timid. I had moved on from all that. Maybe Floyd did get under my skin more than I'd care to admit, but if you make a mistake you don't do it again, do you?

So when Paulie started talking rubbish, I just laughed, 'Okay, Paulie.' He didn't really mention the Lazcano fight to me because he hadn't looked too great himself against

Lovemore. He couldn't have had too many bullets to fire after that, but he made quite a lot of me losing to Floyd and the Mayweather Sr partnership, saying 'You can't teach an old dog new tricks' after I'd said I'd been working on my defence more. 'You're ready for the taking, your best days are behind you,' he said. That was the road he was going down. Part of me wondered if he was right, though I was determined to prove him wrong.

I had two new supporters in tow, as Noel and Liam Gallagher, of Oasis, carried my belts into the ring for the fight back at the MGM Grand in Las Vegas. I had first met Liam when I was going to Atlantic City for Gatti Mayweather. Me and a mate stopped in New York first, and we stayed there for a couple of days; after going to a few bars we wound up in an Irish pub. We found the place filled with people wearing City shirts. 'What's going on here?' I asked. It turned out Oasis were playing at Madison Square Garden and the people in the bar said Liam and Noel were always in and out of there. We went there the next day and from the bar we saw a big group of lads, and there was one guy with a floppy hat similar to the ones I wear all the time and I said to my mate, 'Is that Liam, there?'

Liam got up and swaggered to the toilet, arms out by his sides, as he does, and I was there with a City shirt on and the next thing I knew Liam comes by, lifts the front of his hat up and says, 'Oi, Ricky Hatton. Come over here, you fucker. Come here and have a drink.' My jaw almost hit the floor – people from the band I'd always listened to recognized me. I went and sat with Liam and Noel. Your heroes are always your heroes, no matter what success you might have individually; I'm friends with them both today and privileged to say so. Not just them either – if any of the City players come up to me these days, I'm just on my knees in awe; that's the way it always will be. Noel and Liam can't do anything wrong in my eyes. I'll always see myself as that little kid who stood on the Kippax stand at Maine Road with a pie and a Bovril and listening to Oasis when I was running. I'm still that person now.

We kept in touch over the years, and when I asked if they'd carry the belts in they said, 'Fucking right, we'd love to do that.' It was ticking another box, having the guys I'd listened to all my life do that for me. They were my musical heroes. Before anyone knew who I was I just loved their music and it was unbelievable for me, them carrying the belts in.

There was still much to prove in the ring, though, as I returned to the scene of the Floyd Mayweather defeat, at the same Las Vegas hotel. The tactics were to put the pressure on Malignaggi, use the jab. He's very fast and so I needed to use better footwork and an improved jab. The only chance Paulie had would be if I stood off him, so he could make the most of his hand speed. We had to march him down, catch more shots on the gloves and keep the pressure on. Eventually, we thought I'd be too physical and too strong for him to keep us off.

In the first round he was moving and moving and he caught me with a right cross. He didn't hurt me in the slightest, but the speed of it was amazing. There probably was not much to pick and choose between his speed and Floyd's, although Floyd hit a lot harder.

Then, in the second round, I caught him with a right hook and he was genuinely hurt. I followed up with a barrage of punches and he managed to get through the round but I hurt him again several times as the fight wore on.

But from there on in – from that second round – it was as if he was in survival mode. I don't think he ever recovered. His sole purpose became fiddling and farting his way through to the end, and he must have realized I was not a bad boxer either, not just a brawler. I was as strong as an ox and he couldn't keep me away. So I kept the pressure on and there were a few changes under Floyd Sr, a few more jabs, although generally it was the same me. It was the old me.

I don't blame Paulie for holding as much as he did as the fight wore on, because if he didn't, he wouldn't have made it to the eleventh round like he did. By the time Paulie's trainer, Buddy McGirt, called it off, he'd warned Paulie, 'If you don't throw any punches I'm not going to see you take any more punishment.' I know Paulie is a proud man and didn't want it stopped, but by the end he was not throwing anything, he was just holding and holding and holding. It was quite frustrating for me. That is what happens when you go into survival mode, but when someone who is so strong is charging at you it had to be difficult for him, and I think he knew early on it wasn't going to be his night.

Having seen Floyd Sr in Vegas for the first time a few months earlier I knew he would be able to give me a hundred per cent and I was right to have that belief when you look at the Malignaggi performance. Paulie was a quality fighter and became a two-weight world champion, but it turned out to be a bit of a mismatch – it was possibly my best display since the Tszyu fight.

Floyd took many of the plaudits and a lot of it was down to him. I could have gone with any trainer and they could have revitalized my career to a certain extent, because you get that new, fresh injection, new impetus and you're learning new things and have new people around you. I felt like I had a new lease of life.

When the Malignaggi fight finished, we went to Mexico City to spend time with Oasis and to watch them live. I was on top of the world, back to my best after Malignaggi, with Liam and Noel carrying my belts and then flying out to Mexico. At the concert there were about 40,000 Mexicans; it was unbelievable, and we were in the dressing rooms with the band. Liam was warming up, Noel was warming up on his guitar and they said, 'Come on, let's take you to your seats.' They walked us to the stage and I didn't believe what I was seeing. 'Where's our seats?' I asked.

'They're these.'

Just behind the curtain, out of sight but on the stage, were our seats, a table and four coolers filled with ice, lagers, beers, vodka and Guinness. 'Jesus Christ.' My mates were so happy they were almost in tears.

Then, during the concert, Liam and Noel said, 'Give it up for Ricky Hatton,' and the Mexicans cheered. What a weekend.

I did miss Billy, though. He was the best trainer I ever

worked with, and if I could have stayed with him I would have done; I was hurt that he had started court proceedings against me, whoever was right. I heard later that he went to Vegas for the Malignaggi contest, although he was not actually at the fight. He just sat in the bar drinking. He was hurting, so was I. In many ways he and Floyd Sr were similar as people. As trainers though, their methods were chalk and cheese. Floyd did pads, catching, slipping and rolling shots. Billy did the belt and weight training. Floyd did no weight training. They were at opposite ends of the training scale. When I first met Billy, before either of us had anything, we didn't give a shite about money, it was all about the boxing. When the purses got bigger, and *24/7* came along, Floyd loved the camera and I think Billy loved it as well. They both had massive personalities and, just as Billy always thought he was the best, Floyd thought he was the best. It was uncanny. They were very alike in some respects – and the decision to hire Floyd Sr raised eyebrows – but they were more different as trainers than people.

My ego had been boosted by the Malignaggi fight. It had needed to be, too, because there was a whirlwind from the Philippines called Manny Pacquiao, who had been moving up through the weights and who had his eye on my spot as the world's number one light-welterweight.

CHAPTER 10

Pacquiao

I climbed off the canvas and sat on the edge of the ring. Unsurprisingly, because I had been knocked down, sparring had been stopped. I pulled a towel over my head and cried and cried; I knew Manny Pacquiao was going to beat me, and we were two weeks away from the fight. 'Come on, Rick,' Dad said, trying to comfort me. 'Leave me alone,' I wept. 'Just go away.'

A month before the fight, I had good sparring partners and I was knocking the shit out of them. I was on it; two weeks later they were beating me up. I got dropped by a super-featherweight, Cornelius Lock, who knocked me on my arse.

'Stop, stop, stop sparring,' shouted Floyd Mayweather Sr. 'That's it for today.'

'The penny's finally dropped has it, you dickhead,' I thought. I sat on the ring steps, fuming, put the towel over my head and got lost in my thoughts. No way was I winning this fight. I was sobbing.

'Are you all right, son?' Dad asked again.

My dad doesn't know boxing. But it doesn't take anyone to know boxing to be able to tell where I was. Matthew could see it, Paul Speak could see it, Dad could see it; Mickey Cantwell, a former flyweight champion, who has been a friend of the family for years, could see it. It was a very important fight, and Dad knew how confident I had been earlier in camp and knew how hard it was for me to come to terms with the Mayweather defeat and how I struggled to do so. I think everyone was proud of how I came back from that defeat, and you'd have to be a very, very hard man not to feel some emotion at seeing me that day.

'Just leave me, Dad,' I cried. 'I'll only be a minute.' The fight was just days away.

It wasn't a horrendous knockdown, but Lock knocked me down nonetheless, and he was three weight divisions below me. Previously I had been sparring with Cornelius and had been red hot. But as the fight drew nearer sparring was getting worse and worse. The big Cuban southpaw Erislandy Lara had started having his way with me, too.

People were in my ear, 'Ricky, Floyd's trained you into the ground, this fucker. He's killing you. There's nothing left. You're running up Mount Charleston with those big boots on. You need to have a few days off.' In other camps I would do some longer runs, about eight miles over hills, through fields, down dips – Jesus Christ, they were hard. But we would do four like that in a training camp. With Floyd it was two a week up Mount Charleston, and people were saying they could see, bit by bit, the life was draining out of me. Floyd had me running in big boots – and Matthew, who was fighting on the under-card, was too. In the end, Matthew went, 'Fuck them, I'm not running in those. They're fucking killing me.' Matthew knocked the boots on the head. I wish I'd done that, but me being me I said nothing and got on with it.

Floyd might have suffered from sarcoidosis, the illness that killed comedian Bernie Mac, but he was always in great shape and in great physical condition. His lungs were struggling and he was coughing and spluttering, but we always got the work out and the padwork was top quality – it was just for me there was too much of it. Clearly it had worked with other fighters but with me I felt it had a negative effect. With all of the experience I'd gathered over the years and how I knew my body. I should have said, 'Floyd, I'm not doing this.'

'I know I'm right. I'm the best,' he used to say. I should have said, 'I don't give a shit if you're the best. I know my body. My body is telling me I'm fucked and if I don't have a rest this fucker is going to kill me.' I could and should have done that a couple of weeks earlier but I didn't. I don't blame Floyd. I went through with it, more and more training, and by the time my sparring partner knocked me down it was too late. There was no going back. I had three days off, had a decent last spar, but I couldn't turn it around.

That final session gave me some confidence back, if only a little. It was a good spar; HBO were filming it for *24/7*, and I dropped my sparring partner. I'd desperately needed to have a good one. If I'd had another shit spar I might as well have pulled out – but I would never have done that because all of the fans who had booked their flights and tickets, coming over in their thousands once more. It was just so important to my mental state that I had a good spar before the fight: 'Jesus Christ. Look what I did after having three days off. What could I have done if three weeks earlier I had a week off?' I could have got it back. There's not much you can do three days before the fight.

But it had started badly months before. We had done a month of training in Manchester and that was going to be followed by a month in Vegas, so I had eight weeks with Floyd, and in our first session for Pacquiao he got in the ring in Manchester, put the pads on and I got ready. I punched my gloves together, looked up and said, 'Hang on, Floyd, we're fighting a southpaw.'

'Erm,' he said, 'no, no, no. We will do pads orthodox, we will spar southpaw.'

Stupidly, I went, 'All right, Floyd. No problem. You're the boss.' My brother, Paul Speak, my dad, all said, 'Fucking hell. He can't do southpaw pads? You're fighting a southpaw.' But I don't like confrontation so I went with it, like I do.

Your pads are your biggest preparation for your sparring, and your sparring is your biggest preparation for the fight. So I did orthodox pads and when my sparring partners came it was ridiculous. I had never liked southpaws at the best of times. These were not, however, the best of times.

Manny Pacquiao was the most popular fighter in world boxing. He was on an incredible streak that had seen him end the career of Oscar De La Hoya up at welterweight, and in his previous bouts he had won title fights with Juan Manuel Márquez and David Díaz, at super-featherweight and light-weight respectively, as he tore through the weight classes.

At light-welterweight, though, I was still king. I had never lost at the weight and the convincing manner of the victory over Malignaggi solidified my position as the number one in the division, re-establishing myself after the Mayweather loss. I had been looking forward to the Pacquiao fight, I was so confi-dent I was going to win. Floyd Sr had taken a lot of the credit for revitalizing my career because of the Malignaggi fight. Where I had been aggressive before – like a bulldozer – we worked on improving my hand speed, combinations, footwork and defence, and it worked a treat.

The camp for Malignaggi had been just about spot on, but in the last week of sparring I started to feel a bit weary, but then I got away with it; the last four weeks of this, though, were the straws that broke the camel's back; they did me in. Floyd is a good coach and a lot of his methods I use with the fighters I train now. But it's not just about work, work, work, and that's what Floyd was. There was only one gear. There was no, 'You're looking a bit flat today, Ricky, have a day off and come back on Friday.' Instead, after eight rounds of sparring, he'd say, 'You look a bit tired today, Rick. We'll do ten tomor-row.' Fucking do me a favour – if I was looking jaded or tired, why would I do even more? I will never understand thinking like that, nor will I ever be able to understand why I didn't just say 'No' to him. I blame myself for not telling him I needed a rest.

Left I think this left hook against Castillo was the best I've ever thrown in my career and it was one of my best performances. Referee Joe Cortez stood back and let us get on with it in close.

Below Pure passion. You can see what the performance meant to me. The American journey had been a bit of a disappointment until I stopped Castillo. I needed to impress, and I did.

Right Wayne Rooney and Marco Antonio Barrera carried my belts to the ring. Wayne is to football what I was to boxing. He wears his heart on his sleeve and what you see is what you get. I wasn't sure Marco would side with me against a fellow Mexican, but he said I was his 'brother'.

Top Thousands upon thousands showed up in the rain at Manchester Town Hall and Floyd Mayweather was as original as ever with his Manchester United top on. Fans were singing 'Who are ya?' and he was sticking the V-sign up. That's show business.

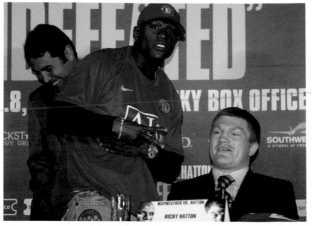

Middle At one of the press conferences, about fourteen weeks out and I probably hadn't even started training. You couldn't get two more different people, it was good cop/bad cop.

Bottom Floyd wound me up, but the more I saw of him, the more confident I was. At the weigh-in, he leant forward and I practically nutted him.

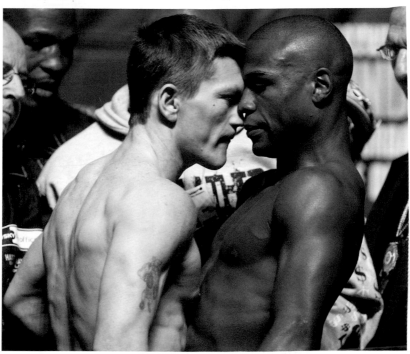

Top It was my work rate versus Floyd nailing me with his hand speed and slippery movement. Once you get in, you have to be allowed to work and I wasn't.

Middle The moment I lost the fight. Floyd ducked beneath the ropes and I missed with a right and still got a point deducted. He was ducking below and turning his back. 'What do you want me to do when he's like that?' I asked Cortez.

Bottom Despite the loss to Floyd, I'm pictured here with Jennifer and my mum and dad in happier times.

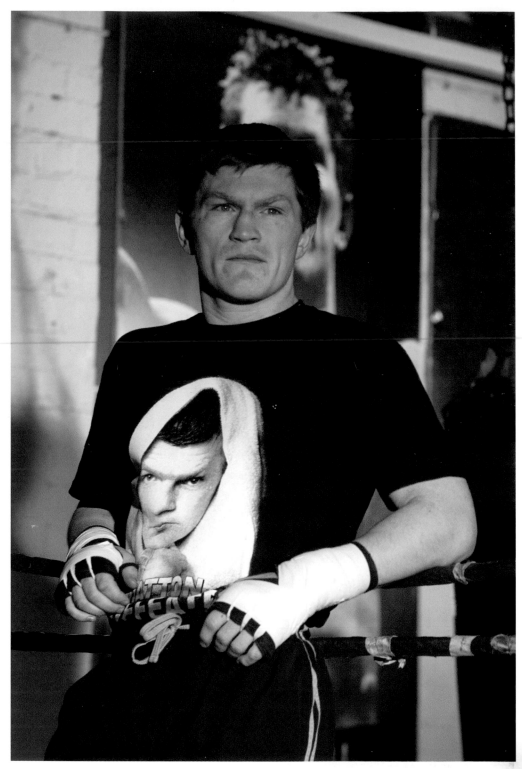

Boxing can be a lonely game. After losing to Mayweather,
I found it hard to get going again in the gym and depression
started creeping in for the first time.

Far left, left and above
Before, After – and After That:
in the fatsuit, looking ripped
and enjoying a couple of Blue
Moons. Not many fighters
have a beer named after them.

Above There were some who said I should
think about quitting, but I felt I was back to
my best against Paulie Malignaggi. As skilful
and talented as Paulie was, he wasn't
strong enough to keep me off.

Left Boxing at Eastlands in front of 58,000.
I think it will be a long time before a fighter
brings in the crowds like I did.

Top I learned a lot from Floyd Mayweather Sr, but I tried to stay focused on the fight while he seemed to want to steal the show.

Middle I was too gung-ho against Manny Pacquiao and he's about to land the lead right hook that knocked me down the first time.

Bottom The most horrifying picture I've ever seen of myself. From the minute Pacquiao put my lights out things went from bad to worse in my life.

Left I shed nearly five stone for my comeback and don't think I ever looked better, even as I fought my demons away from the ring.

Below left My last entrance was an emotional one. Now it's all over, the ring-walk with the fans screaming and singing and the adrenaline pumping is what I will miss the most.

Above right 'Come on Ricky!' I could hear the fans shout. But I just couldn't get up and as Victor Loughlin counted me out, Manchester and boxing went into mourning.

Right My assistant Mike Jackson tries to console me, but you can see the despair and the heartbreak. I can imagine everyone thought, 'Oh my god, where will he end up now?' I feel proud that I've managed to keep things together.

Top, left and above
My family, my world. After so many ups and downs, I'm happy at last with beautiful Jen, Campbell, Millie and baby Fearne.

Some thought my power and size at light-welterweight was going to be too much for Pacquiao, who'd started his pro career as a flyweight – I know I did. They said that Pacquiao had only defeated Oscar because the Golden Boy was drained having to get down to the 145lbs catchweight agreement rather than the 147lbs division limit, but as we did the press tour I was taking nothing for granted. Besides, I was the underdog with the bookmakers.

'This fat, beer-drinking Englishman is going to shock the world again,' I told the press.

Me and Manny met the media at the Trafford Centre in Manchester, before returning to the New Inn, where Manny and I played a game of darts, then we went to the Imperial War Museum in London before stops in New York and Los Angeles. Pacquiao seemed all right to me; I didn't get to know him and I still don't know him, but he was a nice little fella. Obviously he was loved in the Philippines. He was a good fighter and a nice guy, but he was not Mr Personality.

HBO ran another 24/7 series based around the fight, the build-up and our camps, but when Floyd Jr and I did it our series got a TV Grammy award in America. We were just so different, the two of us, because it was me from the council estate and Floyd with all his bling – we were total opposites and the perfect combination. Mayweather, at the press conference was like, 'Look at me. I've got 250,000 on the wrist, 150 on the pinkie, 150 here.' And I said, 'Yeah, but you're a dickhead.' It just worked. Talk about opposites. While I had no strong feelings towards Pacquiao one way or the other, I still thought

Floyd was a dickhead. I couldn't stand him. I really couldn't. I thought he was an arsehole.

I was also starting to form my own opinions about his father pretty swiftly.

We had to stay in a different house when we arrived in Vegas, as the place we'd used for the Castillo, Mayweather and Malignaggi fights was being used – but that wasn't a problem. The team would all meet up to watch HBO's latest *24/7* episode each week and Floyd Mayweather Sr's timekeeping was poor – it was pissing me off. He was terrible, terrible. I'd be in the gym for an hour and a half waiting for the fucker, bandaged up and sitting around. Then, when we watched *24/7*, while I was waiting for him in the gym, he was at the drive-thru having food, Taco Bell or whatever it was. I thought, 'What a fucking dickhead – there's me in the gym, waiting for him.' I couldn't believe it.

Meanwhile, they showed Pacquiao tearing through his sparring partners like a hot knife through butter, and Manny's trainer, Freddie Roach, was closing his gym for three hours a day so he could focus solely on Pacquiao.

Floyd Sr just wasn't the same for that camp as he was for Malignaggi. The fight with Paulie wasn't as high profile but I think when the TV came in for the Pacquiao publicity, Floyd Sr warmed to it. The *24/7* guys were asking me to do all sorts – go for a walk on The Strip, go to karaoke bars because they'd heard I liked them, but I said, 'No, I'm training. I don't want to do all that stuff.' There was, though, a man waiting in the wings who would do everything: Floyd. I don't know whether he thought he was the star of the show or what.

For me, it was just a bad, bad training camp. As a fight nears, you get that bit meaner and nastier. I wasn't. I was struggling and, for someone who suffers with depression, it didn't take much for even the smallest things to play on my mind. One of the oldest sayings in boxing is 'Don't leave it in the gym.' I was there working my arse off and there was Floyd with his poems and his rhymes, 'The best, the rest, nothing to confess, better than all the rest. Better than Freddie joke coach Roach. That's me.' He was calling Pacquiao's esteemed trainer, Freddie Roach, the 'joke coach Roach' in the build-up, but I thought, 'Well, he's not a joke coach, is he? Far from it.' How is he a joke coach – Freddie's a Hall of Fame trainer who's worked with more than twenty world champions. He also belittled Billy in front of the camera; it made me a bit uncomfortable but don't forget Billy was suing me at the time, claiming I hadn't paid him. It wasn't at all nice.

Vegas was under siege from the Brits once more, but anyone who goes into a fight thinking he just needs to get lucky with one shot to win is in trouble. I've always been a little bit reckless and that was my outlook: 'I just want to get one body shot in . . . just one shot . . . This little fart is not as big as me, he's not as strong as me, if I can get one little dig in, it will all be over.'

The only news that really buoyed me that week was that an old friend of mine could be ringside. Back when we left Billy's gym in Salford, and I was boxing at Mottram & Hattersley

Amateur Boxing Club, I met a young boy called James Bowes. Steve Alford was a pal of mine at the time and he ran the club on the estate, so with us not having any premises he said we could share the gym for a bit.

There was a little lad who came in, and he used to watch the boxing with his mum, Julie. 'Can James come in and watch the boxing?' she'd ask. I'd say, 'Yeah, of course. No problem.' He'd come in every day and sit there, dead excited, watching us. Then some days he was there and others he wasn't. Some days he would come in with bandages on his head and I asked his mum what his story was.

James had a rare illness, hydrocephalus, where some of the tubes in his head were blocked up so the fluid wouldn't disperse properly. It created pressure inside the skull so he'd have blackouts, big boils would come out on his head and he would end up collapsing. 'They've not put a time limit on it,' she said, 'but he's not going to have the life we're going to have.'

It was terrible. I started getting a bit closer to him, speaking to him every time I saw him. 'Hiya, James. Are you all right?' When I challenged Tony Pep for the WBU title I asked James to carry my British title belt into the ring and he stood there crying and said he'd love to – he was absolutely made up. I almost welled up at his reaction. The day after the fight he phoned me and said, 'Ricky, everybody saw me on TV. They're asking for my autograph.' He loved it.

For someone who has all of the worries in the world, who's on a short time span, to come in and say I inspired him just took my breath away. Every time he did an interview I had to choke the tears back. 'I'm your inspiration? With all the trouble you've got and you're happy-go-lucky without a care in the world,' I wondered. Over the years we've been out and about quite a few times. We've been to Lapland and once we went to Blackpool, to the Pleasure Beach – I'm terrible for scary rides, I hate roller coasters but he loves them. He dragged me on every one. I felt like I'd fought Mayweather by the end.

Then his mother passed away suddenly and unexpectedly in 2002. Everyone had been so worried about James, but it was his mum, Julie, a picture of health, who got an unexpected illness and died. I wondered how much more James would have to go through. I'd had a few fights in America where, because of his condition, he wasn't allowed to travel. Then, all of a sudden, by some miracle, one of the tubes in his head reopened and he started to enjoy a better quality of life and health. By the time the Pacquiao fight came along he was able to fly. It was brilliant. So I flew him over, put him up in a nice hotel, met him at the airport and he was loving it in Las Vegas.

As he walked down The Strip, fans were stopping him, asking him how he was doing and who he thought would win.

If he hadn't had such a great, supportive family with his gran and his uncle I would have adopted James, no doubt. Everyone knows him in our area and in the end we managed to get a house built for them. He's well loved.

So, as he had done in England many times, he was tasked with carrying my belt into the ring for Pacquiao. The only problem was that when I saw James in the ring at the MGM

Grand it was not the same me he'd met in the ring so many times before.

The fans were out in force, as they had been all week, and the weigh-in was packed again, but as I paced around the ring before the first bell I just thought to myself, 'You've blown it, you've absolutely blown it. You fucking peach, you've left it in training camp. You should have fought this fight four weeks ago.' I was beaten before I got in there. In the first round, before Manny first nailed me, I thought I was just coming into it – looking for my shot. I was even more reckless than usual that night. I hit him with a right hand and he went back.

Then it all went badly wrong.

Being a very good fighter, Pacquiao could tell how wild I was and his eyes lit up, as if he was thinking, 'I'm just going to need one shot here. He's coming in recklessly; his defence is all over the show.' He put me down twice in the first round and the mountain I had to climb became even steeper. I had to see out the round in the end, but I thought if I could pressure him in the second, I could still get a grip on the fight – I could still land that punch.

Lee Beard, who was in the corner with Floyd Sr, said he felt I'd shaken off the knockdowns and I was able to turn the corner if I could get through the next round. That sounded good to me.

I hit Manny with a right hand that put him back on his heels a little bit, but he was practically looking at the floor when he winged over that enormous left hand and bang – one shot – and that was that. There I was, flat on my back. I looked like a shell of the Ricky Hatton everyone knew in there. I was a shell of myself.

I had a feeling Pacquiao was capable of doing what he did. I later saw the horrific pictures of Jennifer, inconsolable at ringside. She was in bits as I lay there, stretched out. I had just been knocked out. I was more than devastated.

I was marching back to the dressing room and Brad Pitt and Angelina Jolie came to see me. 'You all right, Ricky?' Brad asked. I didn't even recognize them. I just said, 'Yeah,' and sulked straight past him. Because it was such a shocking knockout, Angelina had asked to come into the changing rooms to check if I was okay. I didn't give a shit who they were.

It is all very blurry, but I remember young James Bowes coming in. He was really upset, he had never seen me lose before and to see me knocked out in that manner made him very down. 'Don't worry, James,' I said. 'I'm okay.' Physically I was fine. 'I love you, Ricky,' he said, tearfully. 'I love you too, mate.' The fight could have gone better, but I hoped he enjoyed the trip, and I think he did.

Every now and then, to this day, I pop over to his house. He's in his early twenties and he's still very poorly, and I hope he continues proving everyone wrong. He's amazing. When you think all those years ago it seemed he only had a matter of time, he has done so well. What a fighter he is.

In my career, I had been able to beat fighters who were more talented than me because I had such a big heart and a big will, and with them I could perhaps overpower people. After getting destroyed by Pacquiao it was very hard for someone like me to take. I was distraught.

My family were in my dressing room but we had no idea where Floyd Sr was. We later heard he just came in, put on his snazzy suit and trilby, and was off to another press conference. I had barely picked my head up off the canvas and he was on to the next thing he wanted to do.

I was really in a bad way but it didn't set in straight away. The next day there was a pool party at the MGM Grand. 'Go on, Ricky. Put a brave face on,' I said to myself. 'Get a few beers in you.' So I did, but the moment I came home to sunny old England, the bright lights of Sin City disappeared, the cameras stopped rolling and Las Vegas was gone. It all goes. You come back to Gee Cross and your life starts again. Proper life. It was then that everything about Pacquiao and what had happened really hit home.

Once I got home I cancelled all of my functions. I wouldn't talk. I just didn't want to leave the house. I was ashamed, actually hanging my head in shame, sulking. When people said I'd been beaten by the two best fighters in the world it meant nothing to me, absolutely nothing – I didn't care who they were. The depression that had lurked since the Mayweather loss was rearing its head once more. The crying in the gym before the fight was another sign that I was not the same person any more.

I went from bad to worse. It had been a devastating defeat and a spectacular knockout with far-reaching consequences in my mind. The Mayweather fight had started a roller coaster of ups and downs – an emotional express train that I was virtually unable to drive. I was gutted after Mayweather, devastated. Then there was the Lazcano fight, and it wasn't a great performance, and I was thinking, 'Oh my God, this could be it.' Followed by falling out with Billy, working with a new trainer, and then a great performance against Malignaggi, with people saying it was my best since Kostya Tszyu. Finally there was Pacquiao, which was terrible.

That defeat was hard for me to comprehend and even harder to deal with. I had walked through Kostya Tszyu's best shots, been a two-weight world champion and thousands of fans had travelled thousands of miles to see me in a fight that didn't last five minutes. I shouldn't have been in the ring that night, or even near one.

People were starting to call for me to retire and with all that was going for me mentally, I thought, 'They might have a fucking point here.'

CHAPTER 11

Depression

I remember when I first thought that it could be all over and that I might never box again. Me and Jennifer went to Australia after the Manny Pacquiao fight. Australia was always a holiday destination I'd fancied; I have several friends over there but had never been, and as I weighed up fighting again we thought three or four weeks sightseeing in Australia would give us a good chance to relax before I hit the gym again on my return. I would go as far as saying it was the best holiday I'd ever had – I loved Australia and the people. We flew out to Hong Kong and then had the holiday of a lifetime in Melbourne, Sydney, Brisbane, the Whitsundays and Cairns. Surprisingly for me, I actually trained in some of the hotel gyms, but we had such a great time the holiday blues started to kick in when we stopped in Singapore on the way back.

Sat around the pool, Jennifer asked, 'Training Monday?'

'Oh yeah. I know. I don't believe it. I've got to go through all of that shit again,' I replied bluntly. I did want to do it but, at the same time, I didn't. This was the first time she'd heard

226

me react to training like that. Normally, when I've had some time off to regroup, I'm chomping at the bit to get back. This time it was different.

'In all the years I've known you,' Jen said, 'you always have that last drink and turn round and say, "Bring it on."'

All of a sudden it had become, 'I can't believe I've got to go back to the gym.' Still, fighting is what I do and so inevitably when I got home I went back. But the reaction I experienced around the pool in Singapore would not leave me. In the gym I did some training but I just couldn't be arsed, I really couldn't. I was working with Manchester trainer Bob Shannon, who I'd known for years, had always liked and who was training the fighters I was now promoting. 'Bob, can you get the bodybelt on so I can have a blast?' Nothing, absolutely nothing – not even doing some hard rounds – came back to me; it was like rubbing two sticks together hoping for a spark – but it wasn't happening.

'Jesus, Rick, it's over,' I thought to myself. 'It's never going to happen again.' Something that used to come so easily to me, training and dieting – I just couldn't do it. That was it, all gone. It had ended on the worst night of my career and there was no chance I was going to be able to make it right. That's not what I wanted to find out. When I first walked through the boxing-gym door, aged ten, if you'd said to me that in the future I'd win four world titles in two weight divisions, headline in Las Vegas, box at Man City, Noel and Liam would carry my belts in, then I think the ten-year-old me might have thought, 'I will get to do everything I want to do.' But was it enough?

You need hunger in boxing. It's such a tough, hard sport; you have to want it, you *need* to want it. Because when you sit in your nice house with your nice car parked out front and you've got to go back to the gym on Monday, you just don't need it. It's a hundred per cent sport and, to be honest with you, I was thinking, 'Should I give it another go?' I was torn, saying to myself, 'Well, you've done all right, Rick. See how you feel.' But when I did try I just couldn't get going again.

It drove me insane. The further I got from fighting again, the worse I was. I've always had a bit of a drink but when I had a beer on top of how I was feeling, I just felt worse and worse. Before I knew it, I was having blackouts and forgetting meetings. It was unbearable.

I cancelled all my other functions out of embarrassment. Those were bad times, the worst of times. I was in a horrible place, not knowing if I should give it one more go. I did not really know if I was coming or going. I had too much time on my hands, really. I had been sat there sulking. I was there thinking, 'It's never going to happen again,' and I ended up losing the plot, really.

I could never have known what effect this depression would have on me. I don't think anyone could. I would just sit on my own around the house. Sometimes I'd just play darts, have a game of pool, watch a bit of TV and Jennifer would come up and ask me what I was doing up there by myself but sometimes I just liked that. It's all I felt like doing: 'What's left for me in my life? I'm never going to have that feeling you get from fighting again.' I did not like the person I was becoming. I spent my time on my own, in my games room at home, asking myself why and where it had all gone wrong and what I had done to deserve it. I was so lonely.

My games room was filled with memories – good ones – everywhere I looked. It's a big old place with a balcony that looks over my indoor swimming pool, with its Manchester City emblem at the bottom. There are framed pictures of my fights and shiny cabinets with gloves, shorts and pictures of some of the matches that made me 'The Hitman'. There's a Guinness pump at the bar and memorabilia from the sporting and entertainment worlds signed by famous friends all over the walls. In the middle of the room is a pool table with a sky-blue Manchester City cloth. Anyone would love a room like this; well, any self-respecting City fan would anyway. But even things that should upset me within boxing make me smile. I look at the picture of me so badly cut against Jon Thaxton. Horrible, that one, blood everywhere, but it makes me grin, it was a good night. There's the big cabinet with gloves and pictures of the Floyd Mayweather fight tidily placed inside. He was a prick, a bloody good fighter, if a complete pillock. He wound me up, but those memories are surprisingly good ones, although it was heartbreaking to lose my undefeated record. Then there're pictures from the Kostya Tszyu fight, and if I look at them and then close my eyes, I can hear the crowd once more. It's heaven, if only until I reopen my eyes and realize that moment is further away than ever.

Then there was the Manny Pacquiao fight. That is different from the others and the pictures from that haunt me. Me, flat on my back, unconscious in the second round. What a way to go out. After everything in my career, the worst fight of my life was going to be my last. That's a cruel way to leave a sport you have done a lot in. I didn't want that be the last thing people saw, or how they remembered me. I've always been a proud person and a proud fighter, so for someone like me to get laid out like that in two rounds was very, very hard to take.

I couldn't show my face after the Mayweather fight for weeks. After Pacquiao it was months. I sat at home in morbid silence. I didn't know what to do with myself. After a while I'd be restless, stand up, move about, then sit back down again. I was rattling about the house, aimless.

Everything that I had stood for over the last twenty years was gone. I was Ricky Hatton, a boxer. The boy next door, the Manchester lad anyone could have a drink with. A two-weight world champion, who'd taken more than 25,000 fans to Las Vegas – twice. I had all of these great memories around me but it was just depressing. I didn't want them to be memories, I wanted them back. I wanted to smell the Las Vegas casinos again. I wanted to be fit and muscular, to look at myself in the mirror and think 'Ricky Fatton?' They weren't saying that on my fight nights.

I watched the Oscar-winning film *Raging Bull*, starring Robert De Niro as Jake LaMotta, with Jennifer one night. In one bit LaMotta was fighting Marcel Cerdan, and he's coming through the changing rooms, up the arena steps and about to get in the ring. I leant towards Jennifer and said, 'You know what? That's what I miss the most about it: walking to the ring, hearing the crowd.' The roar of the crowd – I missed that more than anything. You can see the passion in the crowd's eyes. You'd look out into the venue and they'd all look at you and scream, 'Come on, Ricky, you can do it.' There's no feeling like it, absolutely nothing. Everywhere I went, the crowds were always so passionate for me – even at the weigh-in for the Floyd Mayweather fight, when more than 8,000 turned up – Las Vegas did not know what had hit it.

You can't replace that buzz. Life became empty without it. I couldn't accept it was over. I contemplated formally announcing my retirement as the depression really hit me. Depression is a horrible thing, and it's hard to explain. I would have given it all up for one more fight, for the hairs to stand up on the back of my neck as I heard the roar of the crowd and 'Blue Moon' one more time.

I suffered badly from depression and then I was drinking too much. But you've got to . . . all of us have got to have something to get out of bed for in the morning. Nearly two years after that night in Las Vegas I felt I had lost too much ground. I had a lot of weight to shift, again, and whenever I tried to get something going in the gym I could feel an emptiness in the pit of my stomach that had never been there when I started training camps before.

A lot of people think my depression came on the minute Manny Pacquiao beat me, when I had to start thinking about retirement, but I don't think it was just those things. I think it started as far back as the Mayweather defeat, two years earlier in 2007, when I apologized to the fans. I reckon that is when the ball started rolling downhill. It really knocked my confidence when I, who prided myself on my heart and courage in the ring, was knocked out. I just wanted to say sorry to everyone. I was thinking about how it impacted on everyone else, without thinking what it would do to me. I felt terrible, that I had let them all down; inside I was not the same person any more.

Eventually, when I did go out, I started getting paranoid. I was just walking into the pub and everyone was looking at me; I'd see someone smiling across the room and think, 'Is he laughing at me?'

'Ah, look at the tough guy who got put on his arse.' That's what I believed people were thinking.

It's very rare for a mate to phone up and say, 'Are you going out?' and me say, 'No.' But that's how bad it got, and it got worse. I went round and round in circles, going over and over again in my mind the things that had happened. In quieter moments, when I watched the Mayweather fight back, I still had a lot of anger towards the referee; I felt really hard done by. Then, when I came back and had the big fight at Man City in front of 58,000, it was really special but I was poor. I won comfortably, but people were saying I was past it, that I had not been the same since the defeat and that I should pack it in. I wasn't having that, but because the way I fought against Lazcano was not great, I had my own doubts. I started to think, 'Jesus Christ, am I gone? Am I finished?' The more I pondered over it, the worse it became.

The Malignaggi fight brought me back up on a high and I

thought it was one of my best fights, but these highs and lows were what I think triggered the depression. That yo-yo effect can really mess you up. That's the problem with having such big highs. The lows eventually match them in their magnitude.

It wasn't the right way to think because I had family and friends and I was fortunate with everything I'd done in boxing, but I couldn't help thinking, 'What's left for me in my life? It's just going to be shit from here on in.' That's what I thought. Once that depression gets hold of you, it doesn't matter how tough you are, how many fights you've had or what you've got in the world. You're struggling. It is the hardest thing possible to cope with.

I started going out again. I don't even know why – I was not even enjoying myself, just getting more and more drunk. I was losing myself in Guinness after Guinness. I didn't care what I looked like, who I was with, what I was doing. I was on a suicide mission. I just wanted to self-destruct. I put on loads of weight, more than ever before. I didn't give a shit what I looked like – I was fifteen stone and I didn't care.

I went through a lot of money. I've got loads of pals so there was always someone to drag out. Before I knew it, I was going out Thursday night, Friday night, Saturday, Sunday night, Monday . . . It was absolutely crackers. Out night after night, drinking more and more.

There is always a reason. There has to be a trigger.

It starts in the taxi on the way home and I think about things. There is no small talk with me and the driver. I sit quietly. So does he. I get myself more and more wound up, into such a state that I cannot think straight. The front door of my house is like Fort Knox, so without wanting to disturb anyone inside I walk through the back door and into the kitchen. Water? No. Snacks? No. Not another beer, either.

Jen's upstairs. Everything is quiet and it's just me. I quickly reach for one of the carving knives in the holder on the island in the middle of the room, grab it and hold it at my wrist.

They might think I had been the life and soul of the party in the pub earlier but they could not see this torment. Nor can they feel my hurt.

I lift the blade in my hand and terrible thoughts come to the front of my head. How could I have let everyone down? Why does it have to end like this? If there is not going to be a happy ending, perhaps I should end it sooner rather than later.

This has not happened overnight. This 'thing' has eaten away for a long time, no one thing happened to make me think I would go and slit my wrists. No.

I try to make sense of what happened. The more I try, the harder it becomes. The more I drink, the worse it is. I look at the knife in my right hand and look at my left wrist. I perform that several times, wondering which hand will blink first before they meet. I cannot see beyond tonight, I am living this nightmare in the moment. I am not thinking about a funeral, nor about what I will leave behind.

'Come on, Rick. Come on, Rick. You can do it. No one gives a fuck about you. Do it. Do it. Do it,' repeats a voice. I try to reason with it but seem to be losing the argument. The ongoing debate sees me totter to the sofa, and I plonk myself down, knife in hand. I'm comfortable. It's quiet. The serenity is restricted to the setting, however. My overactive mind is in turmoil. I feel it is made up, too. I raise the knife to my wrist, and begin the act of committing suicide.

The cold blade makes contact. I break the skin, pierce the flesh of my wrist. I just want to die. But I can't go ahead with it. I don't know why I can't do it. I don't know what stops me. I'm millimetres from slitting my wrists and then, for some reason I can't explain, I back out. I can't do it and do not have the courage to do it. Then I drop the knife and burst into tears.

Along with being so pissed, everything goes dark. Whether I'm in a daze or asleep I don't know.

Jen comes down and there I am. I am not moving. There is a knife on the table, blood on my wrist and the sofa now has blotches of crimson on it. She tries to stir me but I do not respond at first. She shakes me by the shoulder, panicking. I mumble something as I come round. 'Rick, what are you doing? I didn't know it would come to this. Come to bed.'

I don't think anyone saw this coming. While I was out, my friends still thought I was happy. 'What a laugh Ricky is,' they'd say, not able to tell it was a smokescreen.

Even Jennifer doesn't really know how I am actually feeling. I hide it from her too. She marshals me upstairs, and I pass out in the bed, still fully clothed. I have survived.

Until next time.

*

The suicide attempts happened on four, five, six occasions. I can't remember exactly how many times. They aren't exactly nice memories.

I have since spoken to relatives of people who have been in the same position. Their loved ones had times like I went through, nearly doing it, getting close, getting closer and then, one day, they've done it. If they hadn't been able to do it at first they kept trying, kept trying and then they've done it. That's all it takes. Some people have done it straight off. Others have been a work in progress, getting closer each time – and that was me. I was drinking more and more and getting more depressed, and the more depressed I got, it seemed the closer I got to going that extra yard. It only takes that one night, but thankfully it never happened for me – I just could never finally do it.

Sometimes Jen would go out shopping, come home and I'd be sat there stone-cold sober just crying, with the knife. 'I want to do it, Jen. I want to do it.'

Saying it and doing it are two different things, I know that. I'm sure there are a lot of people who say it and don't really mean it. I did mean it. I'm just glad that I did not have one of those nights where I finally did go through with it. Thankfully I never had the courage to.

Jennifer ended up saying, 'You need help, Rick. You need help. I'm sick of coming downstairs and finding you here with a hang-over and a kitchen knife next to you.' It must have been horrendous for her, but even then her pleas were falling on deaf ears. I was self-destructing, one day at a time. By now it

wasn't just the highs and lows I'd experienced, nor was it Pacquiao, retirement or drink. I'm sure cocaine was not helping,
either.

I turned to drugs, hoping they might make things better,
shortly after the Pacquiao fight. The first time, I didn't even
realize what I'd done, I was that bladdered. I was massively
drunk. I'd been out drinking from about noon, and by teatime
I was legless and said I was going home. I was knackered. Then
I went into the toilets and just said to two random lads, 'Ah,
give me some of that.'

My friends told me I was stupid and the next day I didn't
even know I'd done it until they said, but I was in that bad a
state I didn't care.

Sometimes I would go out and be the life and soul of the
party, and I'm sure people thought, 'He's having a good time,
isn't he?' But I wasn't. It was a smokescreen. Then, as the night
wore on, I would just be sat there, glum, quiet, not saying anything and just fobbing people off if they asked me if I was okay.
Some of my mates would turn round and say, 'Ricky, get a grip,
you.'

I would ask 'Why, what's up?' They would say, 'Last night
you were taking drugs off someone.' I said, 'Fuck off, you're
joking.' 'Honestly, Rick, you were. Sort yourself out.' It's not
like I had a dealer I was buying from every night – it was every
now and again when I was that pissed; I was out and I didn't
give a shit. I would do drugs with complete strangers, I just
didn't care. The long and short of it was that every time I went
out I just wanted to drink myself to death.

I went out and was drinking more, and I was having more blackouts. Even when I wasn't drinking I was losing days on end. I could hardly remember a thing. I was going to my own boxing promotions and I was half pissed because I couldn't face being at a boxing match. I mean, I wasn't on the front row rolling about, but I had to have a couple just to get over that. What it led to was nothing short of a nightmare.

If I was in the right frame of mind, I would not have taken drugs. Not a cat in hell's chance. But I was that down, I didn't give a fuck who saw me, who I was with or what I was doing. I was on the bottom rung. Or I thought it was. Turns out things could and would get much worse.

Me and Jen were out in London on a Saturday night when I got a frantic call from Paul Speak.

'Wahay, I'm in London, in a pub,' I laughed. He asked if we could talk. In fact, he said, 'Fucking go outside. I need to speak to you. Now.' When I was out, he said, 'Ricky, it's on the Internet here and it's going in the *News of the World* tomorrow that you were in a bird's hotel room taking drugs.'

I told him where to go. 'No chance,' I said. I genuinely didn't believe it. I didn't know I'd done it. I wasn't calling his bluff. But when it came out in the paper, I cast my mind back and remembered little bits and pieces.

I went back into the pub and I was white. 'What's up?' Jennifer asked.

'Erm, Jennifer. There's going to be something in the paper tomorrow. Apparently it's me taking drugs.'

'Where were you taking drugs?' she asked.

'Well, don't lose your rag. I was in a hotel room with a bird.'

She was devastated. I said, 'Jennifer, I don't believe this. I can't believe it myself. Before you shout and bollock me about something I don't remember, let's see what it says.'

Paul drove all the way down from Manchester to London that night, picked us up and we went back, and no one said a word, the entire the way back. I was just devastated and I can only imagine how Jennifer was feeling. I couldn't believe it.

When it came out in the paper the next morning I was disgusted and heartbroken. I don't even really remember the night in question. That's how bad a state I was in, and I thought, 'Oh my God. I've worked so hard on my reputation as a good lad, a good boy of British boxing. I flew the flag, was down to earth and a boy next door. Now it's all gone.' Now I was something else. I thought I'd ruined my career. I thought I had ruined everything. It was all gone: reputation, career and legacy – in one fell swoop.

When I was in the hotel with that woman I don't even remember it. It was hard for me and Jennifer, but the *News of the World* made it out to be a nine-month affair. They made it out to be something it wasn't; they showed pictures of me and this girl in the bathroom, but it didn't show that there was a load of other people in the next room. I think Jennifer could forgive me because she could see I was poorly. I issued a statement through publicist Max Clifford that I was 'distraught and devastated'.

'He's not blaming anyone else,' Max told the press, 'but

obviously we know how difficult it can be for people when they are not at the top any more. He's in a very bad place.'

Jen ranted and raved and I had to take it but I was very, very poorly. She had actually asked me to retire before the Pacquiao fight, and after that defeat she wanted me to call it a day even more. When I tried to come back and I realized it wasn't there, I was that down about it that I didn't have a clue what I was doing. Jennifer stood by me. She lived with me through all of that, through the training camps, and when she told me to retire before the Pacquiao fight, she said, 'Do you even know what you are trying to achieve any more? You've achieved all of your goals.' I did not. I didn't have a clue. I didn't know what I was doing half the time. She could see, bit by bit, that I was not the man I was; I was crumbling, but ultimately she stood by me through thick and thin.

My mission to self-destruct was all but taken out of my hands by what came in the paper. It was the kick up the arse I needed. I really needed it. I wish it had never happened, but without that maybe I wouldn't be the man I think I've become today. Maybe I wouldn't be here at all.

Thankfully Campbell was at the age where I don't think he really knew what was going on. I said, 'Campbell, you know the things that have been in the paper about Daddy?' and he said 'no'. And I just said, 'You know, just about me retiring, and sometimes papers write silly stuff, don't they?' and just left it at that because he obviously didn't know.

When the shit hit the fan, or rather the *News of the World*, I spoke with my dad, and he said I should stay in the Priory in

Altrincham. Sometimes you've gotta hit rock bottom before you get your finger out your arse and you think, 'Right, Rick. You need to do something now.' I was angry about it, but it was now time for damage limitation. I also had to get out of Jennifer's way because she was going to bleeding kill me.

The Priory was about half an hour away from our home. Part of me thought I needed to go, part of me didn't, which probably did not help with my experience there. People go to the Priory for several problems. It can be for drink, drugs, depression, but nine times out of ten they all come hand in hand. More often than not, drink can lead to drugs and both can lead to depression. Then, when that story was in the paper, I thought, 'Yeah, I probably do need to speak to someone now.' It certainly wasn't a drug problem; I was down, depressed, drinking too much; I just did not know what I was doing. I couldn't remember days on end. I didn't care if I drank until I died. That's how bad it was getting. People were saying, 'Ricky, you're not coping well, son.'

'I'm fucking all right,' I'd snap. I was the life and soul of the party, or so I thought, but it was a lie. I was feeling the complete opposite.

I didn't find it easy in the Priory, either. It was hard because I felt the focus was on what they perceived to be my drink problem, while I felt the issue was my depression. They would say, 'You've got a drink problem.'

I would say, 'No, I haven't. I'm depressed.'

They said, 'No, the drinking makes you depressed.' I was in

there with alcoholics who had inducted themselves because their drinking was out of order. I felt I was there for a number of reasons. I had been in a girl's hotel room, I had depression, was drinking, found that out in the paper, then Jennifer was giving me earache, asking, 'What's happened here?' and I didn't know.

I met a lot of wonderful people in the Priory, patients and staff, but was repeatedly told, 'You're an alcoholic, Ricky'; and I was saying, 'You don't even fucking know me. What do you mean I'm an alcoholic?'

'See, denial. That's the first thing an alcoholic does,' they said.

'Do you know my story?' I snapped. 'Yeah,' they went. 'We've seen it in the paper. You wouldn't be in that position if you didn't drink too much.'

'Fucking rubbish,' I said. I lost my temper a few times with people when I was in there. I was sitting in meetings and I was thinking that none of the others in there had been embarrassed in front of millions like I had. I had fallen off a cliff of fame and celebrity, and plummeted into a wilderness that I didn't feel many people could relate to. As far as I was concerned, others were there because they were drinking too much. I didn't feel that the staff saw the bigger picture with me. We are all individuals, but I felt at the time they'd made their minds up before I'd opened my mouth. I struggled; I didn't think it was for me or that I needed what other people there required.

'Look at them,' I'd think, taking in my new surroundings, 'they don't know what it's like.' As I sat amongst them I was acutely aware how individual we all are and how problems are all different.

When I came out I didn't drink for weeks and I was still depressed. I was still fucking crying, I was still fucking suicidal and I still wanted to fucking kill myself – and I hadn't touched a drop.

Obviously it took a while for me and Jennifer to get back on track after everything. A good while. Although I knew it was a bad time for me, I knew it was horrible for her. She had been on the two-year roller coaster with me, everything: Mayweather, the self-doubt after Lazcano, Pacquiao, the drink, the nights out, the depression, the *News of the World* stuff and now rehab. She lived through it all.

But having reached the bottom, there was only one way to go, and that was up. Somehow things felt better when I started training again, so I stopped drinking; I had good days and bad days. For a long period I was okay.

Several months went by before I could bring myself to watch the Pacquiao fight on tape, though.

I was in the house on my own one day and I finally put in the DVD. It was just as shocking as I'd heard it was but I had started to feel better about myself.

I was going to Bob Shannon's gym and working with his lads and getting a buzz out of training them, taking them on the pads and showing them moves here and there. I got a trainer's licence from the British Boxing Board of Control – they'd stripped me of my licence to fight after the *News of the World* story – and started to think that the best thing for me now I couldn't be a fighter was to bring one through the ranks and get him the opportunities I'd had. There was the occasional wobble but the ship seemed to be steadying. I was promoting my shows, training my fighters and things were going well. I was doing well.

There were occasional triggers that would set me off. Me and Jennifer went to the Manchester Arena to watch David Haye fight Audley Harrison, and the crowd started roaring and I was nearly blubbing again, thinking it should have been me up there. I still wanted it. I stood there in the audience as it roared and I started welling up. I said, 'Listen, Ricky. You're not gonna fight again. You're holding on to something that's not there any longer.'

People used to say to me, 'You having one more fight, Rick?' I used to reply, 'Well, you never know.' But I did know – I couldn't do it any more and it was driving me potty, wanting to do it but not being able to. I stood there in the crowd that night and all I could hear was a voice in my head as the penny dropped. 'Ricky,' I thought. 'You need to retire. What are you doing to yourself?'

A few months later I went to the Sky Sports studios to do some expert analysis for a bill featuring Marcos Maidana and Érik Morales, light-welterweights fighting in Las Vegas – my weight class and in the city I was synonymous with. As the presenter Dave Clark introduced me, Sky had packaged a highlight reel of my best memories in Vegas and that nearly set me off. Then they turned the camera on me, live, and I was choking back the tears. I still couldn't let go but I realized I needed to and finally, in July 2011 – two years and two months after Pacquiao and having survived everything that had followed – I met with members of the media in a London restaurant and announced my retirement.

I told them that it was the end and that I was in a good place. Me and Jen had a baby on the way, due in September, and I was ready for a fresh start. Letting go had been the hardest thing, I said, but it was time to do that and face up to the fact I would not fight again.

Unfortunately, I was in a bad way at the time. Maybe I meant it, maybe I did not. I thought by announcing my retirement formally it would stop the nagging that carried on inside me about fighting again. It would be one less thing to worry about – but it was quite possibly the worst thing I could have done.

Saying I was going to retire and facing up to never being able to do something you love again are two very different things. I went into a worse place because I called it a day when I didn't want to. My heart was telling me, 'Go on. Give it another go. You can do it. You love it.' I couldn't imagine life without it. In those two years, even though I did not have the motivation and I'd put on the weight and there were drink and drugs, I was thinking to myself, 'I've still got it. I've still got it.' But I didn't have it, or if I did, I couldn't find it. No matter how hard I tried.

Having everything means nothing when depression takes a hold of you. You don't think, 'Look what I've got.' It's all 'I'll never do this, I don't want that.' It's all negative and it takes everything within you to shake it off.

It's been the toughest fight of my life.

Or at least it was. When I eventually got into court with Billy, in December 2010, things got far worse.

CHAPTER 12

The Lowest Ebb

That December I found myself somewhere I never wanted to be: in court with Billy. I was shocked to see him. He had a big, long beard, looked terrible and was overweight and I wasn't far behind him in that respect.

I said stuff in the courtroom to Billy that I would never have said if I had known what I know now. He and I had a lot of good times. I could see us one day sitting down and talking about the old days but, knowing him like I do, it wouldn't surprise me if he said, 'Listen, you said too much in that courtroom for me to go back now.'

The fall out with Billy is a part of my career that was a real downer because I loved him and I hope he reads this. He was more than a trainer and to end the incredible road we travelled on together on such bad terms like that is massively upsetting. For a while I thought Billy was ungrateful and there was bad blood between us, but now I see things a bit differently. Time can allow a different perspective sometimes. I don't think we will ever be mates again, but I'll always be grateful for what he did for me. I wish him and his family nothing but the best.

Eventually, Billy and I settled out of court and that day I walked straight from there to the pub. I felt ill. At that time I was in the middle of a major falling out with my dad over money. It's the thing no one wants to fall out about. I am not going to go into details because the two people who matter – me and him – know exactly what happened and why it is an issue. We had a confrontation and whatever the rights and wrongs, I said I needed him to do certain things that I thought were fair or lose me. Whatever his reasons he chose his path and he has to live by his choices, as do I and my family.

If that wasn't enough, things became more complicated and strained over the months that followed. In September 2011, Jennifer and I had a baby girl, Millie-Meg Hatton. When Millie was born I wasn't speaking to my mum and dad because of the money issues but Jennifer phoned my mum and said we'd had a girl and invited her to the hospital. She came, I'm there, and my mum and dad came in and they were fussing over Millie. They did not say two words to me. No 'Congratulations, Son. We've had our problems but isn't she beautiful?' Nothing. To be fair, I did not say anything to them.

My mum had always wanted a girl. 'I'm sick of boxing gloves and football boots,' she'd say, 'I want a little girl.'

I said to Jennifer that Millie still deserved to see her grand-parents, who were a ten-minute walk from our house: 'I don't have to get on with my mum and dad but they can see her whenever they want – you can take her up the hill to see them.'

Every week, Jennifer, who'd had a C-section, pushed Millie up the hill so they could see her. A couple of weeks before Millie's first Christmas, my mum gave Jennifer Millie's Christmas present. Two weeks before Christmas. I thought that was strange. You'd give the grandkids their presents on Christmas Day, wouldn't you? 'Aren't they going to want to see her on Christmas Day?' I asked Jennifer. 'Well, you don't know. They might be getting all their jobs out of the way,' she said. 'I don't think so. I don't think they're going to bother,' I replied. She said I was jumping the gun because I wasn't getting on with them.

Christmas Day came and there was nothing. No phone call. Nothing. Campbell came round late in the afternoon and he'd been over to my mum and dad's for a Christmas party. I said to Jennifer, 'So the rest of the family are up there having a party with Campbell and they, on Millie's first Christmas Day, have not wanted to see her or phoned to wish her a Happy Christmas?' The whole family had been up there.

A couple of days later Jennifer called my mum and put the phone on loudspeaker in the kitchen, asking my mum why she'd not been in touch. She said her phone had been on charge all Christmas day, but Jen wouldn't have that as an excuse for not seeing Millie. Then Mum said it was about me and my dad not speaking and that it was my fault. Jennifer wasn't having that, either: 'Don't blame it on your relationship with Ricky. It's not a Ricky–Carol–Ray situation. This is a Millie–Carol–Ray situation,' Jennifer said.

She told my mum that two weeks after her C-section she

had been pushing Millie up the hill to see her, despite the advice of her family and the doctors, but she'd still done it. My mum replied, 'It's not like it's the end of the world, is it, Jennifer?' We couldn't believe our ears. The conversation took a turn for the worse and I told Jen to put the phone down.

The next day, Jen got a text off my mum: 'What's happening with Millie?' That was what we'd been asking the day before but they'd had their family gathering and only now could they squeeze Millie in? I told Jen not to reply and the next day we got a text that said, 'This problem will not go away.'

It was a horrible period. It added to my depression and I hit an all-time low.

It felt like it was me and Jen against the world. I was more isolated than ever and I took no pride in what was going on with my family. I didn't talk about it to anyone.

We had always been one and the same, a family unit. There had been the TV show, portraying us all as one small happy family and Matthew, my mum and my dad were a big part of everything I'd done. Family had always meant the world to me. Then, when the difficulties with my dad came along it seemed almost everyone took his side.

Out of all of us I had the first apartment on the complex in Tenerife years ago and, as I started doing better, I bought a bigger apartment and gave the other one to my mum and dad. When things got even better, I got an even bigger apartment on the top floor and gave the other one to Matthew – it's not like I was tight. Some people might get taken out for meals, I buy apartments in Tenerife.

After the falling out, when me and Jennifer were in Tenerife sunbathing on the roof we could look over the balcony and could see both my mum and dad's place and Matthew's. We didn't feel comfortable there, even if they weren't around; I hated it, I didn't like it on the balcony, I didn't like walking down the street in case I bumped into them – so I moved my apartment. I bought them the apartments and I was the one who ended up moving.

It was the same at Manchester City. A group of us, me and a few friends and relatives, had chipped in for a box. We had it for a few seasons and then we all got season tickets together. Before the fall out, my dad got a season ticket as well. I renewed my season ticket the following season, not thinking he would do the same, but he did. I was going to the football and watching City and he was sat a couple of seats down from me.

The only positive in all of this was it had somehow helped give me a fresh focus – a new perspective on things. I was in the gym with my fighters, Craig Lyon, Adam Little, Ryan Burnett and Sergey Rabchenko, and the weight was coming off me. From nearly fifteen stone, the pounds dropped off. I started running, more weight came off and I could see some cheekbones reappearing.

Friends started asking me if I was going to make a comeback, and in my mind I believed I might be able to, but it was not the first thing I was thinking of. As I posted training pictures on Twitter, more and more people asked if I was coming back. It became more of a possibility, as I got into better shape with each day and every training session – I was both looking better and feeling better. I was not drinking, was watching what I ate, while training hard and regularly was having a therapeutic effect.

About five months had passed since my mum had texted Jen. There was not a phone call, no one knocking on the door asking to see Millie, nothing. I was finding everything so difficult to understand – how could this have happened?

I was never won over by the Priory (I know they do good work but it just did not work for me) and Jen suggested I should look to go somewhere else. She found out about a place called Sporting Chance, a private and specialized facility for elite sportsmen and women who have demons to face. It's in Hampshire and was the brainchild of former Arsenal footballer Tony Adams, who'd publicly confronted alcoholism. It takes just four people at a time, and it is fair to say I didn't want to go.

I hadn't been able to shake the depression and different things would set me off, like my dad driving past me in the car, or something else. It could only be something minor but I would struggle to cope. Even when I've been in good places I've still had bouts of depression and suicidal thoughts, and when something has upset me, I've just thought, 'Life doesn't matter any more,' and loosely that meant going to the pub and getting absolutely shit-faced.

Jennifer was saying, 'Why don't you go and speak to someone?' and I would fire back, 'I don't fucking need to speak to someone. What would I do that for? I haven't got a drink problem. I haven't got a drug problem.' She said, 'But, Rick, every time something upsets you, you turn to drink and you go on that warpath of wanting to drink yourself to death. It's all connected and they will probably talk to you about how best to deal with it.'

We reached a decision that I would go to see someone who knows about sport and who knows how to deal with sports people. At Sporting Chance they taught me how to cope better when things flared up; they'd had people there with drink problems, drug problems and gambling problems, and they were used to dealing solely with sportsmen at the top of their game.

At the Priory I'd felt I was in with a lot of people who had to go in there because they had a drink or drug problem; none of them had the problems I was dealing with. They had their own specific subjects. Sporting Chance is used to dealing with sports people and they treated me differently perhaps because they knew where I was coming from a little bit more.

Just because you've become successful at your particular sport doesn't mean life is always a bed of roses. It really isn't. When all of a sudden it's gone, it's not easy, and it was nice to go in there and speak to people, sportspeople, who have the same problems. I was in a good place straight away.

Let's be clear, I don't think you ever get rid of depression. The best way I can describe it is it's a bit like a wave machine at an aqua park. One minute the waters are all calm, then something can trigger you off and it can be the smallest of things but a ripple can turn into a tidal wave, which in my case leads to me at times going on a bender and wanting to drink myself into oblivion. By the time I went to Sporting Chance I had practically made my mind up about making a comeback, but I wanted some clarity before a final decision. They helped me learn how to cope better when problems arose, but another appeared while I was in there.

Having not heard from my family for five months, I got a solicitor's letter saying that, as grandparents, my mum and dad would like to see their granddaughter; that they didn't want to go down the court route but that they might do that. As far as I was concerned they hadn't bothered on Christmas Day, then not for five months, and then they sent me a solicitor's letter about my daughter while I was trying to clear my head – steam was coming out of my ears. If I'd have been back in Gee Cross I don't know what I would have done.

I felt that even when I go away to a place to try and sort my problems out and get better, they still can't let it lie. Of course they did not know what was going on with me, but then I guess I felt that was rather the point. Whenever I think I'm getting somewhere, something else raises its head. I was so down again, tears were flowing like a waterfall and thank God I was in Sporting Chance with the right people around me. Sporting Chance did a massive amount for me, teaching me how to deal with so much, and I will always be eternally grateful to them. I'm in a better place now because of my time there and I came out of there feeling fresh, despite what had happened.

Around a month passed and I replied to my parents, through solicitors, and said we did not want them to have contact with Millie. We had never stopped them seeing her, as far as I was concerned they had just not been arsed. I know that sounds harsh and I am sure they see it differently, but it is how I feel. Despite the issues between us, Jennifer had made the attempt to keep them involved. It was all such a mess. The letters went back and forth and I put a few home truths in them. It was bitter and horrible, as things often are when you get solicitors involved. I did not want any of it, but did feel the need to defend myself.

For the next month or so I buried my head in my training and, as speculation intensified, I made up my mind about my future and called a press conference to make an announcement. I was going to come back. We booked a conference suite at the Radisson Blu Hotel in Manchester and on Friday 14 September 2012, I was faced with convincing the world that not only was my return to the ring, at the age of thirty-three, a good idea and that my mind was fully on the job at hand, but I had to hide the fact that I was in turmoil over everything that was happening with my family.

As I prepared for my own fight, with Bob Shannon at his gym in Openshaw, I was still training my boxers every day at my gym. The buzz was back.

The press conference is tomorrow, the worst days are behind me and I'm excited as I go to the gym, tapping the steering wheel to the radio, pulling up in my usual parking space alongside Hatton Health and Fitness. It's mild outside, fine for the tracksuit bottoms and T-shirt that I'm wearing as I prepare to train my fighters. I turn the ignition button off and walk round the car to take my kitbag from the boot.

As I open it up I hear the angry revved engine of a four-wheel-drive vehicle hurtling into the car park. It brakes sharply and comes to a stop behind my car, trapping me in. It's Dad.

I wonder if he has been waiting for me to come here, but before I know it he's storming round the front of his car and shouting at me. 'All that stuff you've written about your mum in that solicitor's letter is a fucking disgrace!' he yells.

I'm unprepared, but manage to fire back, 'You tell me what part of it is a lie, then?' I carry on taking my gym bag out of the boot and hold it by the handles in my right hand. Dad is still fuming and we exchange a few words. He is angry – furious – but I stand my ground.

Then he swings at me. He punches me in the face, catching me on the cheek.

'Dad, do not do that again,' I ask, although I can see he is still fired up. 'Don't fucking do that again.' He's enraged so I hold him up against my car, hoping the storm blows itself out, but when I let him go he comes at me and cracks me in the face again. 'Dad, this is your last warning.' I can see he will not listen and that nothing I can say will stop him; he swings a leg at me, trying to kick me.

That's it. It has to stop.

I block it and crack him with my left hand, causing him to fall against his car. Seconds pass but groggily he comes defiantly back at me. 'Do it again. Do it again!' he shouts. I still have my kit bag in my right hand. I think to myself quickly, 'I know what he's up to. He wants me to fill him in, here.'

'Go away,' I reply, forcefully.

Finally, he scurries back around the car and speeds off. The whole thing lasts barely a minute. I'm shaken up. I'm in bits, actually, and I walk into the gym shaking my head, trying to fathom what has just happened. I think to myself how I'd just had to crack my dad because he'd attacked me – there is no pride attached to doing it.

I walk into the gym, shell-shocked, still shaking, and one of the employees looks at me, stunned. We phone Paul Speak and tell him about it. A former policeman, he will know what to do. We review our CCTV footage and watch the whole sorry sight unfolding again. Then the phone rings and things start going from really bad to far worse.

Paul had a voicemail from my mum saying that I'd chinned Ray and that they had witnesses. We'd seen it on CCTV and we were thinking, 'What witnesses has she got?' We were the only ones there and we had it on tape. I had the best witness: the camera footage.

I was in a dilemma what to do. If I sat there and waited for the police to come and take me to the station, or waited for them to come and speak to me in front of the world's media at the press conference the next day I would have no control over when they would speak to me or how they would interpret it. Rather than the headlines reading 'Ricky Hatton's making a comeback' they would be 'Ricky Hatton chins his dad'.

We phoned the police, they came round to the gym and I showed them the footage. 'I don't want him arrested or anything like that,' I said, 'just tell him to stay away from me.' But after they saw the attack they said it was a clear-cut case of assault and they had to proceed. So they went to his house, arrested him, took him to the police station and showed him the footage, where he admitted he had attacked me first and then they gave him a caution.

Of course, I could have pressed charges but I didn't want to. He put some cock-and-bull story in the papers about not wanting me to make a comeback. I was looking fit and well and, instead of being happy for me, he chose to do this the day before one of the biggest days of my life.

The ironic thing about this was the solicitor's letter I had sent to them had gone three weeks earlier. So you would have read the letter, reacted and gone straight round there, not left it until the day before the press conference. But that's why you have solicitors' letters, to stop stuff like that from happening.

The press conference went ahead as planned, and I managed to convince almost everyone that it was the right thing for me to be doing – and it was. The incident was low key, although of course everyone wanted more information.

There were brief reports in the papers about the confrontation with my dad, just stating that a sixty-one-year-old male had attacked a thirty-three-year-old in Hyde and was cautioned.

The rot had set in with Matthew a while back, too. He had sat on the fence and didn't get involved with the family dispute and that frustrated me.

After Dad attacked me in the car park, I never had one phone call from Matthew, saying, 'Jesus, Ricky, what's happened there?' Nothing. It was in the papers, everyone knew. If he'd attacked Matthew I would have gone straight over there, Matthew was closer to me than anyone.

It was a horrible position for him to be in, I know that, and I would never ask him to choose between me and my dad and my mum, but I feel I've not needed to, as his actions have been clear. A few people have stayed in the middle of the split but I don't feel Matthew has. He never phoned me, he never went out of his way to speak to me . . . He still sees them, goes on family holidays as if nothing's happened. I just feel like saying, 'Bloody hell, Matthew. What planet are you on?'

It is not the only thing I feel let down by Matthew about. When I was promoting Matthew we got a fight sorted for him for the WBA interim title against Ismael El Massoudi, and Eddie Hearn put in an objection at the last minute because his fighter, Kell Brook, was ranked above him. I had booked Bowlers, the Manchester venue, I'd got the tickets and posters printed and it was taking time to get it sanctioned, but I'd had it on good authority from the WBA it would go ahead because there was not much time and Brook wouldn't have been able to get ready in three weeks.

'Just hang fire,' I said to Matthew – but out of the blue he pulled out. He said he'd been training for eight weeks and if the fight was not even sanctioned it might not happen. 'Matthew,' I said, 'you've got an interim world title fight. It's there for you. You've been training eight weeks. You only have to wait a few more days.' He still withdrew. There are two sides to every story and I knew he could not see it all coming together in time but he should have had more faith.

I was paying El Massoudi about €200,000 to come over to defend his belt, for my brother. I had already done that for him to get the European title shot against Gianluca Branco, the veteran Italian. I got him opportunities by investing my money and for him to turn around and go 'I'm pulling out', I couldn't believe it. Matthew would have made less than the champion but sometimes that is how it works, you take less to get the opportunity – that's how it was with me and Kostya Tszyu. He would have made decent money, I would have put an undercard together and, all in all, the show would have set me back about £250,000, and for my brother to pull out I felt let down.

An article appeared in the *Manchester Evening News* with Matthew slagging my company off, saying the fight hadn't been sanctioned. I felt it was a disgrace and that, although I'd done nothing wrong, I needed to look at my company. To put that in the paper, I was really disappointed. He slagged the business off when the firm had done a lot for his career and his finances. This was the company that had put food on the table for his family for years and just three or four weeks earlier I'd given him the apartment in Tenerife. Then he went to another promoter. I don't mind that he left me because he went to fight Kell Brook, and Matthew has always fought the best opponents possible and Kell was the best in the country.

Me and Matthew don't speak any more which is, without

doubt, very upsetting. I am sure he has his side of the story, but I don't know what it is because we have never spoken about it.

The family is split now and I don't see him. It's a shame but if you ask me if I'm disappointed in him then I would have to say 'Yes.' Everyone is in an awkward situation, really. I don't see my Uncle Paul, I rarely see my Uncle Ged, Auntie Margaret, never mind my mum and dad or Matthew. I feel for the others because they're in a horrible position and they don't know what to do. If they come round to see me I don't want them being moaned at for seeing me.

Matthew has done really well in his career when you think he turned pro just to give it a go after about fifteen amateur fights. I'd thought that because he'd spent less time in the amateurs he would be a late bloomer and he'd come into his peak later than most. I said, 'Keep at it, keep at it and you'll come good.' He kept at it and went on to win a European title and fight Saúl Álvarez for a world title. It just shows any aspiring pros or kids from the local boxing clubs that it can be done because he's done so well.

When I look back, I can't remember the last time my dad told me he loved me. I have no doubt he was proud of me but things had changed. I don't remember going round to my dad's house and it being about anything but business. Even my mum used to turn round and say, 'Ray, can we have a day off from boxing today?' Sometimes I would phone him up and he would start listing everything he'd been doing in the business. I said, 'Dad, but I've rung you.'

He would pause. 'Oh, all right, what's up?'

'I'm just phoning to see how you are, Dad.'

When I think of being a father, as much as anything else it's about telling your kids how much you love them – I tell Campbell, Millie and Fearne exactly that, every day. It's emotional support. Emotional security. For the last fifteen years I don't think I had a dad – I had a business manager. I really don't mean that to sound horrible but, it is how our relationship became.

I've kept out of his way, I don't speak to him, I don't talk to him, I've moved my apartment, my season ticket at City, he sent a solicitor's letter, I sent one – since then I've tried to do everything right to keep myself to myself. I can't do any more than I have done but it's the split with my family that's eaten away at me the most.

It's split the whole family. We'd all been so close. They'd all been to Vegas for the fights, we'd all been on the cruises. We'd had so many happy times together. All of us. I just don't see the others now.

I dwell on things. That's what depression does to you. You dwell on them, and I harp on about things and take things personally.

People think it was the Pacquiao fight that sent me over the edge; they think it was the *News of the World*; they think it was the drink, the drugs. Perhaps it was all of those in part, but this, this was the fucking biggest killer for me.

CHAPTER 13

Redemption

'You're a freak of nature,' Billy Graham and Kerry Kayes used to tell me. 'You can't lose three stone, win a world title, come back, lose three stone again and beat Kostya Tszyu, lose three stone again, move up in weight, move down in weight and keep losing several stones for each fight – because sooner or later you're going to hit that wall. You're getting away with it, but it's not going to be like that forever.'

That is what happened on the night of the comeback, wasn't it? My body wasn't the same as it was years ago.

'Ricky, you're going to have to start looking after yourself a bit better,' they'd say. That was years ago, and if you think of everything I had been through, it was a warning I had never heeded – I'd always been able to get away with it. As the weight dropped off for my comeback there was no reason to suggest things would be any different when I got back into the Manchester Arena ring for the first time since I had defeated Tszyu seven years earlier.

My opponent was Ukrainian Vyacheslav Senchenko. He

had lost his WBA welterweight world title in his previous contest, to my old friend Paulie Malignaggi, but it was the only fight he had lost in twenty-six bouts. He was good, and the minute I proved I still had plenty left, I wanted to be fighting for world titles. That wouldn't be possible if I was fighting Mr Bean – you have to fight someone who will get you rated.

I enjoyed training with Bob and my guys in the gym. It was brilliant. I loved it again. It was clicking and I don't think I'd ever looked in better shape. The change was monumental, internally and externally. Physically, after three and a half years out, and having this time lost four-and-a-half stone, I can imagine people thinking, 'How does this dickhead do it?'

But you couldn't see the damage that I'd done over the years. Sooner or later it was going to catch up on me, like Billy and Kerry said it would. People like them, as well as journalists, had always raised concerns about it, but when I kept winning and winning, they couldn't really keep saying and writing he's fat and pissed in the pub again. They'd already done that story dozens of times, there was no point doing it any more.

This fight was something different though. It was not just another fight for me. This was about redemption, a chance to change what I believed public perceptions were of me.

I'd always loved Roberto Durán, and I respect him more than you can imagine, but, for a while, before he ended up having major surgery to help his weight, he was huge. People were amazed that he was in such bad shape, but no matter what Roberto does he will always be my hero. I was looking at him once and he had this dirty horrible T-shirt, jacket and jeans on and it looked like he'd not had a wash in about a fortnight – he could have walked in with a bin bag on and I would have admired him – and I thought, 'Look at the size of him.' I bet people had looked at me in the same way.

I didn't want that any more. If I'd retired and sat on a beach somewhere and just carried on getting fatter and being a drunken fucking idiot like I was, people wouldn't have had any respect for me. But with people being able to see I was coming back, at thirty-four, after the Manny Pacquiao defeat, after all the troubles I'd had, I thought they might say, 'Good for him.'

The big question was, of course, was I coming back? It was a big decision, huge. People had always told me I'd had a great career, but I'd got to the point where that didn't mean any-thing to me. They asked why I couldn't leave it, but there was more to it than that. No one wants to end their career the way I did – destroyed after my worst night. I didn't want to retire; it's just the hunger wasn't there. All things considered, when you pile that on top of it, it had been a horrible three years. But being a father again, working with my fighters in the gym and being able to pass on my knowledge changed my mindset – I was filled with a passion to make people proud of me, and I wanted Campbell and Millie to be proud of me and to make British boxing and my country proud again. I didn't want people feeling sorry for me, saying: 'What a career he had but didn't he go and blow it.' I wanted everyone to be proud of me once more.

It was not just about a comeback. The last thing people saw of me in the boxing ring was me flat on my back against

Pacquiao and that story in the paper. Fat, overweight, sweating, in bars and nightclubs and ultimately in a hotel room. 'Can I believe I looked up to that man there?' they must have said. I couldn't blame people for thinking it, but I still wanted to be the People's Champion and I did not think I was any longer. This was about redeeming myself and redemption was more valuable to me than any world title. People will forgive you and if they see you're making an effort – they will believe you.

I had started using Twitter when I was still in my depression and I tweeted a picture of me, Jen and Millie when we were out for Sunday lunch. 'Why don't you just get AIDS and die you fat bastard?' someone replied.

I would fire back – I didn't really know how Twitter worked at the time. I didn't realize there would be so many trolls and how personal the abuse could get and I wasn't ready for it. I'd get up in the morning and look at what I wrote the night before and think, 'I can't believe I sent that.' I didn't like the person I was at the time – my responses weren't newspaper-worthy but it was hardly PR-friendly. There were a lot of good wishes on Twitter but some of the hurtful things were really horrible. I suppose I got used to it and, as I got better, I could relax about it rather than get involved in arguments.

When I first turned round and mentioned the comeback to Jennifer she was not for it at all. She's not a boxing fan and she first wanted me to pack it in after Maussa, then again before Pacquiao. But she saw how I'd knuckled down, how I got myself in shape, and she saw me physically disappear from the fifteen stone I was to being healthy, sounding more positive and after I had started my training camp, sparring and doing the pads with Bob, she couldn't shut me up. I was buzzing once more. She'd seen me at my worst and lowest. It's nice that people out there cautioned me about getting hurt or tarnishing my legacy, but you need to have been in and around the four walls of our house over those last three years to understand why I was doing it. I had reasons that the public just didn't know about.

I had so much drive because I felt I'd pissed everything I'd done against the wall.

I know there were plenty of negative whispers. I could hear them. Whether it was in the papers or on the Internet, the mood gradually started to change a bit. There were some who said, 'Fair play to him for coming back and giving it another shot.' I thought, 'Hopefully I will come back with a vengeance, put in a good performance and prove all the naysayers wrong, as I always have done.'

My career was about to start again; already there was exciting talk of me facing Britain's top light-welterweights and welterweights, Amir Khan and Kell Brook. Khan would have probably been the easiest fight to make because he was with Golden Boy and with all the work we'd done with Golden Boy it would have made sense. Brook's ability was not in doubt; good boxer, good puncher with good skills. But I thought there were question marks over attributes that you need if you're going to get to the highest level. He had never been in the trenches, tested his heart or stamina late in a fight. He was slick, quick and talented – with a decent punch – but his talent had not yet turned into world titles. Then there was talk of a two-fight deal with Malignaggi, who held the WBA welterweight belt, having dethroned Senchenko. A former opponent with a title, we could have done a fight in England and one in the USA, and that seemed a likely option. I'd watched them all since I'd been off, from the comfort of my settee, and thought, 'Come on, Rick. What are you doing sat here?' But three years was a long time to be out and there was no point talking about them until I could show everyone what I had left.

I knew there would be questions about the fight with my dad at the press conference. Stories appeared in the papers that morning but the detail was thin. It was tough convincing everyone that day that my mind was solely on the fight because it wasn't. It was emotional to say the least, and I nearly didn't make it – when I went to leave the house I said to Paul Speak, 'I'm not sure I can keep it together, here.'

At the Radisson I started talking about how I'd let my family down, how I had let my community down and how I let British boxing down. I felt my bottom lip going and I was getting emotional but thankfully I made it through. All I wanted was for people to give me a chance when I finally stepped back into the ring, on 24 November 2012. That's all I asked – the chance to prove there was life in the old dog.

When you think I was suicidal and sometimes waking up in the morning with a knife, where I'd been trying to summon up the courage to 'do it' and never did, thank God. When I looked at those days and reflected on the size of me, I was actually bursting with pride to be back up there in front of the media, and I meant every word when I said I wanted people to be proud of me. I wanted my redemption.

By the end of it, I think people who were maybe unsure of the comeback knew why I was doing it. I felt that even if the worst was to happen and I was to be defeated, then it wouldn't have been like the Pacquiao loss, on my back after two rounds. If I was beaten then my training camp would still have been better than it was for Pacquiao. There were simply too many question marks after that last defeat for me to be sat on the settee, content with just retiring. People couldn't appreciate what demons and ghosts I had going around in my head; they needed to be put to bed if I was ever going to live without boxing.

The next time I retired I would make sure it was for the right reasons and knowing I could do no more.

Despite a double-dip recession and money being tight everywhere, more than 18,000 tickets sold in two days after they went on sale. That was before we announced an opponent or the undercard. It was a full house after a week or so. I couldn't have been more proud – after everything – that people were still interested in me fighting. You can put good shows on and good fights and, as a promoter, I know how hard it is to sell them. It made me teary-eyed but it didn't detract from the main goal – that I wanted to bounce back with a vengeance because I felt I had ruined my career and ruined my life.

It wasn't simply about winning the world title, it was bigger than that for me. I didn't come back to fight six-rounders – I came back to fight the best. The fight was signed at welterweight, never my best weight, but I was older now. I wasn't sure my body had another ten stone weigh-in in it. I doubt it does.

I was training with Bob because I didn't want to be far from Jen and Millie and I could still train my own fighters, too. I was running with my guys in the early morning, training them before lunch in my gym and going to Bob's to train in the afternoon. Bob used a fair few of Billy's old methods. He used the bodybelt and we were doing weights, circuits and some gruelling runs. I had seen the work he had done with Matthew and his own fighters, Denton Vassell and Prince Arron, and I always knew he was a caring trainer. Bob said to several journalists that he was looking after a British institution; if nothing else, that was a reminder of my age.

In the gym I was not missing a trick, it was like I had not been away. The weight fell off, sparring was sharp and my timing was on from the start. 'You look like a young man again,' Bob would say.

I found myself able to almost eat what I wanted, but I didn't want rubbish any more. It was a lifestyle choice I was making. Why would I eat junk, because what goes into your mouth is your fuel and where you get your energy from. With about a fortnight to go I was only around a stone over the weight. In the old days I was a stone over on fight week.

The media interest was intense, the training hard and the Manchester Arena was jam-packed. With all of the hype about me possibly fighting for world titles again, I read somewhere that if my comeback was successful, and I wound up back topping the bill in Las Vegas, it would be the best comeback since Elvis. The fight was on Primetime in the UK and on Showtime in America. The atmosphere was unlike anything I'd experienced – whether it was the Tszyu fight, the thousands of supporters in Las Vegas or 58,000 at the City fight. This was different.

But after Senchenko landed that body shot in the ninth round, the night was turned on its head. The fans were pleading with me to stand up but I just thought, 'I'm sorry guys, I can't.' I was trying to breathe in through my nose and gave it one last shot by trying to take breath with a big gulp with my mouth open.

It was the worst thing I could have done, and when the referee Victor Loughlin waved it off I had to fall over on my side. The pain more than doubled. I just couldn't get up. There was only about five seconds left in the round.

It was heartbreaking; I couldn't do anything about it. You could hear a pin drop initially, when the fans realized I would not beat the count and the fight was over. But moments later they were in unison, singing 'There's only one Ricky Hatton.'

I draped my arms over the ropes, looked out disconsolately into the crowd and shook my head. Some kept on singing but near on 20,000 people had gone silent. Some looked stunned. There were people crying. If you've suffered with depression for years the last thing you want to see is people disappointed in you. I just broke into tears. Then I did an interview with TV, which I made a pig's ear of, and the first thing I cried was: 'I'm not a loser.' I cringe to watch it back but I looked into the crowd and felt like apologizing again, saying: 'I'm so sorry. I told you all I was going to come back and win another world title. I just couldn't do it.'

I had been beaten for the first time in England, let alone Manchester. For the first time, I had been defeated by someone who was not a pound-for-pound legend. I was thirty-four and talk of big British fights with Khan and Brook, of more huge nights in Las Vegas, of fighting my old victim Paulie Malignaggi, was silenced. (Malignaggi was ringside – he must have been the second most gutted man in the arena.) I cried. In front of all those people, I wept and there was nothing I could do to stop it, even though I tried to curl my lips upwards to fight my natural emotions.

Even in my heyday I couldn't have been any more prepared. But it doesn't matter what you look like on the outside – it doesn't reveal what's on the inside. I might have looked perfect, but an X-ray reveals the damage you've done over time. And although I looked physically fit, I'd had a career of hard fights; even some of my six-rounders at the start of my career were tough because that's how I boxed. I'd fought the best, I'd been up and down in weight, drinking, and then there were drugs in the bad patches, and you can't tell what kind of damage all that had done. Round nine against Senchenko was when it all finally caught up with me.

Having burned the candle at both ends – having lost nearly five stone to get back into fighting shape and after putting my body through hell to do it – I had to die by the sword, having lived by it. To get done with a body shot like that – that told me. From a boxing and technique point of view, I was done. But to lose to a body shot, it was just an acceptance that, 'Yes, my body has given up on me now.'

Everything in my heart before told me I was going to come back better than ever; a fighter knows when it's not there any more, he just won't always admit it.

After the fight, I was in the vast dressing room with Jennifer and a handful of members of my team, and I looked into the huge, wide mirrors in the bowels of the Manchester Arena. My face was swollen and bumpy. The left-hand side was black, blue and purple and there were bulges over and under my eye, causing it to start closing. I didn't say anything, but spent a few moments staring at the mess looking back at me, and I told my team I would be ready to see the media shortly. 'It's just not there any more,' I thought to myself.

Some of my team were saying, 'Don't make any hasty decisions at the press conference; you were winning the fight,' and I had to interrupt and say, 'Look at my face. Look at the state of me. How many times do my family have to see me like this, getting beat, getting knocked out?'

Then I asked my director of boxing, Richard Poxon, 'A few years ago, would I have walked through Senchenko?' He said: 'Ricky, in a heartbeat.' What did that tell me? It was time to move on. 'It's just not there any more,' I said to myself over and over. 'I've found out now.' That was that: there was peace, finally.

This was more than a boxing match. Yes, I would have liked to have been a world champion again but ultimately I wanted to make people proud and, even though I ended up on my knees, I like to think I achieved that. The media who covered the fight twice gave me standing ovations at the post-fight press conference. I'd never seen them do that to anyone before and I'd like to think that was their way of thanking me for the journey we had all been on.

'We found out tonight, it wasn't there any more,' I told them, matter-of-factly. 'I gave it my best. I was heartbroken in the ring and I was crying, and no doubt I will go home and cry tonight, but I'm happy. I found out. I needed to find out if I could mix it up at world level and I got my answer. I can't. I thought I was four rounds up at the time of the stoppage but I knew. I don't need anybody to tell me. If I don't draw a line in the sand now and end my career, I never will.'

When the door closed on the makeshift media room I took the lonely walk down the long Manchester Arena corridors with my assistant trainer, Mike Jackson. In my dressing room, Jennifer was waiting for me and she hugged me again. My left cheek had swollen further still.

It had been my encore performance and now I had to leave centre stage, my home, as I no longer belonged there. I gave it my best shot and it was just not there, I wished it was but it wasn't. Fighters will always search for excuses, I should know because I've been there. But there was none: I was too old, had put on too much weight between fights and had not lived the life of a disciplined, professional prizefighter outside training camp. There had been too many hard, draining battles.

During the after-fight party at the Hard Rock in Manchester, Jennifer was saying, 'Your eye's closing, should we go home? I doubt you feel up for seeing people.' I said, 'I never expected a feeling like this. I feel up to seeing people; I feel happy, content. I did myself proud, didn't I?' And I didn't feel like I wanted to hide away from a party, even a few hours after a loss.

Some might have thought I would have gone straight to bed sulking and been in turmoil but I talked to everyone and thanked them for coming, and I think everybody turned round and thought, 'Good for you.'

Despite the tears and the emotion from the fight – and there were plenty of tears – very soon afterwards I felt okay. I went out on a mate's stag do the night after in Manchester and we celebrated just like I did when we beat Kostya Tszyu. When I went through my bad times, I'd think about how I was never going to hear that roar of the crowd again. Hearing it that one last time sent me into retirement happy and content. I didn't win but it ended on a good vibe. It was the best thank-you the fans could have given me.

Now, in retirement, I feel really proud. I thought if I was beaten it would have been a little harder to take, but it's been easier than I could ever have imagined. Ultimately I wanted to come back to make people proud of me and find out if I still had it. I've got the answers and that's why I'm happy to go into retirement, build a family and do what I'm doing.

I wasn't destroyed like I was against Pacquiao. I could finally say, 'All right, I'm happy with that now.' I can watch boxing today and enjoy it. I can look in the mirror and say, 'Listen, you have not got it any more.'

It's time for a fresh chapter in my life; one that does not involve me punching people or getting hit for a living.

CHAPTER 14

Being Happy

People have said my lifestyle made me and broke me – the hard fights, the late nights, the drinking, all the weight I put on. Maybe they were right. Those same people said it was because I was a Jack the Lad, not going to red carpet events, just going down the pub, playing darts, going to City, going out with the lads on a Friday and Saturday night. Going to watch the boys play for their local teams on a Sunday morning, and then out on the piss with them all day, but then this is why the people loved me. In all, I reckon I lost around seventy stone in my career. In one year, when I fought four times, I lost two and a half stone per fight; that's ten stone in a year, my entire body-weight. I had no shame. But if I'd lived my life differently, would 25,000 to 30,000 have gone to Vegas?

Las Vegas is some place, by the way. I always dreamed of fighting there. When I go back to Vegas it's amazing; even today in the casinos the croupiers nod at me and people sing 'There's only one Ricky Hatton' or 'Walking in a Hatton Won-derland'. They must be sick of it now over there! You'd think

I'd be yesterday's news, so it makes me feel proud; it's not bad for a guy who hardly knew a world existed beyond the council estate he was brought up on. It's not like it's round the corner, you're over the other side of the world and people treat me so nicely. Me and Jennifer have been to Vegas several times since my last fight there, and when we've asked for tickets to shows and offered to buy them – for example, at the MGM Grand – we're told, 'Ricky, your money is no good here. The MGM Grand has never taken as much money as it did that weekend you fought Floyd Mayweather. These tickets are on us.'

I presented an award in Vegas not long ago and I went for something to eat and drink at the Crown & Anchor British pub off The Strip with one of my pals; when I asked for the bill, it was the same thing: 'Your money is no good here. We took the most money in the history of the Crown & Anchor whenever you were in town. Don't you dare.' When we went to leave, and I asked them to call for a taxi, one of the staff gave us a lift. I'd never have thought travelling there would be anything like that.

When I first started off, I wanted to be a world champion more than anything else; the only other things that interested me were supporting Manchester City and listening to Oasis. I ended my career having won four world titles in two weight classes, I've boxed at Man City's ground, where I'm on first-name terms with the players – and I still get star struck – and I'm mates with the Gallagher brothers, Liam and Noel. Being a Man City fan meant that when City were going through some financial issues a few years ago there was speculation in the paper that I was going to buy the club (it's a far cry from where City are today). Fans said to me, 'The club's in trouble, Rick. Why don't you invest some of your money and buy us a player?' There was a right back who played for us, Sun Jihai, and when the club was struggling I was asked, 'Why don't you buy Sun Jihai, that can be your contribution to the club?' I couldn't believe it. 'Fucking hell, how much do you think I've made?' I will always love City but no way could I do that.

After City won the league in the 2011–2012 season, when Sergio Agüero basically clinched it with the last ball that was kicked that season, I was in one box and Liam was in another. When Agüero scored, Liam was running around his box, saw me, and ran towards me with his arms out, shouting out as he ran over, 'Fucking have it. We're fucking having it tonight, Rick. We're going out.' We went for a drink at his box. I was pissed and Liam swaggered out, and we posed for pictures. You couldn't have wiped the smiles off our faces and I could just tell people were thinking, 'I bet those two will have a good night tonight.' We painted the town blue.

Nights out for me are rarer now, though. I have my family, my businesses and my fighters to train and promote. My fighters are vital to my business – any promoter will tell you, you have to invest in talent. When Frank Warren signed me up, there was no guarantee I was going to end up where I did and that's the gamble Frank took as a promoter. I have to do the same; you've got to invest in someone, *hopefully* they will get to the big stage and *hopefully* you will get any winnings back. That's promoting. So I have invested my money in fighters, a few champions. I had to get them fighting and I had to get some dates from Sky for the fights to be broadcast, and in order to get those dates, I had to double up title fights on my bills because I had fewer dates than I'd have liked. I thought because my shows were so good they would give me more dates, but they didn't. They cut me from the schedule.

I've got good fighters who I've invested in and I've got a good stable together, among them some titleholders, and then when my dates were cut I thought, 'What do I do now?' It would have been dead easy for me to say, 'Right, that's it. There's no revenue coming in so I'm going to knock it on the head.' But I haven't, I've stayed at it, and all of my fighters are still getting work, fighting title fights.

I've realized that I'm not that different from Frank in many ways – just because things don't go right I'm not one to chuck the towel in. I saw this happen with Frank – just when you'd think he might have trouble and he's not going to be the same force, he comes back and delivers. I'm sure when I lost my Sky dates people thought I would be gone like a cool breeze, but that's not the case – I'm made of stronger stuff than that.

I was upset at the time by the split with Sky – of course I was – and it has made the already hard business of promoting even harder. When you think of how big boxing is in the Sky Sports empire, my part of it was so minute, but they decided they wanted to go with one promoter, Matchroom, who do a high percentage of Sky Sports programming across the board with snooker, darts and fishing. It's understandable, so there are no complaints about that. But where I feel hard done by is that I never got a phone call or anything personal at all – a brief email went to my director of boxing, Richard Poxon, saying they weren't going to renew the dates, and wishing us all the best. That was it. It's a different ball game as a promoter though. I had 8,000 people turn out at my weigh-ins – if I could sell that for a show now, it would be unbelievable. No one said it was easy and I know for a fact it's not.

Ultimately my success has cost me my family. It breaks my heart, what has happened with them. They have been in a number of papers over the last few months talking about our split here and there. It's always, 'a family friend said . . .' or 'a source close to . . .' but it is never nice. There was a story where it was written that Mum and Dad had sent Millie a birthday present as an olive branch; but they'd agreed, through solicitors, to have no contact. At the end of one of the articles it said my businesses were losing money and I've got a load of hangers-on, but these were businesses that my dad started. I have since got rid of the TV company; the equipment we had was not good enough and the wage bill too high and we were overpriced. We've made a few changes with the Health and Fitness facility and we're now making money, and we have sold the clothing company on to another firm – it's their area of expertise – and that is going from strength to strength. Financially, I am secure. I will probably never spend all my money, and my children are my beneficiaries.

Although I lost to Senchenko, I still feel I could win another world title. If I'd picked an easier opponent, I could have done it all over again. There were people like the old Australian lightweight banger Michael Katsidis and veteran contender Lovemore Ndou mentioned as possible opponents, and perhaps if I'd selected someone like that – a confidence booster – and then gone for Senchenko, then I could have gone on from there. I feel there was a world title in me. But the comeback was not all about winning another title; I'd loved to have done that, but it was about finding out what I needed to find out, and I got what I wanted from it. I'm quite chuffed with how I've held it together, in retirement. If I'd won and squeezed over the finishing line, I'd have been tempted to fight on, so maybe the best thing was to suffer a defeat like that, a knockout defeat to make me realize. A knockout defeat brings the reality home.

But I wouldn't change it for the world. My boxing idols, Nigel Benn and Roberto Durán were there that night. Nigel Benn was everything to me as a teenager; when I went to Old Trafford and looked at the size of the crowd when he fought Chris Eubank, little did I know that fifteen years on I would be doing the same at the City of Manchester Stadium. The teenage Ricky Hatton sat there in awe, thinking Nigel Benn could do no wrong, so to do what I've done, and finish in front of Nigel Benn himself, makes me very proud. I've come a long way.

Roberto Durán was my other hero. Roberto had been to my gym before in Hyde, been to some of my fights and we've done a few sportsman's dinners together; when he heard I was visiting his country (for a WBA convention at the end of 2012) he got in touch with Paul Speak. He said he would pick me up at the airport and I couldn't believe it. Roberto Durán? Picking me up at the airport? You're joking. Imagine your hero picking you up at the airport. When I got off the plane I expected him to be outside the airport with a car but he was right there at the gate, shouting, 'Ricky, Ricky, come this way.' There was a massive queue at passport control and he just whisked me round the side while the immigration people yelled at him, 'Roberto, Roberto, passport, passport. He needs to show his passport.' Roberto just spun round, raised two fingers and told them to fuck off. He took me right through. How famous are you when you don't even have to go through passport control in your country? Incredible.

One of the questions I get asked most is, who I would like to have fought in history? I answer Roberto, because as he was my hero it would have been nice to share the ring with him. I'd like to have found out just how good he was. I feel like I've fought pretty much everyone in my era, but I always wonder how I would have got on against Puerto Rican warrior Miguel Cotto, or the always-exciting, but sadly late, Arturo Gatti. Those are the fights I wanted to be involved in, proper tearups. I struggled badly coming to terms with the losses to Mayweather and Pacquiao, but time is healing those wounds because when I retired and knew I wasn't going to fight again I could actually deal with it better. At the time, it was devastating. Even the Senchenko pill is not as bitter now, knowing there will be no more comebacks; against him I got the peace of mind I set out for. The more people try to change my mind now, the more likely I am to go back to a darker place, so while I'm still happy, I just want to leave it be.

Some fighters have health issues after long careers. My first boxing fight was when I was ten or eleven and my last was when I was thirty-four. When you see what happened to Muhammad Ali, the obvious one, it's heartbreaking. But if everyone had the attitude, 'Oh, what if something could go wrong? Damage could happen to me down the line', then boxing would cease to exist. It's the risk all of us take when we put our boxing gloves on.

I've seen what happened to Muhammad Ali in person. A lot of high-profile boxers have visited my gym – I've been very fortunate that way. Durán, Evander Holyfield, Lennox Lewis, David Haye and many others; but shortly after Pacquiao, Muhammad Ali's people asked me if I would speak at Old Trafford because Muhammad was doing an appearance there, at a dinner. 'Absolutely,' I said. 'Of course I would.' 'How much would you want paying?' they asked. I said, 'Want paying? To go and speak in front of one of the greatest men who has ever lived? Please don't insult me. It would be an honour to speak in front of him.' I was happy enough just to meet him and have the chance to speak in front of him. His people said they would like to show their gratitude in some way, that they'd heard I'd opened a gym and Muhammad would come and make an appearance. My jaw hit the floor faster than my head had hit the canvas against Manny Pacquiao: 'It would be great for him to come to the gym, providing he was okay and healthy enough to do it. If he wakes in the morning and for whatever reason can't do it, then he should not come,' I said. Muhammad Ali doesn't come to England much any more, let alone to Hyde.

When he came to the gym – what that did for the community and the area, will go down in Hyde history. Word got out, the streets were cornered off, the police were out in force to hold people back as others clambered up the lamp posts and onto the roofs of houses to get a look – and I don't blame them. It was something else: Muhammad Ali in Hyde, incredible. He didn't speak much, he was clearly very poorly, but he could communicate with his movements and eye contact – and he could flick a jab at you.

He arrived at the gym in a wheelchair but when he got to the entrance he said something, asked them to stop, stood up and started walking. I asked, 'What did Muhammad say there?' He'd said, 'Get me out of this wheelchair. I'm not getting pushed in Ricky Hatton's gym.' It was an amazing experience, if tinged with sadness throughout. It certainly put things into context for me. You think of things that might be going wrong in your life and everything that has happened, and then you see a man like Muhammad Ali in a wheelchair, struggling to walk and to talk, then you see things in a different light. It made me feel differently about my own circumstances.

People close to me said, 'You're depressed? Look at Muhammad and see what you've got to be depressed about.' They were right – but I don't think the people who said I shouldn't make a comeback were. I made that comeback and whether you thought I was right or wrong to do it, I made it. How many fighters come back time after time after time? The one thing with me is when I realized I didn't have it any more I could look back and say, 'You know what, that'll do for me.' It's not like I need reminding any more.

Health-wise no one has a crystal ball; we can't look into the future. No one knows what's coming down the line because I have had a lot of hard fights and my defence was not my best attribute. I don't recall my nose ever being badly broken during one particular fight, although I know it's been swollen after some of them. The damage to it was probably just an accumulation of punches. It's bled and my eyes have been puffy the next day, but now one nostril is more blocked than the other. I said I'd get it sorted when I retired but I haven't got round to it yet. Even though I've had a lot of hard fights, was involved in a lot of wars and had the brutal Pacquiao knockout, when people speak to me I don't think I come across as a stereotypical boxer. I can be sensible, I talk very well, I'm knowledgeable about the sport and I don't slur my words, and if you didn't know me and spoke to me on a regular basis, I'd like to think you would say, 'Wow, I didn't know he was a boxer.'

I am grateful for what boxing has done for me. Granted I worked hard at it, but when I think that Jen and my children have the house we have now, with a swimming pool and a lovely garden to play in, I feel I'm giving my kids a life that not many people can dream of and I won't move from there now.

My house is called The Heartbreak, mainly because I was an Elvis fan (though it could be called The Heartbreak now for different reasons). I was in Vegas, looking through the tacky memorabilia shops, and saw a house sign that read 'Heartbreak Hotel' so I bought it and stuck it on the side of my place. We started calling the house The Heartbreak and that's what it became known as. When I moved to the house we're in now, which is one I had my eye on for a while, I had it officially registered as The Heartbreak.

It's a decent-sized house at the end of a road, next to a farm and with a field behind it. The field is on a slope, so when it rained all the water used to run off that field into the garden. The back garden was like a marsh, boggy with trees and bushes everywhere, so we cut everything back and sorted the drainage out; now the water runs down to a stream where I keep my carp. I love my carp and we have a natural spring and a nice garden for Campbell to play in. I feel very privileged when I sit in the garden and look at the house, the garden, the pond with my fish in and a bridge going over it, and a treehouse in the back for Campbell and Millie. It is a lovely area for them.

It's a nice family house, but we extended it, and re-bricked it so that we made it just how we wanted it. In my games room, I keep all of my memorabilia. However, when I look around, at my belts and my achievements, I think the highlight of all of them might have been my MBE, which I was awarded in 2007.

From an early age, when I was winning schoolboy trophies, I knew that I was pretty decent at boxing and I thought I could do well; but going to Buckingham Palace, and receiving my MBE from Prince Charles – it's beyond the realms of fantasy. I'm still the boy from the council estate, you see. In all of my years I have probably not moved further than a six-mile radius from where I was born. We had a couple of years where my dad had a pub in Marple, but apart from that it was always Hattersley, Hyde, and Gee Cross. When I started doing well for myself I never wanted to move, I just bided my time to get a house in the area close to my mates, close to my family and close to the pub. I'm happy in Hyde.

Five years after the Senchenko fight I will be eligible to be voted into the International Boxing Hall of Fame. Like the MBE, that is another accomplishment that would be above and beyond my dreams of what might happen in boxing. A world-wide of panel of experts makes the decision, but I would be delighted to get in and have a plaque on the walls in Canastota in upstate New York. That would go alongside the best achievements of my life. But that's not my decision and everyone will have an opinion. Some will think I should be in there, some will say I shouldn't. That's what makes boxing great, because it's open to interpretation.

Alongside my MBE and belts, I've got my memorabilia framed and hung on the walls. There are the gloves and wraps from the Kostya Tszyu fight; a frame with my amateur certificates in; my bronze medal from Cuba. I always kept the gloves I fought in and got my opponents to sign them. There's a great picture of me and Kostya the day after our fight – the size of his jaw is incredible – and that is the fight I will always be remembered for, so that means a great deal to me.

I think that was my best win. That said, when you beat someone like him in the manner that I did, I think that, even though it was my best night in some ways, it was the worst thing that could have happened to me because you just think,

'Fuck it, I've gone through Kostya Tszyu. I'll go through any-one.' You forget the subtleties where you come in: jab first, move your head, change the angles. After that, part of me thought, 'I'll just steamroll everyone here. No one's going to be stronger than me.' That's how my fighting went. Everyone saw him as a punching machine and when I went through him and he stayed on his stool at the end of the fight, I think my style changed because of that success. Things were never the same after that fight, that's for sure.

I'd like to think I'm the People's Champion again. I hope I am. When I'm asked what my greatest achievement was, it wasn't a particular fight, punch, title, victory or night – it was the fanbase I had, and how they loved me. That's one of the reasons why making a comeback was so important. I was always known as the People's Champion – laugh-a-minute, goes to the match to watch City, has a pint, has a game of darts, doesn't have a bad word to say about anyone – and I think that's why I was liked. Then, when I had all of my troubles, I lost my most important title, and things went so badly for me. I've admitted to taking drugs, I've admitted to drinking too much, and hopefully that is a story we can move on from now. It's a part of my life I'd like to move on from. It did become a proper problem for me, with people saying I was an alcoholic, but if that's the case, why is my drinking on track now? There are reasons I did what I did. I have triggers that have set me off and there's stuff I've done I'm not proud of, and things I don't want to go back to.

When people see me now, training my fighters, in the gym

every day, I can say it was a problem at the time. Is it something that could raise its head again? I don't want to think so – it was linked to my depression; if something sets me off, I go out and get pissed – lots of people do that. I've always taken things people say seriously; if you cross me I take it to heart. If people say, 'Ricky, you're shit, you are,' I let it get to me. My friends say, 'Who cares what they think? Who cares what everyone else thinks?' But I'm not that type of man; it means a lot to me. That's why, when I got beaten by Mayweather, the first thing I wanted to say was sorry. A lot of people find that strange but, if you know me, it's not. I did feel sorry – I felt I'd let everyone down; being the person that I am, when people said there was no shame in it, I didn't understand what they were talking about. Even though I was so successful, I have a bit of a defeat-ist attitude; if you cross me, I'm going to lash out.

I would like people to remember me as the no-airs-and-graces lad who came from the council estate, whose career had a lot of highs, a lot of lows and a lot of speed bumps along the way, but someone who found happiness. That's what hap-pened. With great highs come equally deep lows, and I've had all of them. To be honest, I could have not been here. I could have turned into something really bad but I'm fighting my demons.

Things would niggle me but I've learned now that when a problem comes along I can sit down and talk about it; I don't keep it to myself. It's the same with Jennifer. If I've got some-thing on my mind I will go in and say it, whereas before I would go away and brood on it for days – and if you do that, it eats away at you. It doesn't matter how hard or macho you are, sometimes you've got to get things off your chest, and if you don't it can send you loopy. I thought that People's Champion title had gone and I hope I've got it back in the way I returned, lost all the weight and picked a good opponent. I'm not naturally slim so I have to work at my weight, and it's nice when people say, 'Jesus, Rick, you're keeping it off.' People don't expect that. I'm never going to be skinny, am I? But I can keep an eye on it.

After I retired, I did *Let's Dance*, a BBC show for Comic Relief. If I'm honest, I never thought I was going to win it – I'm not a dancer. I had to do a twirl, a dance and this and that; I thought, there was no way I was going to get it right, so I felt like I'd really achieved something – remembering the moves, the back roll and the routine. Having thought there's no way I'd do it, I did it, even though the part where I was meant to fly around the studio didn't happen because they didn't attach the cables in time. I don't think reality TV is for me but never say never, I've learnt that.

Jennifer has been everything to me. As I was going through all my bad times and my depression, my mum and dad were nowhere to be seen; then they were a big part of me feeling the way I did. It was just Jennifer who was there. She can see that I have been poorly, she knows exactly what has happened to me, that I have been unwell; she's put up with a lot when she could have kicked me into touch a long time ago. She's stood by me, she's been an absolute rock. I'm still the same fella she fell in love with all those years ago, no doubt, but through everything I think I'm quite a damaged person.

It was horrifying seeing Jennifer so upset when I saw the tapes back of the Pacquiao and Mayweather fights like that. The cameramen zoomed in on her screaming and crying – I'd love to know who shoved the camera in her face when she was at her world's worst. After the comeback, I definitely knew I didn't want to put her through any more than she had already had to go through; it was not fair on her to keep seeing me like that. There's no more pain for me or for her. Our highs and lows ultimately determine the person you become, and I'm a stronger person because I've had those lows. Jennifer has brought me back from the brink so many times, she's my soulmate. She's seen the best and worst of – and with – me.

From getting beat by Pacquiao, to retiring, to being in court with my best mate, Billy, to wanting to commit suicide, to finding that out about my dad and him attacking me . . . sometimes I have sat in my games room when I've been drunk and just lost the plot, crying and shouting at the wooden beams over my head, 'What have I done? What have I done bloody wrong to deserve this?' It's been one thing after another. I've been trying to get myself on the straight and narrow, which I am, but just when I get over something there is something else that comes along. I'm left wondering when it will all end. I just want to be happy for a bit, now. I feel sorry for myself, and I'll continue to do so because all I ever wanted was to work hard, be the best I can be and provide for my family – and the wealth that I've got I've shared it with my family.

My faults and my problems are ultimately what have made me as a person. If anyone tells you life is easy, they're liars because it isn't. It's very hard and we all have ups and downs, but it's the man you turn out to be after the ups and downs that counts.

Real life is not 50,000 fans at the City of Manchester Stadium. It's not 25,000 fans running round Las Vegas. It's not having world titles lifted above your head. Life's a lot harder than that. They are just things I was fortunate to do and achieve, but real life is when it slows down, after all those highs have been and gone and real life plateaus out. Because after those highs, I would think: 'What have I got to look forward to now? My life is going to be shit.' But I've come through it, I've had the highs, the lows and the good times. I don't blame anyone who's had similar experiences going off the rails, because you think it's going to last forever and it doesn't; when it doesn't you can lose the plot. The main thing is you can get yourself back on track.

I love the musician Johnny Cash, who I've got a tattoo of on my left arm. He was a bad man, a rebel. He nearly lost all his family, his life turned to shit and he came good. I like his music. I like the words because they're all very deep and he's a bit of an inspiration to me. He nearly lost everything and everyone and turned his life around. I love 'Walk the Line', perhaps his biggest hit, because that's what I've got to do – I've got to walk the line. When someone suffers with depression and you put all of the things that have happened to me into the mix, I'm still trying to be upbeat, positive and get on with life. I just want some middle ground. I've been generous with my money, I've looked after my family, my kids are going to be sorted and I've worked my arse off so my family is taken care of – but it feels like they've all shit on me. It's sad when you think about it.

While I'm happy, just leave me be. My family is now Jen, Millie, Campbell and our new baby Fearne, that's it. I feel very proud of the job Jen is doing with bringing Millie and Fearne up; she is a pure mum.

Jen's family have been brilliant with me. Jennifer's mum, Meg, dad, Kevin, her brother, Adam, and her sisters, Kate and Lauren, have been really good to me. Adam has a son, Alfie, too, and we have an open-door policy so they come over and let themselves in whenever they want. You can imagine Jen's parents, seeing me in turmoil, in a bad way, out drinking too much and in the paper and pissed everywhere. It's not nice to see the boyfriend of your daughter crumbling, self-destructing. With the *News of the World*, how difficult that was for her family as well as her. If it was in the papers that a lad had done to Millie what I had put Jen through, I would have wrung his fucking neck, I really would. 'What've you been doing to my daughter?' But they know about my depression, what I've been through and they've been patient with me and stood by me as well and I will be eternally grateful to all of them. I think they all sympathized with the situation and her family mean a great deal to me. We have family meals together, and when it's someone's birthday we have a big party; it's a big occasion and we open presents together, and it's something I'm really pleased to be included in.

Aged twelve, Campbell came to see me training my boys one day, then he wanted me to take him on the pads and now he's a gym regular. When I go to the gym to watch him – at the Louvolite, where I started almost a quarter of a century ago (they still have a lot of the same methods they used when I was boxing there) – and I am stood on the balcony looking over and watching him, I stand on the exact same spot where my dad used to watch me when I was Campbell's age. I feel a bit emotional every time I go and watch him; if I had a choice I would rather he didn't box, but it's what he wants to do so I will support him – it's the best sport in the world.

Anybody and everybody who walks through the gym door wants to be a champion, but even if you don't achieve that, whether you have a hundred and one fights or one fight, generally you come out of boxing a better person. When the lads come in it's, 'Come on, guys, start stretching; get your ropes out; get your gloves out. Oi, put your rope away, you; where's your bandages, whose are these bandages? Tidy these up. Who's sparring?' Then, to start sparring, you touch gloves and there's respect and manners. It's life skills and discipline. There were two lads at my amateur boxing club and they absolutely hated each other. They would fight, argue and kick off in the playground every day, but at the age of eleven or twelve they started going to the boxing club and sparring with each other and they became best mates. It's another boxing cliché, but boxing turns thugs into gentlemen. It teaches you to respect others. It keeps you fit and channels your aggression, so I can't turn round and say I'm disappointed Campbell has started boxing. He looks just like me – he's a real chip off the old block.

I would play it by ear in regards to how involved I become if he wants to do it. When we get back from the gym I always give him a little bit of one-to-one in the house, dos and don'ts, and I do a bit of work with him in the gym, but I let the coaches do what they do with him. It would be disrespectful of me if I started sticking my oar in. They're doing a great job with him. I never let him come to my fights, though. Not even the Senchenko one when he was a bit older. You never can tell what is going to happen. I remember one time Ensley Bingham fought Mpush Makambi for the IBO middleweight title; he had moved up in weight and I had my trainers and second's licence back then and I was working the corner with Billy Graham. I remember all of Ensley's kids were there, aged between about thirteen and eight, with their mum, and Ensley got knocked out. We went back to the changing rooms to see the doctor and I could see his children crying with their mum and his family, and I thought it had to be heartbreaking to see. Everyone is different but I didn't want Campbell to be in that position. Each to their own. Lots of fighters have their kids there and there's no right or wrong; it's a personal choice, but you never can tell what will happen.

In fact, Campbell was bad enough when he was younger. He's always been into wrestling and the WWE, and they have often involved me when they have done big shows in Manchester. Campbell has loved seeing me 'fight' Chavo Guerrero and get in the ring with people like John Cena and Triple H. The

Undertaker and Batista visited Billy's gym once, but I once had to square up with a seven-foot monster they called the Big Show and Campbell, who was only young at the time, was blubbing in the front row, thinking the giant was going to kill me.

Sometimes fame has been difficult. I can only take the blame for my own actions, but with what happened in the *News of the World* I was in a really bad way and certain people took advantage of it, didn't they? The *News of the World* was one. I think to myself, 'If I wasn't famous nothing would have come of that.' What isn't nice about fame is that someone's always trying to have you over and people want to shit-stir – some people are always going to try and stitch you up. There are pluses and minuses to it all. When you make an appearance somewhere or you're at a sportsman's dinner and you see all of the fans who say how much they have followed you – and that some of them even came to Vegas – and when you go to schools and you see the children – money can't buy that. When I was a kid I would look at Nigel Benn the same way people now look at me and it makes me very proud. But I honestly wouldn't care if no one knew me. I still do the same things in the same places. Having a pint in the same place, getting pissed in the same pubs and nothing has really changed.

I try to live that way – normally. You grow up, have a family, work to be a good parent, work all your life so you can see your kids and grandkids grow up and know that financially they will be okay. I think that's the best thing you can possibly do – as a father – to know they've been taken care of. I've done that. I've worked hard for everything I've got. I have the best partner I could ever have. I have three lovely kids. We live in a lovely house that I've worked hard for. We've got a holiday home in Tenerife we can go to and, if the kids want to go to college or university, I know I can provide for them. Their kids and grand-kids will be okay and I will grow up and see my children and their grandkids. That's my role as a man ticked.

That's how it is for me. I'm content. I'm happy. I hope the bad days are behind me. I've had some amazing things happen to me in the last twenty years that some people won't experience in a lifetime. And I'm looking forward to the next twenty years. Onwards and upwards.

The depression will never leave me now. I accept that. It will always be there. It's about how I handle it and cope with it from now on, and I am getting better. Two-week benders now last two days. I can talk to people about my problems. It is an ongoing struggle but I am trying my best and I will continue to do so. Problems will always raise their head, but I'm in a happy place.

I've experienced enough wars for a lifetime. There have been wars in and out of the ring, with the scales, with drugs and depression, with drink, with Tszyu, Mayweather, Pacquiao and the others.

Now it's time for some happiness and peace.

Picture credits